Environmental Justice
and the New Pluralism

Environmental Justice and the New Pluralism

The Challenge of Difference for Environmentalism

DAVID SCHLOSBERG

OXFORD
UNIVERSITY PRESS

OXFORD
UNIVERSITY PRESS

Great Clarendon Street, Oxford OX2 6DP

Oxford University Press is a department of the University of Oxford.
It furthers the University's objective of excellence in research, scholarship,
and education by publishing wordwide in

Oxford New York

Athens Auckland Bangkok Bogotá Buenos Aires Calcutta
Cape Town Chennai Dar es Salaam Delhi Florence Hong Kong Istanbul
Karachi Kuala Lumpur Madrid Melbourne Mexico City Mumbai
Nairobi Paris São Paulo Singapore Taipei Tokyo Toronto Warsaw
with associated companies in Berlin Ibadan

Oxford is a registered trade mark of Oxford University Press
in the UK and in certain other countries

Published in the United States
by Oxford University Press Inc., New York

© David Schlosberg 1999

The moral rights of the author have been asserted

Database right Oxford University Press (maker)

First published 1999

British Library Cataloguing in Publication Data

Data available

Library of Congress Cataloging in Publication Data
Schlosberg, David.
Environmental justice and the new pluralism : the challenge of difference
for environmentalism / David Schlosberg.
Includes bibliographical references and index.
1. Environmental justice—United States.   2. Environmental policy—United
States.   3. Environmentalism—Political aspects—United States.
4. Pluralism (Social sciences)   I. Title.
GE180.S37   1999   363.739290973—dc21   98-41320

ISBN 0-19-829485-9

1 3 5 7 9 10 8 6 4 2

Typeset in Stone Serif
by Best-set Typesetter Ltd., Hong Kong
Printed in Great Britain
on acid-free paper by
Bookcraft Ltd.,
Midsomer Norton, Somerset

For my daughters, Mira Enya and Valerie Violet

Preface

This project began in Oregon, overlooking the majestic mountains of the Cascade Range. It concludes during a snowstorm in the shadows of the San Francisco Peaks of Northern Arizona. In each place, and at each time, I could describe the beauty of the natural environment I was lucky enough to be surrounded by. But the environment in both of those idyllic settings was more than the natural beauty; in both places, environmental injustices abound. During the work in Oregon, a monstrous semiconductor manufacturing plant rose out of what was once wetlands in my community, destroying creeks and wetlands, spilling toxic acids, soaking up tax breaks, and threatening nearby schools and neighborhoods. And now, environmental groups, community groups, and Native American tribes are working in coalition against plans to bury low-level radioactive waste at a sacred site in the nearby California Desert, as well as against plans to ship nuclear waste through my present community, on their way to storage near other Native American nations.

Through both my studies and my personal experience, I have been exposed to numerous understandings of the concept of 'environment', as well as a variety of forms of resistance. The challenge for all of this difference in environmental movements, of course, is in developing political ethics, practices, and demands that are both encompassing and just. That challenge was the motivation for this project, and what I explore here are notions—in both the realms of theory and practice—that have evolved in response.

I owe a great deal of thanks to a great number of people for their help on various parts, in numerous stages, of this project. My greatest single debt is owed to John Dryzek, who introduced me to the concept of discursive democracy which has, in turn, led to the whole range of questions inherent in pluralist discourse and practice. John's comments on the text, and on many of the theories and theorists I address, were always succinct and insightful. Discussions with him were invariably fruitful, especially those laced with his trademark wry humor fed by award-winning homebrew. At Oregon, Deborah Baumgold, Irene Diamond, Dan Goldrich, and Greg McLauchlan pushed me in numerous directions. Irene was the first to suggest I look at the early pluralist literature in my examination of difference in the environmental movement, though I am sure she had no idea where it would lead me. Dan fought to keep my theoretical work relevant to contemporary movements, and his own dedication to, participation in, and evaluation of the movements he studies was both inspiration and motivation.

Throughout the project, I have had the fortune of the aid of numerous academics and activists alike who have had an effect on my thinking of both theory and practice. Whether in interviews, discussions, presentations, supplying materials, or in responses to the written work, I have benefited from the input of: Magdalena Avila, Wanda Ballentine, Santina Baumeister, Joseph Boland, Steve Brittle, Bunyan Bryant, Leslie Byster, David Carruthers, Pamela Chiang, Sumi Cho, Avigail Eisenberg, Tupac Enrique, Danny Faber, Kathy Ferguson, Mike Glavin, Jennifer Gleason, Roger Gottlieb, Doug Heiken, Tim Ingalsbee, Bern Johnson, Josh Karliner, Timothy Kaufman-Osborne, Robert Knox and the staff at EPA's Office of Environmental Justice, Denny Larson, Sanford Lewis, Mike McGinnis, Ron Mitchell, Alan Moore, Richard Moore, Mary O'Brien, Devon Peña, Chris Rootes, Peggy Saika, Ted Smith, Noël Sturgeon, Liz Taylor, Nate Teske, Kaylynn Sullivan TwoTrees, and Mike Welsh. Faulty memory and bad note-taking keep me from mentioning many others; apologies for those inadvertently excluded.

I am forever grateful to the Political Science Department at Northern Arizona University for providing me with a home supportive of, and conducive to, my dual interests in political theory and environmental politics. Those here who have offered specific assistance in the refinement of some of these ideas include Geeta Chowdhry, Sheryl Lutjens, Sheila Nair, Larry Preston, Mary Ann Steger, and Carol Thompson. Graduate students at NAU have also prodded me in various directions; thanks especially to Martin Nie, Richard Tahvildaran-Jesswein, Paul Vaughn, and everyone involved in the dissection of Chapter 5 in my Graduate course on Politics and Ecology.

Heartfelt appreciation goes to Dominic Byatt of Oxford University Press for his constant support of the project. A special thanks to Doug Torgerson, for his thorough, constructive, and, of course, positive review of the manuscript for OUP; Doug fully engaged the text and offered numerous valuable suggestions on both substance and organization. Thanks also to another—again valuable reviewer for the Press Les Thiele.

Barbara and Stewart Schlosberg—Mom and Dad—have been right there through it all. Their enthusiasm for my work has never wavered, and has been a constant source of energy. Sheila Clancy, my wife, partner, and *media naranja*, must get credit for her faith, support, and encouragement to stick with it, even in the depths of graduate school uncertainty and despair. She continues to this day, not letting me slack in parental duties and insisting I come out sledding, even as deadlines approached. Finally, I borrowed a tactic from an old professor, and I tried to induce my daughter—with chocolate—to take the blame for the mistakes herein. But she knows a raw deal when she hears one (and also knows she can get chocolate from me anytime), so the standard disclaimer about all fault for mistakes, omissions, and various oversights falling on the author alone will have to apply.

For financial support at various stages of this project, I thank the family of Neil Blackman, the Oregon Humanities Center, the University of Oregon Department of Political Science, the College of Social and Behavioral Sciences at Northern Arizona University (especially Dean Susanna Maxwell), and the Organized Research Committee at NAU.

D.S.S.

Flagstaff, Arizona
March 1998

Acknowledgements

I have drawn from some previously published work in constructing the larger argument here, and I thank the publishers of those articles for permission to recycle my own thoughts here. My essay 'Challenging Pluralism: Environmental Justice and the Evolution of Pluralist Practice', from Roger Gottlieb, ed., *The Ecological Community: Environmental Challenges for Philosophy, Politics, and Morality* (London: Routledge, 1997) was an initial foray into the relationship between pluralism and environmental practice, and bits of it appear throughout the book, especially in Chapter 1. Elements of Chapters 3 and 4 appeared in 'Resurrecting the Pluralist Universe', *Political Research Quarterly*, 51/3 (September 1998). Chapter 5 appeared, in an edited form, as 'Networks and Mobile Arrangements: Political Innovation in the U.S. Environmental Justice Movement', *Environmental Politics*, 8/1 (Spring 1998).

Contents

Abbreviations

CAFE	Community Alliance for the Environment
CCHW	Citizen's Clearinghouse for Hazardous Waste
CERCLA	Comprehensive Environmental Response, Compensation, and Liability Act of 1980
CHEJ	Center for Health, Environment, and Justice (previously CCHW)
CRT	Campaign for Responsible Technology
ECO	Environmental Careers Organization
EDF	Environmental Defense Fund
EPA	United States Environmental Protection Agency
LCHA	Love Canal Homeowners Association
MELA	Mothers of East Los Angeles
NAFTA	North American Free Trade Agreement
NEJAC	National Environmental Justice Advisory Council
NEPA	National Environmental Policy Act of 1969
NRDC	National Resources Defense Council
NWF	National Wildlife Federation
RCRA	Resource Conservation and Recovery Act of 1970
SMO	social-movement organization
SNEEJ	Southwest Network for Environmental and Economic Justice
SVTC	Silicon Valley Toxics Coalition
SWOP	Southwest Organising Project
TSCA	Toxic Substances Control Act

Part I

Environmentalism and Difference: The Pluralist Challenge

1

Introduction: The Environmental Challenge to Pluralism

There is no such thing as environmentalism. Any attempt to define the term in a succinct manner necessarily excludes an array of other valid definitions. 'Environmentalism' is simply a convenience—a vague label for an amazingly diverse array of ideas that have grown around the contemplation of the relationship between human beings and their surroundings.

The twentieth century has seen quite a growth of environmental concern, and this growth has not just been embodied in an increase of people joining various environmental organizations. The growth has been, more importantly, in various meanings of what environmentalism is, the numerous identities and discourses that have developed, and in the expansion of actions environmentalists have taken—personally and politically—to help bring their views toward realization.

The founding story of environmentalism in the US is itself based on difference—the distinction between the romantic preservationist represented by John Muir and the efficient conservationist embodied in the forester Gifford Pinchot. But even that narrative excludes an entire realm of urban environmentalisms that developed and expanded at the same time. Strands of this form of environmentalism focused on municipal waste and sewage, public health, and industrial-caused illness (Darnovsky 1992; Gottlieb 1993; Melosi 1980). All of these foci have evolved, and new ones have arisen, in the broad growth of environmentalisms in this century.

Presently, the environmental field includes not only romantic preservationists, efficient conservationists, public-health advocates, and environmental illness victims, but also deep ecologists, greens, bioregionalists, animal liberationists, advocates of permaculture and organic agriculture, ecofeminists, religious evangelists, social ecologists, steady-state economists, neo-Malthusians, neo-Luddites, neo-Hobbesians, ecological technology promoters, nature consumers, indigenous rights activists, spiritualists, planners, conservation biologists, environmental health professionals, environmental justice advocates, environmental lawyers, gaians, ecosocialists, nature writers, worker-health advocates, eco-anarchist youth, and more. Even within such categories, diversity is often vast—for example, within sustainable development, deep ecology, ecofeminism, and environmental justice. It would take a study much longer than the present one to identify and explore both the large and subtle differences among them. And this is not my present task.

The argument I make in the following chapters assumes the diversity in the movement. The problem is that past attempts to classify, explain, or analyze environmentalism have excluded and marginalized significant parts of the movement. But it is not just academic examiners that are guilty of this type of exclusion. The major groups of the US environmental movement, in taking on the role of interest groups in the liberal pluralist model, have also excluded and marginalized many positions, and limited what counts as a valid environmental perspective. It is in this context of exclusion—by both examiners of and practitioners within mainstream environmentalism—that I address the issue of difference in the movement. The question is not how to categorize, describe, explain, or advocate certain notions of environmentalism. Rather, this study focuses on two key concerns. First, how can we acknowledge and recognize, rather than deny, diversity? Second, how can that diversity be politically organized in a manner more inclusive than the liberal, or mainstream environmental, model? In responding to both questions, the focus here is on innovations in both political theory and environmental activism. New pluralist theory—both critical and radical—centers on political strategies for encompassing and including difference. And the environmental justice movement has forced the environmental movement more generally to face difference. That movement serves here both as an example of differences within contemporary environmentalism, and as a nascent embodiment of a new form of pluralism in practice.

Environmental justice and the new pluralism posit a challenge to both conventional liberal pluralism and the practices of the major groups in the US environmental movement. It is the development of this challenge, again, in both theory and in practice, that I explore in this work.

Problems with Conventional Pluralism

The critical pluralism that I engage in both theory and practice differs radically from the more commonly understood and dominant paradigm of pluralism in political science since the 1950s and practiced by much of the environmental movement since its resurgence in the 1960s. Before I move on to the main questions at hand, I need to make the argument that the existing diversity of environmentalisms is ill served by the current political strategy that dominates the environmental movement: the model of liberal pluralism. That will serve as the second assumption of the present study.

After a brief period of articulation of liberal pluralism in the 1950s and 1960s (Banfield 1961; Dahl 1961; Truman 1960), the model, along with its methodology and practice, has been repeatedly criticized. The responses were numerous and broad. Here I mention only a few issues that are relevant to the current study.[1]

Liberal pluralism is defined by its emphasis on groups as the key unit of political action; these groups act out of the desire for self-interested economic rewards. And, importantly, the model stresses open access—the penetrability and heterogeneity of the political system (Dahl 1961; Lindblom 1965; Truman 1960). The model assumes that interest groups are homogeneous and easily defined, making it possible for representatives to represent accurately myriad holders of the interest. It also assumes, and celebrates, the notion that if interests are organized well, and are supported by ample resources, participants with those interests will find success (Dahl 1961).

Lowi's (1969) critique of interest-group liberalism, which he calls a 'vulgarized' version of pluralism, laments the fact that the model negates what he sees as the traditional mode of political life—a focus on philosophy, morality, and dialogue. Instead, he argues, this existing form of pluralism focuses on the rituals of the competitive process. The management of interests has replaced the more noble notions and practices of politics. As the pluralist critic Wolff

---

[1] I return to criticisms of this generation of pluralism in Ch. 3.

eloquently notes, '[t]he genius of American politics is its ability to treat even matters of principle as though they were conflicts of interest' (1965: 21).

The absolute necessity of resources to express interests in the competitive system was also a point of contention. Critics argue that liberal pluralism equated the extent of resources in one's possession with the expression of the intensity of interests (Lowi 1969). As such, the most well-funded interests became the most consistently successful. Underfunded interests were seen as unpopular, and the lack of their success was attributed to lack of support.

This is one reason why criticisms of the pluralist process focused on the denial of diversity and the exclusion of certain groups. Wolff (1965: 42) argued that the system simply does not represent the interests of tens of millions of Americans. Liberal pluralism does not justify this, he notes; it simply ignores it. Wolff (preceding Lowi here) argued that part of the problem is the inherent conservatism of the model—that once certain groups are established, diversity is frozen: 'The application of the theory of pluralism always favors the groups in existence against those in the process of formation' (p. 41).

With such limited and frozen participation, pluralism—in both theory and practice—became, in Connolly's words, biased. A biased pluralism is one in which 'some concerns, aspirations, and interests are privileged while others are placed at a serious disadvantage' (Connolly 1969: 16). There was no protection, in the model or practice, for unrepresented minorities, whether racial, cultural, ideological, or class-based.

In addition, critics focused on the nature of the interactions and participation within interest groups. As Kariel argues at the beginning of his study of pluralism, 'the organizations which the early theorists of pluralism relied upon to sustain the individual against a unified government have themselves become oligarchically governed hierarchies' (Kariel 1961: 3–4). One of the original functions of interest groups—mediating between individuals and governmental decisions—became impossible, as groups outgrew their originally envisioned size and mission.

Even as the theory of liberal pluralism was soundly attacked, and some of its original formulators began to have doubts and changes of heart (see especially Lindblom 1977, 1982), the political practice continued. As environmentalisms expanded in their second wave of popularity in the 1960s and 1970s, various parts of the movement explored diverse political models. By the 1980s, the major groups in the movement had settled comfortably into their roles within liberal pluralism and into their representative interest-group offices in Washington, D.C.[2]

Over the past twenty-five years, the major groups of the environmental movement have modelled themselves along conventional pluralist lines, styling themselves as interest groups among many.[3] These groups have become quite successful, in terms of the model. Memberships and fund-raising have grown, access to the decision-making process has increased, an increasing number of mainstream environmentalists have moved into various nodes in that process, and policies were successfully negotiated (at least early in the process).

The zenith came as Bill Clinton and Al Gore were elected in 1992. After twelve years of exclusion and constant attacks by the Reagan and Bush administrations, the major groups were ecstatic. The Vice-President was the author of a best-selling book on the environment (Gore 1992), and more than twenty staff members of the major environmental groups entered the new administration, including Bruce Babbitt, former head of the League of Conservation Voters, and George Frampton, former president of the Wilderness Society. Those

[2] Numerous authors speak of the 'waves' of the environmental movement in different ways. I take the more broad historical approach and see the first wave as the initial growth of both conservationism and urban public-health concerns early in the century, the second wave as the massive upswing in interest in the 1960s and 1970s, and the third wave as its institutionalization in interest groups. This book analyses part of the fourth wave: the move back to the grassroots and alternative forms of organizing. Other authors want to distinguish more thoroughly between the conservationist focus early in the century and the more radical response to the degradations brought by industrialization in the 1960s and 1970s. I have two responses to this: (1) much environmental concern early in the century *was* in response to the degradations of industrialization: the progressive municipal house-keeping, or sewer socialist, movements which culminated in the development of the public-planning and public-health professions (Gottlieb 1993, Hoy 1995, Melosi 1980); the second wave was not necessarily more radical than the first, but there was a forgeting of the radical, and urban, past of environmental issues: (2) the radical and critical nature of environmentalism in the 1960s and 1970s was reined in by the institutionalization of the movement in the 1980s. Contemporary grass-roots environmentalism(s) resist that institutionalization, and that innovative resistance is part of what I wish to examine here.

[3] By major groups, I refer to many of those who were part of the 'Big Ten', or 'Green Group', of the 1980s, including: Natural Resources Defense Council (NRDC), National Wildlife Federation (NWF), Environmental Defense Fund (EDF), Sierra Club, National Audubon Society, Wilderness Society, and Friends of the Earth (FOE).

inside were finally friendly, and the doors were left open for their old acquaintances. Brock Evans, lobbyist for the Audubon Society, exemplified the euphoria of the time, commenting 'I can't tell you how wonderful it is to walk down the hall in the White House or government agency and be greeted by your first name' (quoted in Dowie 1995: 179). As an interest group in the model of conventional pluralism, the environmental mainstream had reached the highest pinnacle of success. Or had they?

The first two years of this supposed success story saw an Everglades plan favoring developers and sugar growers, support of bovine growth hormones, the first moves towards a repeal of the Delaney Clause's zero tolerance for carcinogens, the ousting of reform-minded Bureau of Land Management director Jim Baca, a political plan for Northwest forests that failed to take science seriously, the start-up of the heavily opposed Waste Technology Incorporated incinerator in Ohio,[4] a retreat on grazing price reform, retreat on elevating the Environmental Protection Agency to Cabinet-level, defeat in attempts to reform the 1872 mining law, the divisive battle on the North American Free Trade Agreement—and much more.[5] The 103rd Congressional session was generally acknowledged to be the worst on environmental issues in two decades. All of this, of course, was before the Democrats lost majority control of Congress, and the Republican-led 104th Congress attacked environmental protections head on.

Criticisms of the major environmental groups and their organizing model had been growing long before the problems with the Clinton administration became obvious. And they exemplify the problems earlier critics saw in the model of liberal pluralism. Much of the reproach focuses on the lack of diversity in the major groups, in terms of both ideas and participants. The insider, conciliatory nature of the Beltway process left many individuals and groups dealing with resource and wilderness issues frustrated. Their exits from the process in the early 1980s became the impetus for some of the more radical environmental organizations—some well-known, such as Earth First! and Sea Shepherd Society (Foreman 1991; Scarce 1990), others less so, but just as dedicated, such as the Native Forest Council. While many of the complaints from this school of *émigrés* on the lack of diversity

---

[4] This start-up was particularly angering to the anti-toxics movement, as Clinton and Gore had pledged to oppose the plant during their 1992 election campaign.
[5] See the discussion of the evolving relationship between the environmental mainstream and the early Clinton administration in Dowie 1995, ch. 7.

in the movement were limited—focusing solely on philosophical and strategic differences—the growing grassroots movements enthusiastically eschewed the pluralist model.

The emergent environmental justice community raised the issue of the lack of diversity to a new level, focusing on both the white, upper-middle class nature of the mainstream organizations and their avoidance of issues of concern to people of color and urban dwellers (Shabecoff 1990; Taylor 1992). While the lack of minority representation in the offices and on the boards of the major environmental groups was a focus, the more telling complaint centered on the movement's focus on natural resources, wilderness, endangered species and the like, rather than toxics, public health, and the unjust distribution of environmental risks. These issues of interest to low-income communities and communities of color had been left off the environmental agenda; the new movement's bringing them to the fore helped to expose the bias of the major groups' concerns (see Bullard 1994*b*).

In addition to the lack of both diversity and attention to environmental inequities, the *form* that mainstream environmental organizing has taken has angered grassroots activists attentive to resource and environmental justice issues. Specifically, critiques have addressed the centralization and hierarchical structure, the lack of democratic and community participation, and the general evolution of the major groups into professionalized interest groups practically indistinguishable from their adversaries. All of these concerns have made the mainstream at best alienating, and at worst irrelevant, in the eyes of many grassroots activists and critics (see e.g. Cockburn and St. Clair 1994; Dowie 1991, 1995; Gottlieb 1990; Montague 1995).[6]

The argument here is not just that the mainstream of the movement has failed in many ways, and become subject to criticism; it is also that the very form the movement has taken, styling itself in the

---

[6] Jeff St. Clair's (1995) description of the mainstream groups, part of a talk on the influence of major funding organizations on their agenda, is the most comprehensive lambasting of the movement I have seen: 'Somewhere along the line the environmental movement disconnected with the people. Rejected its political roots, pulled the plug on its vibrant tradition. It packed its bags, it starched its shirts and jetted to D.C. where it became what it once despised: a risk aversive, depersonalized, overly analytical, humorless, access-driven, intolerant, statistical, centralized, technocratic, deal-making, passionless, sterilized, direct-mailing, jock-strapped, lawyer-laden monolith to mediocrity.'

fashion of an interest group among many in the competitive political arena inside the Beltway, has led to that failure. In sum, while environmentalism's initial foray into the liberal-pluralist model produced much of the environmental policy in place in the US, it has failed, more recently, on two key counts. The first is the failure of the major groups to continue to secure gains within the model and to satisfy even the limited interests it represents. And the second is the obvious inadequacy of these groups in representing the diversity of environmental interests, identities, foci, and forms of action. In the grassroots, especially in the environmental justice movement, new demands and new forms of organizing attempt to address both of these failures.

Environmentalism and Difference

The argument of this study is that a return to pluralism—in its origins and its recent resurgence—might help to move political theory and practice beyond the limitations and exclusions of the conventional model of pluralism. A 'critical pluralism', defined in the following chapters, offers a way of understanding the construction of diverse understandings of and reactions to the reality of environmental degradation, and suggests political forms and practices that can encompass these differences. Attention to the differences inherent in the response to the environmental crisis can illuminate the reality and origins of that diversity, as well as illustrate the democratic potential of a new form of pluralism.

A number of authors have addressed what they see as the democratic potential of the political response to environmental problems and risk (e.g. Beck 1992; Dryzek 1995, 1997; Giddens 1994). All discuss the benefits of the decentralized, self-coordinated, and networked action that is common in grassroots environmentalism. But the reality of differences in environmental experiences is often absent from these discussions. Beck, for example, understands environmental risk as inherently egalitarian: 'smog is democratic' and 'risks display an equalizing effect' (Beck 1992: 36). The environmental justice movement, focused as it is on the unequal and arguably classist and racist distribution of environmental risk, is a persuasive

counter to Beck here.[7] But there is more missing in Beck than attention to the inequitable distribution of risk. Beck assumes that we all
experience risk in the same way. On the contrary, attention to some
real-world examples would have shown a world of difference.

Take the seemingly simple example of a polluted river. The
Willamette River, which flows near my old home in western Oregon,
has its origins in one of the purest bodies of water in the world; by
the time it flows into the Pacific, after joining the Columbia, it is one
of the most carcinogenic rivers in the US. This pollution is not as
singular an objective reality as it sounds; it is experienced differently
according to situation. Recent Asian immigrants in Portland, who
fish for food, experience both the pollution and environmental law
enforcement in a particular way. The risk is experienced differently
by parents whose children swim or play in the river downstream
from a paper mill which spews dioxin and other toxins into the
water. Those experiences differ from the biologist who studies skel-
etal deformities in fish, which affect 95 per cent of the squawfish
population in some stretches of the river. Finally, that pollution is
understood and experienced differently by a lobbyist for a major
environmental organization who is trying to draft compromise language for revisions in the Clean Water Act.[8] The experience and
knowledge of the same event differs, and, contrary to Beck, the risk is
not equally distributed across these experiences.

Part of the democratic potential of grassroots environmentalism is
in the *recognition* of these different experiences. The environmental
justice movement is based on the acknowledgment of diversity; it
is one important way environmental justice distinguishes itself
from mainstream environmentalism. Bringing out alternative environmental discourses that have not been equally heard—the
pluralization of environmentalism—is a central project of environmental justice. The key lesson to be learned from an examination of
the movement is not that environment or risk is the one unifying
commonality of modernity, as Beck argues, but that environment

[7] The literature which specifically examines the existence of environmental
inequity is quite broad. See e.g. Bullard 1993*b*, Lavelle and Coyle 1992, United
Church of Christ 1987. For a discussion of the criticisms of the inequity approach,
and a response, see Goldman 1996. Szasz and Meuser (1997) offer a constructive
overview of the literature.

[8] As many in the environmental justice movement argue, these different experiences are often based in cultural differences. See especially B. Lynch (1993).

offers a way of understanding the origins of one dimension of difference within modernity. In addition, the potential of contemporary
environmental politics stems from the inherently pluralistic and
democratic political practices developed by the grassroots—practices
that take difference as their core and attempt to recognize and bring
them into the political process.

The Justice of Environmental Justice: Equity, Recognition, and Political Participation

One cannot talk of the environmental justice movement without
discussing the notion of justice that is at its core. Obviously, the
justice in environmental justice refers, in one key respect, to the
inequity in the distribution of environmental risks. Here, the call
for environmental justice focuses on the problematic distribution of
environmental ills, which mirrors the inequity in socio-economic
and cultural status.

But 'equity' does not fully encompass the desires of the environmental justice movement. In fact, many in the movement were quite
critical of the EPA's first report on environmental justice issues,
entitled *Environmental Equity: Reducing Risk for All Communities*
(USEPA 1992). While many criticized the EPA for its focus on 'equity',
as opposed to *in*equity, a major concern was the lack of attention
paid to activists and academics who had been involved in environmental justice issues, and a lack of concern on the part of the EPA to
involve affected communities in resolving problems of environmental justice.[9] The concept of *recognition* was missing from the EPA's
definition. It was the narrow focus on 'equity' that was one of the
central critiques; the report, and the process of its development,
failed to recognize and represent diverse concepts of justice in the
environmental justice community.

The justice demanded by the environmental justice movement is
really threefold, and begins with two central issues: *inequity* in the
distribution of environmental risk, and *recognition* of the diversity of
the participants and experiences in the environmental-justice movement. As Nancy Fraser has written, these are really the two major
issues of justice in recent social movements. 'Justice today', she

---

[9] See the comments of the external reviewers to the 1992 report (USEPA 1992: ii).

argues, 'requires *both* redistribution *and* recognition' (1997: 12). Justice also requires an understanding of the way in which unjust distribution and lack of recognition are tied together. Unfortunately, Fraser notes, theorists have generally insisted on a dichotomy between the two concepts, by focusing on one or the other (pp. 11–15). The argument here, however, is that the environmental-justice movement, through its focus on both distribution of environmental ills and the recognition of the communities involved, illustrates the very real possibility of getting beyond such a theoretical impasse in political practice.

For the environmental justice movement, this integration of distributional equity and recognition comes in the form of the demand for more *public participation* in the development, implementation, and oversight of environmental policy. In a sense, the movement argues that *procedural* equity is a way to address both distribution and recognition. Through public participation, activists and communities may accomplish both more equitable distribution of environmental risks (or, more ideally, a decrease in toxic exposure and environmental risks for all) and the recognition of various communities, cultures, and understandings of environmental health and sustainability. So the demand for a more open, communicative, and participatory political process is how the environmental justice movement brings together—and attempts to address—the issues of distribution and recognition. The movement's concern with political participation and more open policy-making processes is central: justice is seen as an issue of equity and of recognition.

While there has been much written on the distributive element of environmental justice, there has been less on the specific issues of recognition and a participatory political process in the movement. Robert Lake (1996: 162) has complained that the movement itself 'generally overemphasizes issues of distributive justice' and 'adopts an unnecessarily truncated notion of procedural justice'. But there is much within the movement's literature and its political action to demonstrate the very key focus on recognition and participatory process. Benjamin Chavis, who coined the term 'environmental racism', includes 'the history of excluding people of color from the mainstream environmental groups, decisionmaking boards, commissions, and regulatory bodies' in his definition of the term (1993: 3). Dorceta Taylor's (1992, 1993) work on the necessity of *inclusion* of anti-toxics and environmental justice activists in the environmental movement appeared alongside evidence of environmental inequity in the two earliest collections on environmental justice (Bryant and Mohai 1992; Bullard 1993*a*). The Principles of Environmental Justice, adopted at the First National People of Color Environmental Leadership Conference in 1991, include elements of recognition of difference and mutual respect, as well as political participation and self-determination. The National Environmental Justice Advisory Council (NEJAC) includes a subcommittee on public participation, which has developed a Model Plan for Public Participation (USEPA 1996*a*). The structure of public participation in environmental policy-making has been central to the movement from Love Canal (Gibbs 1982) to current discussions of brownfields redevelopment (Lee 1996). Issues of public participation in the political process are integral to the environmental justice movement, and central to the very definition of environmental justice. This is not to say that process is *more* important to the movement than the inequitable distribution of environmental risks to people of color and low-income communities; rather, a focus on process is seen as a method of addressing *both* the inequity and the recognition of these communities.

Pluralism in Theory and Practice

Finally, it is crucial to examine the evolution of pluralism in *both* theory and practice. While a number of political theorists have focused on particular aspects of the critical pluralism I describe (see Chapters 3 and 4), none brings together all of these issues and none thoroughly examines these concepts in the practice of an existing social movement. Works by Ulrich Beck and Beck with Anthony Giddens and Scott Lash (Beck 1992, 1995; Beck *et al.* 1994) address the democratic potential of the response to ecological problems, but fail to focus on the potential of *difference* in this response, and do not address the evolution of democratic practice in environmentalism as they remain, above all, in the realm of theory. These works then lack attention to real-world experiences and practice—witness Beck on the equity of risk. Recent literature on democracy and difference (Benhabib 1996*a*, Phillips 1993, Young 1990) illustrates the same problem. Much of this literature calls for various representational systems that will result in the inclusion of more diverse voices. But closer attention to the relationship between diversity and democracy in social movements such as the environmental justice movement, for example, would have shown an interest not just in equitable *representation* at the level of the state, but in ongoing diverse *recognition* and *participation* at a variety of levels and a number of practices of environmental policy-making, organizational politics, and community life. Attention to a movement based, in part, in the recognition of diversity will help to shed light on the hands-on ways activists and community members have realized some of the potential of difference, plurality, and democracy. Social movements and political practice offer more than just fodder for social theorists. In addition to spurring some political and social theorists in new directions, they are living examples of evolving political relationships and reflections which can be examined to illuminate a variety of ongoing theoretical issues.

On the other hand, though there is much literature in environmental justice, the vast majority of that literature is dedicated to demonstrating the problems of environmental inequity and bringing the movement to a larger audience. Very little of the environmental justice literature focuses on, and relates the movement to, larger theoretical issues, such as the importance of acknowledgement of diversity within, or on the evolution of political practices and demands of, the movement. My focus in this project, then, is not just to examine developments in the realm of pluralist theory, but to explore how the environmental justice movement embodies new forms of critical pluralist practice.

Pluralism, defined as a politics based in the recognition of difference, has evolved in both theory and practice. The critical pluralism that I describe in the following chapters poses a challenge to the conventional model of liberal pluralism, offers a promise of inclusion and participation to those alienated by the political processes engendered by conventional pluralism, and illustrates the democratic potential of the acknowledgment of difference.

Preview and Plan

Unfortunately, attention to the environmental movement does not guarantee a sense of respect for its diversity. Chapter 2, therefore, is dedicated to a study of the limitations inherent in various approaches to the study of environmentalism(s). The argument there is that many examiners are more interested in building explanatory models than in understanding the diversity of environmentalism; hence, many models are built on a foundation of exclusion.

I move on, in Chapter 3, to examine a genealogy of pluralist approaches to multiplicity and difference in the twentieth century. William James (1976 [1912], 1977 [1909]) began his study of pluralism with a 'radical empiricism' that is opposed to a more singular, monist position. James argued that our experiences of empirical events diverge, and one explanation could never encompass all of those experiences. More recently, Donna Haraway's (1988) description of 'situated knowledges' and 'embodied objectivity' resurrects James. She argues for 'epistemologies of location' where claims of knowledge can only be considered partial. The argument here is that a return to such original notions of pluralism helps to validate the diversity of experiences and knowledges that grow out of the variety of ways we are all situated in any number of experiences, including environmental degradation.

The acceptance of multiplicity as the precondition of political action is central to the new generation of theorists and activists I call critical pluralists. In political and social theory, a range of authors has finally begun to respond to a lament broached by Mary Parker Follett in 1918. Pluralists early in the century had acknowledged difference, she noted, but they had not gotten to the heart of the question: what is to be done with this diversity? In Chapter 4, I examine some of the contemporary responses to Follett's question and construct a list of *practices* necessary in order to build political relations across difference. These get at issues of justice beyond the material, concerning both recognition and participatory process. I argue that agonistic respect (Connolly 1991), attempts at intersubjective understanding (Benhabib 1992; Habermas 1970*a*, 1970*b*; Honneth 1992), inclusive, open discourse free from domination and the possibility of reprisals (Dryzek 1990*a*; Forester 1989; Habermas 1984, 1987*a*), and the development of a particular form of solidarity are all crucial to the practices suggested by a new generation of pluralist theory.

Agonistic respect exceeds the bounds of past pluralist notions of 'tolerance' of others. The evolution from toleration to agonistic respect includes the democratizing ingredient of the 'cultivation of care' for the positions and responses of others. Tied to this agonistic respect is a re-evaluation of political discourse. The partisan and resource-oriented nature of communication in the last generation of pluralism led to various distortions of process and the exclusion of numerous positions. A critical pluralism notes these problems and advocates a more open, participatory, and intersubjective process of communication.

Solidarity is a more complicated matter, one that has vexed pluralism through all three generations. The problem centers on the process of reconciling difference with the need for concerted political action. I focus on how the notion of unity suggested by Follett was discarded by the second generation of pluralism, but is now mirrored by numerous contemporary theorists, including Rorty (1989), Haraway (1991), and Deleuze and Guattari (1987).

The central claim of this work is that the diverse and fast-growing environmental justice movement in the US embodies these newly emerging concepts and practices, and so I turn to the movement for examples of this critical pluralism in practice. Chapter 5 examines how, in practice, organizing based on the validity of multiplicity has increasingly taken on the form of alliances and networks. The Citizen's Clearinghouse for Hazardous Waste (CCHW)[10] and the Southwest Network for Environmental and Economic Justice (SNEEJ) serve as illustrations here, as they have both consciously and deliberately organized in a manner distinct from the liberal pluralist model. The emphasis on networks of semi-autonomous local groups, rather than large-scale organizations based in Washington, D.C., illustrates the importance of recognition and participation *within* the movement, and not simply in movement demands on governments and corporations.

Chapter 6 explores how the environmental justice movement has taken on some of the communicative and participatory demands and practices of critical pluralism. The movement has been critical of the communicative methods of the mainstream—the top-down organizational structure and its one-way nature of communication, and the lack of attention to issues of public participation in policy-making (see e.g. Bullard 1993*a*; Di Chiro 1992; Krauss 1994; Miller 1993; Moore and Head 1993; Szasz 1994; Taylor 1992). Issues of communication have been a central focus in the development and demands of environmental justice. Accepting the diversity and the situated experiences of individuals and cultures has fostered the use of, and

---

[10] Now known as the Center for Health, Environment, and Justice (CHEJ).

demand for, a variety of innovative communicative processes. Internally, the movement has attempted to employ more open discursive processes, paying particular attention to communication within and across diverse groups. Externally, the movement has made demands with regard to issues of communication and more discursive and participatory policy-making on government agencies, particularly the US Environmental Protection Agency (EPA).

It is important to note that much of the literature that I examine in these two chapters comes from sympathetic advocates of environmental justice, both participants and academic participant-observers. I rely primarily on the literature of the movement—pamphlets, newsletters, commentaries, articles, edited collections, meeting proceedings, internet mailing lists, and websites—in addition to discussions with activists and advocates. There is a wealth of data available, and it is a wonderful source for academic inquiry. Still, it should be noted that there is very little reportage from non-leaders or non-spokespeople within the movement, and a limited amount of literature available on the practices of the movement from beyond its borders—from either academics or other environmentalists. I saw my task as exploring and laying out an evolving form of political practice that is inherent in the environmental justice movement and reflected in its literature, but that has not been fully developed from within, nor addressed from without. While I lay out the stated political desires of the movement from its own literature, I attempt to retain a critical approach to that literature. In this vein, I will on occasion note places where the practices of environmental justice do not always live up to the aspirations of the critical pluralism I discuss.

In concluding, in Chapter 7, I begin an evaluation of critical pluralism in practice. *Begin* because both critical pluralism and the environmental justice movement are young, and a thorough evaluation will have to be done over time. At this point, however, we can explore the successes of the model and the movement, as well as some of the possible problems it faces now and in the future. In this initial attempt at evaluation, I address a number of questions about the value and sustainability of critical pluralist practice in the environmental justice movement, as well as the possibility of the expansion of such practices into the larger environmental movement.

Both pluralism and the environmental movement have evolved tremendously in this century. The myriad ways people define and experience 'environment' gives credence to a form of pluralism that takes diversity seriously. Acknowledging this multiplicity, however, calls for a form of organization, methods of communicating, and institutional design quite distinct from the model of liberal pluralism on which the mainstream of the environmental movement has been based. The purpose here is to explore how both the theory and practice of a new form of pluralism acknowledge difference and develop relations and actions across that difference.

2

Approaches to Difference in the US Environmental Movement: Classification Schemes, Hegemonic Definitions, and Singular Motivations

In the vast literature of what can be called political ecology, most examiners have dealt with political reasons for environmental problems, suggestions for environmental policy, critiques of policy approaches, surveys of public attitudes, or suggestions for a 'new' politics. But comparatively little has been written on the environmental movement in the United States—the large-scale following and variety of political actions environmentalism engenders. The work that has been done on the environmental movement generally falls into four areas. Examiners offer particular versions of the movement's history; they look at environmentalists and attempt to classify them by types; they take environmentalism as a whole and attempt to forge a singular definition; or they focus on particular motivations for environmental concern and action. With all of the growth and diversification evident in environmental identities and political action over the course of this century, very few examiners of the contemporary environmental movement can discuss it without resorting to some sort of simplification scheme. The academic community's attempts to understand or explain the environmental movement is based on the exclusion of diversity—the vast majority attempt to herd a broad movement into ideological corrals incapable of holding the whole.

What is generally missing in examinations of the environmental movement is attention to the evolution of variety and diversity in environmental theory and action, as well as the range of innumerable motivations for developing environmental concern. The sense one gets from much of this literature is that the diversity of the movement, its actions, and motivations, is a hindrance not only to understanding environmentalism, but to the success of the movement as well. My argument, rather, is that the myriad motivations and the variety in the movement help us examine the widespread and insidious nature of environmental damage, and the diverse experience of that damage. The reason for so much diversity in the movement—in its history, theory, action, and motivations—is simply the variety of problems, conditions, and experiences that instigate responses and forge resistance. Ultimately, I argue that various environmentalisms evolve out of diverse situations, and that a single definition of the movement, its motivations, or its aims, is not only impossible, but unnecessary and counterproductive. Rather, if the environmental movement is to be successful, the recognition of the various backgrounds, definitions, and political acts of environmentalism—and their innate validity—needs to become a practice of both the movement and its study.

Before getting to this argument, and in order to illuminate it, I will critically examine the current state of the literature on the environmental movement. The methods of classification, the attempt to forge an environmental vanguard, and the myriad claims to unlocking the motivations of environmental actors will be addressed. First, however, I want to take a brief look at the limits of standard histories of the environmental movement.

Histories of Exclusion

Histories are always an exercise in framing, and histories of environmentalism are no exception. Standard histories of the US environmental movement (such as Fox 1981; Nash 1982; Petulla 1980; Sale 1993; Shabecoff 1993) frame the movement in such a way as to make some voices much more audible, and some issues much more visible, than others.

Most standard histories include the familiar figures of the romantic and transcendental age. Emerson and Thoreau, with their understandings of the beauty and power of nature beyond its resource value, are examined to set the stage for the movement. Immersed in the experience of a transcendental nature, John Muir began to

publicize the plight of the wilderness as more and more of it fell
to the axe, the mine, or the dam. Hence came the birth of a movement and its first major organization, the Sierra Club. Along with
Muir came his nemesis Gifford Pinchot, first chief of the Forest
Service, who represented the conservationist 'gospel of efficiency',
and aimed to replace the existing destruction of the wilderness not
with transcendental awe, but with rational economic planning by
technical experts. The conflict between these two figures is the origin
story in all of the standard histories of the movement (see e.g. Nash
1982). Their encounter over the building of a dam in the Hetch-
Hetchy Valley near Yosemite is the defining battle of the movement,
between two different visions of the relationship with nature. And it
is this continuing battle between preservationist and conservationist
ideas and personalities which constructs the trajectory of environmental history.

What is usually absent in these accounts are issues of class, of race,
of the role of women in the movement, and of relations with the
working and urban poor. While accounts have surfaced of the role of
women in conservation (see Merchant 1985), these discussions have
not reached many of the most recent historians of the movement
(see e.g. Shabecoff 1993). Only Fox (1981) delves into the distasteful
history of the racism of some conservationists, around issues of
immigrant hunting habits and civil rights.

These histories are more likely to define key events in the movement around the battles of wilderness and resources, rather than
those in urban and industrial environments, and as such, they nar-
rowly define a much broader movement. Mentions of Alice Hamilton, the premier investigator of occupational hazards in the US, or
Lewis Mumford, a harsh critic of the urban environment, are almost
entirely absent.[1] Contemporaneously with the early preservationists
and conservationists, an environmental movement grew in the cities
that was unconnected to wilderness and natural resources. Industrialization brought with it the need for the resources of nature, ration-
ally controlled or not, but it also brought more industry and
centralization to the cities. Environmental problems grew in urban
areas: sewage and wastewater, varieties of solid waste, clean water and
air, and noise, along with the health problems associated with
them—all became issues central to the municipal housekeeping and

[1] Gottlieb (1993) is the notable exception here.

settlement movements which focused on the conditions of daily life in urban neighborhoods (see e.g. Melosi 1980).

Environmental organizing around these urban issues, as well as workplace safety and health, and the special injustices faced by the poor, women, and minorities, are simply excluded from the standard histories. Certainly, the links between urban and occupational environmental ills and the loss of wilderness and resources were drawn only tenuously early in the century.[2] One would think that as urban and non-resource issues have come more to the forefront of the environmental movement, recent attempts at history would be more open to the existing diversity, but this is not necessarily the case. Recent histories, including those of Sale (1993) and Shabecoff (1993), continue the tradition of excluding or slighting large portions of the movement, even as these become areas of the most intense organizing in the US environmental movement.

These continued exclusions in the understanding of the past translate into exclusions in the contemporary movement. Concerns with urban issues, pollution, and environmental injustices are treated as 'new' portions of the movement, emerging only after Rachel Carson's *Silent Spring* in 1962 and Earth Day 1970.[3] They are seen not as a part of the traditional movement, but as outsiders pushing to expand the realm of environmentalism. Even as the focus of environmental awareness and activism began to incorporate and integrate the urban and occupational ills of industrialization with the abuse and destruction of wilderness and natural resources, the major organizations were slow to follow. Industrial, urban, and toxics issues, and their advocates, are then either ignored or placed behind the traditional issues of resources and wilderness in the agendas of the major organizations.[4] Hence, the need for civil-rights and environmental justice

[2] The most interesting example of this was the Progressive Party, led by Theodore Roosevelt. Jane Addams, who advocated for municipal housekeeping in Chicago, delivered one of the speeches nominating Roosevelt for the presidential ticket in 1912. After defeat in the election, the Party established a 'Progressive Service'—a type of shadow Cabinet—which brought together urban and resource environmental issues by including a Department of Conservation headed by Gifford Pinchot and a Department of Social and Industrial Justice headed by Jane Addams (Gottlieb 1993: 66).

[3] See e.g. Hal Rothman's characterization of 'A New Set of Concerns' in the 1960s (Rothman 1998: 84–94).

[4] See the priorities outlined in the Big Ten's *Environmental Agenda for the Future* (Adams *et al.* 1985), and note especially the lack of toxics, urban, or environmental justice issues in that document.

organizations to lambast the policies and practices of these major groups.

There are, however, some signs that the reality and worth of diversity in the movement is beginning to be recognized—at least by academics. On the historical front, 'stories less told' of the past are beginning to be re-examined, and a refusal of narrow definitions of the present has increased (see especially Darnovsky 1992; Foster 1994; Gottlieb 1993). These broader histories have two key goals. First of all, they draw our attention to the long histories of problems of urban pollution and show the parallel problems in the past and present: urban crowding, water quality, sewage and sanitation, solid and hazardous waste, air emissions, and occupational and public-health issues. Rather than seeing these problems as newly emerging in the 1960s and 1970s, or as infringements on the long-standing dominance of resource and wilderness issues in the movement, these accounts allow us to see the long history of our contemporary pollution, toxics, occupational health, and environmental justice problems.

In making links with the past, the purpose is also to broaden the conception of contemporary environmentalism. By breaking down the barriers between the various environmentalisms of the past, a revised history helps break down those barriers today. By examining the long histories of urban, workplace, and racial environmental problems, those issues no longer look new and outside the 'traditional' environmental movement. These new histories help to shift the boundaries of contemporary environmentalism (Darnovsky 1992: 28) and put pressure on the mainstream to acknowledge movement diversity from the past and in the present.

Classifying Variety

The simplification of the movement continues in two other common academic responses to the variety in environmentalism. Some examiners attempt to establish a classification scheme in which one can place all the different sorts of environmentalists. Others attempt to draw all this diversity together and forge a singular common identity.

For some, all of the arguments occurring in the environmental realm up to the present can be traced back to the expression of the two very different but long-standing traditions. This view asserts that the split between more traditional and conservative conservation groups and the more radical parts of the environmental movement today is simply a manifestation of basic differences between the utilitarian and romantic attitudes that began at the turn of the century. Different types of action in the movement are explained by positing that the 'romantics' inspire the more democratic strand of the movement while the utilitarians remain 'non-challenging'. This scheme is echoed in numerous works. Sandbach (1980) divides the movement into 'ecological/scientific' and 'humanist' branches. Devall and Sessions (1985) distinguish their brand of 'deep' ecology from more mainstream 'shallow' environmentalism, making the connection between deep ecology and past figures in the preservationist movement. Petulla (1980) goes a step further into a tripartite scheme of biocentric, ecological/scientific, and economic/efficiency branches, dividing the more professionalized aspects of the movement.

Another common dichotomization is an 'us versus them' scenario. The Sprouts (1978), for example, simplify the conflicting postures in the environmental debate into the existing 'exploitive posture' versus the 'mutualistic challenge' of ecologists. Milbrath offers this same type of scheme in his *Environmentalists: Vanguard for a New Society* (1984). His model of the environmental movement puts people in one of two camps: supporters of the 'old' paradigm, and supporters of the 'new' (1984: 23). The 'new' paradigm seems to be a vast ideology with little or no internal dissent—Milbrath tosses together a variety of contemporary environmental identities such as deep ecology, social ecology, and geocentrism into a single environmental 'vanguard', downplaying their differences as they struggle together in the face of the likewise singular, old dominant paradigm. It is not that Milbrath does not see the differences and variety in the movement—he offers two different classification schemes based on the desire for environmental and social change—but these schemes depend on sympathies one might have about the 'old' paradigm or the 'new', rather than on the variety of views, ideas, critiques, and identities spawned by the movement itself. Milbrath then retreats even from this limited acknowledgment of difference back into a reassertion of the rearguard/vanguard split.

Other authors, such as Cotgrove and O'Riordan, begin with the same type of fairly obvious or easily visible split between the 'traditional' and the 'radical' forms of environmentalism (Cotgrove 1982:

5), or the technocentric versus ecocentric themes within the movement (O'Riordan 1976: 1). But rather than simplifying from this point, both of their works go on to lay out the numerous differences and divisions in the movement. Cotgrove describes what he sees as differences in major *goals* of normative change or more general value changes, as well as differences in predominant *strategies* of mere personal transformation or larger societal manipulation (1982: 11). In a similar vein, O'Riordan begins to examine how some areas of the environmental movement expand the normal realm of political action, from advocacy and policy lobbying to more direct and participatory forms. While neither of these works, as attempts to examine the whole of 'environmentalism', focus specifically on the movement and its political strategies, they begin the process of understanding the environmental movement, including its various action components, as a very heterogeneous and differentiated beast.

The most thorough of the classification schemes is the attention Schnaiberg gives to the contemporary environmental movement in his 1980 work on *The Environment*. Schnaiberg (1980: 336) argues that the

modern 'environmental movement' is sufficiently diverse that a question arises as to whether it is really proper to label such diversity with a single name. Environmental organizations and their memberships differ often in their choice of concern over particular environmental withdrawals and additions, in their analysis of the social causes of such ecological changes, and in their prescriptions for appropriate social changes.

In dealing with the differences among groups, Schnaiberg distances himself from other more dichotomizing authors. He breaks down the movement into four different profiles: cosmetologists, meliorists, reformists, and radicals. The first two of these profiles emphasize consumption issues and voluntary consumer action. Cosmetologists are mostly concerned with aesthetic problems, such as littering, and criticize 'people' for being careless. Meliorists, on the other hand would be those concerned with the growth of waste in general; they tend to call for large-scale recycling. The latter two profiles locate problems in the sphere of production and emphasize broader sociopolitical solutions rather than voluntary consumer-oriented ones. Reformists recognize the ecological problems that come with production and call for a variety of political and economic incentives to reduce them, while radicals stress the inevitability of exceeding ecological limits in the growth orientation of advanced industrial production and call for vast economic and social restructuring.

Schnaiberg's analysis is important because he undertakes a broad dissection of the various groups by their own definitions, tactics and critiques, rather than remaining content with the old romantic/ utilitarian opposition. He moves away from the tendency to dichotomize the myriad groups in the movement or to prescribe a singular or particular ideology for its success (though his sympathies admittedly lie with the radical alternative technologists). Still, his fourfold classification scheme continues to minimize differences and exclude some forms of identity and action. With this, Schnaiberg misses the opportunity to make the link between the movement and his otherwise thorough examination of the varied genesis of environmental problems.[5]

Defining the Environmental Vanguard

Milbrath (1984), in addition to his dichotomization, exemplifies another common approach to the study of the movement—the explicit attempt to forge a new, singular paradigm of environmental politics, in his case led by a 'vanguard'. This type of attempt to round up and mould the variety of environmentalisms into a consistent, sound ideology is offered in a couple of different ways. While it is obvious that different types of environmentalism attempt to get others to come over to their views (the deep ecologists, for example), the phenomenon described here is one that attempts to see similarities in the variety of environmental*isms* and produce a singular, encompassing image of environmental*ism*.

Likewise, Robert Paehlke, in his *Environmentalism and the Future of Progressive Politics* (1989), understands the varieties of ideas and practices that may be alluded to when discussing 'environmentalism'; but he goes on to attempt to draw many of them together into a singular ideology (much like Milbrath's), which he asserts to be the foundation of any future progressive politics. Toward this end, Paehlke lays

---

[5] It should be stressed that Schnaiberg was writing in 1980, before the expansion of interest and participation in the environmental movement during that decade. It is possible that he would include more classes in his system at this later date. In fact, much of Schnaiberg's more recent work focuses on the effects of industrialization in numerous issues and battles. See Gould *et al.* 1996.

down a construct of environmentalism that is drawn from the ideas of many individuals 'only a few of whom might accept the whole perspective' (1989: 3). The reasoning behind this is the quite common tenet that there is a tendency to closure in ideology that is in some way inevitable, 'since one cannot come to a coherent political view without shutting out something of other intelligent versions of reality' (p. 5). The problem here, however, is what is shut out. While the aim is to develop a strong environmental and progressive politics, the first step is the exclusion of a portion of the existing movement.

Paehlke builds past environmental ideas and present views into an environmental ideology in a very singular sense, arguing that it is a program aimed at a 'majority appeal' focusing on the 'medium term' (1989: 243, 253). While he mentions the importance of this environmentalism remaining more 'open' and 'adaptable' (pp. 5, 177) than past ideologies, Paehlke lays out what he sees as key value assertions of 'environmentalism', including respect for other species as well as democracy and autonomy among our own (pp. 144–5).

Unfortunately, his system leaves out ideas that are important to some in the movement, while not acknowledging the difficulties other activists or scholars might have with his list. For example, in asserting this overarching value system, Paehlke downplays potential and actual conflicts over values (e.g. ecocentrism/technocentrism, spirituality), issues (e.g. population, multiple use) and tactics (i.e. lobbying, boycotts, or direct action). His singular value system also appears to be internally contradictory: Paehlke includes the value of 'humility' regarding the human species to other species, but not humility of humans toward each other's differing ideas. While Paehlke shows concern for this issue elsewhere (Paehlke 1988), a key problem remains: if his final value of autonomy in the movement is to be taken seriously, how can one assert such a singular environmental value system for all participants?

While Paehlke attempts to develop a progressive environmentalism by extrapolating from what he sees as key *values*, Bryan Norton has argued in *Toward Unity among Environmentalists* (1991) along the lines of similar *policy* desires. While noting the advantage of using different strategies or values in different contexts or to different constituents (pp. 191, 205), Norton both describes and pushes for a convergence towards consensus on policy issues (p. 187). He complains that the single greatest weakness of the environmental movement is its inability to form a single, long-term plan for the future;

but argues that the movement can encompass a real pluralism in values while pushing a united policy front organized around 'quality growth' (p. 119), the acceptance of some types of economically justifiable pollution (p. 134), and 'common sense' limits on conservation (p. 153). In so doing, he both derides and ignores those with policy objectives outside his 'unity' (e.g. a whole range of deep and social ecologists, and advocates for environmental justice).

So we have on the one hand an argument for a singular system of environmental *values* which leaves open the question of policies and tactics, and on the other hand an argument for consensus on *policy* that accepts the moral pluralism of the movement. Both approaches accept some diversity, some contextuality, some variety in responses to environmental conditions—yet both authors argue for the need for a singularity or consensus on one or the other of these aspects of the movement. This practice of recognizing the movement's diversity, followed by criticisms of it and subsequent efforts toward synthesis is common in the recent literature (see also Caldwell 1990; Callicott 1990; Young 1990). According to these views, a particular picture of 'progressivism' of values, a moral monism, or a consensus on policy is the necessary precursor to the success of the environmental movement.

The problem here, again, is simply what is left out. With all his concern for the 'adaptability' of an environmental politics, Paehlke still insists on the 'tendency to closure' that will inevitably shut some out (Paehlke 1989: 5). Others are not quite so gracious in their exclusions. Walter Rosenbaum, for example, discusses the 'diversity of viewpoints, social support, and political strategies' within environmentalism, but limits his discussion of this diversity to the core coalition of the Group of Ten (Rosenbaum 1985: 70-1)! Robert Goodin argues quite frankly, in the preface to his *Green Political Theory*, that his aim is to show 'what positions greens *should* take, given their core concerns—whether or not they actually do . . . This amounts, politically, to an attempt to rescue greens from themselves' (Goodin 1992: p. viii).

In sum, classification and hegemonic definitions in the literature on environmentalism minimize the variety within the movement; and they do this under the assumption that diversity is a weakness. This assumption is necessary for action only within a limited notion of liberal pluralism, and is problematic if one believes that the variety is the basis for a new form of pluralism.

Environmental Motivations

In addition to attempts at limited histories, classification, or singular definition, a fourth common approach to the study of the environmental movement is to examine the motivations of environmental activists. Rather than focus on types of environmentalists and environmental policies, this approach emphasizes the root causes of environmental concern. The basic question asked is why or how environmental activism arises. Some researchers look at the values of the actors. Are they post-material, or simply consumerist? Others examine the types of political or social alienation or deprivations those who turn to environmentalism are faced with. And still others examine the precursors to the movement—what resources are available to them that enable action?

In assessing the values of actors within the environmental movement, numerous authors refer to Inglehart's 'post-materialism' (Inglehart 1971, 1981, 1990). Those with post-material values emphasize quality of life, community, self-expression, and human and political rights rather than issues of sustenance and security, since the latter basic needs have presumably already been met for the majority in Western industrialized nations (Inglehart 1971: 880). Post-materialism has been used to explain why the new social movements, including environmentalism, are less class- or economically based than past movements, such as labor or Marxist struggles.

In addition to the new values at the base of these movements, post-materialism can be used to explain the growth of the movements in general, as well as the expansion of political tactics within them. Inglehart argues that post-materialist values are expanding as the population that originally organized around them continues to age and pass these values on to their followers and offspring (Inglehart 1981, 1990). These new post-materialists continue the willingness to engage in political protest beyond the boundaries of standard institutions (Inglehart 1981: 891)—moving from electoral and legislative practices to protests, boycotts, and direct action.

But not all examiners of the environmental movement agree on this post-material thesis. Samuel Hays (1982, 1987), for example, examines the *materialist* base of the environmental movement. The growth of the environmental movement after the Second World War, for Hays, was due simply to the growth in material consumer demands. While he recognizes that later years have been marked, at times, by a social movement with social roots and new social values, Hays argues that these values still reflect a market mentality, a desire for environmental amenities. Post-war environmentalism is part of the more general growth of consumer culture's demands for more products. Hays sees 'environmental values as part of evolving consumer values' (1982: 22). Clean air and water, mountains and deserts to explore, forests and rivers to enjoy—all these Hays labels simply 'consumer wants' (p. 17). Environmentalism, then, is simply the fight to expand the consumption of environmental amenities, not a new social movement struggle for the broader demands of post-materialism.

But while the post-materialist thesis includes an attempt to explain the expansion of political tactics, Hays cannot explain why it is that 'consumers' take on increasingly more radical actions, such as product boycotts, other changes in consumptive habits, and even direct action. Nor can Hays's materialism account for why many of the actions of contemporary environmentalists implicitly and explicitly criticize aspects of a consumer identity, e.g. the criticisms of a culture of wasteful consumption, the gospel of unbridled economic growth, and the very notion of human-centeredness.

Some environmental organizations and practices do, in fact, fall under the consumerist definition that Hays asserts—demands for better national parks and healthier food are part of a long-standing consumer tradition in the movement—but there is much more at work in the movement as a whole. Likewise, the post-material thesis must acknowledge that many in the environmental movement *are* simply looking for material gain and more parks or wilderness to 'consume' during retreats and vacations.[6]

In addition to the focus on values to explain the motivations and varied actions of the environmental movement, other authors concentrate on the variety of political and social alienations faced by these actors. In the political realm, the emphasis is on alienation both from the input of political decisions and from the outcome of these decisions.

Herbert Kitschelt's (1986) work, a study of the difference in the actions of anti-nuclear groups in different nations, is a good example

---

[6] Inglehart acknowledges that the dualism of material/post-material is most likely artificial. He notes (1981: 885) that he is not dealing with pure materialists and post-materialists, but a continuum of people whose emphases are in one direction or the other, and vary in strength.

of an analysis that focuses on alienation from political input. The differences between the tactics of these groups are to be understood in terms of what Kitschelt calls 'political opportunity structures'—the degree to which political systems are 'open' or 'closed'. When political systems are 'open' and weak, Kitschelt argues, they invite assimilative strategies. Movements attempt to work with the accessible established institutions of these systems through lobbying, petitioning government bodies, and influencing public policy through partisan politics and referendum. When access is limited in more 'closed' political systems, movements are more likely to adopt more confrontational and disruptive strategies such as public demonstrations, civil disobedience, and site occupations which are obviously orchestrated outside of established institutional political channels (pp. 67–8).

What is useful in this argument is the acknowledgment of the importance of movement variation; what is problematic is that Kitschelt deals only with variation *across* nations, and not *within* them. Kitschelt does not in any way acknowledge the variety of strategies in the US, where the anti-nuclear movement has clearly embodied a wide spectrum of action strategies (see e.g. the work of Epstein 1991). Kitschelt argues that US groups are assimilative in their strategies, given the supposed 'open' political system of this country. Even after acknowledging that many US groups have practiced direct-action strategies, Kitschelt argues that these were simply an 'imported . . . aberration' (1986: 68). In his attempt to develop a simple model, Kitschelt has simply failed to recognize the reality of political action of anti-nuclear groups in the US. Direct action against nuclear facilities has been a major component of the movement, and these types of actions have been a central strategy and common practice, not aberrations.

Still, there is much to be gained in applying the concept of political opportunity structures as a factor in political action if we drop the all-encompassing notion of the US as an 'open' system and instead deal with the *perceptions* and *experiences* of the system by individual actors and the various groups comprising the movement. We can then hypothesize that those who perceive or experience *openness* in the political system opt for more reconciliatory strategies, while those who perceive or experience a more *closed* system would choose more confrontational methods. Cotgrove, in a similar vein, asserts that 'where belief in the reasonableness of the political system, and its openness to reasoned argument and debate, break down, the normal channels of petition, protest, and pressure group tactics come to be seen as inadequate' (1982: 82). The key here is 'belief'. If beliefs about the openness of the political system vary, then there is no contradiction in both reconciliatory and confrontational methods being used either in the movement as a whole or by one particular, though diverse, group.

But perceptions of the relative openness of the political system for varieties of input is only one side of the perception of political alienation. It is not only frustration with the *process* of political systems that might be alienating, but disagreement with the *outcomes* as well. Robyn Eckersley, for example, contends that it is not alienation *per se*, but 'moral and intellectual disagreement with the results of conventional politics' that motivates participants in the environmental movement to expand their tactics (1989: 213). Freudenberg and Steinsapir give political alienation as one of the reasons for the expansion of the grassroots, anti-toxics wing of the movement (1992: 29). Many in these movements had not previously identified themselves as environmentalists, let alone activists; they had been private citizens, homeowners, mothers, etc., becoming involved in the anti-toxics movement when they lost faith in government or business to address their concerns satisfactorily (see e.g. Cable and Cable 1995; Gibbs 1982; Krauss 1994; Pardo 1990).

Numerous actors in various areas of the environmental movement have attempted conventional political routes, met with limited success, and then moved on to other strategies. Claus Offe discusses how 'those who use nonconventional practices of political action do not do so because they lack experience with (or are unaware of) available conventional forms of political participation; on the contrary, these nonconventional actors are relatively experienced in, and often frustrated with, conventional practices and their limitations' (1985: 855). Movements frustrated with the status quo of political practice, then, engage in 'challenging the boundaries of institutional politics'. The growth of the direct-action tactics of the movement—from deep ecologists in the forests to environmental justice activists in the cities—emphasizes the frustration with institutional processes and the lack of satisfactory outcomes.[7]

Moving beyond political frustration, some theories of motivation

---

[7] This frustration played a large part in the formation of radical organizations such as the Sea Shepherd Society and Earth First! (Scarce 1990: 24), in addition to the growth of the environmental-justice movement.

begin to expose the possibility of diverse motivations. A number of critical theorists have begun to examine more broad social alienations, which, they argue, lead to new social movements such as the environmental movement. Some argue that these movements are part of a broader politics of postmodernism, a politics constructed in part from a new awareness of the dangers of societal rationalization and a frustration with the 'meta-narratives' used to justify this rationalization (White 1991). Others argue the same point with their feet squarely in the modern world (e.g. Habermas 1981). The point in discussing new motivations and forms of politics is not to label the environmental movement 'postmodern', but to argue that conditions in the modern world have led to changes in political practices and articulations and to suggest that at least some parts of the movement have become an expression of this new politics. As a model of explanation, both postmodern and critical theory can be applied to new social movements in order to account for more diversity in the environmental movement than other attempted explanations of environmental motivations.

Laclau and Mouffe (1985) serve as an example here. They describe a variety of what they call 'new antagonisms' in the social realm. Laclau and Mouffe posit a method of understanding social movements with a new theory of the political subject—one who is constructed by a multiplicity of subject positions articulated by increasingly rationalized and hegemonically developed social practices. Because the practice of rationalization has reached beyond the economic sphere into nearly all aspects of everyday experiences, how people respond to issues such as the environment is affected by the variety of positions and identities they occupy in these increasingly diverse, yet rationalized, areas of their lives.

A number of other critical theorists elaborate on this notion of increased rationalization and the variety of alienations that may spring from it. Clause Offe describes how more and different social movements, and more and different aspects within different movements, come to evolve as more administration and regulation reaches into new areas of individual identity (Offe 1985: 845). Jurgen Habermas (1981, 1987*a*) discusses what he calls the 'colonization of the lifeworld'—the organization and domination of various social and political structures and interactions by instrumental discourse and practices—a rationalization without representation. He writes specifically about new social movements, including the environmental movement, as forms of resistance to this colonization. The environmental movement in particular acts against 'developments that visibly attack the *organic functions of the life-world* and make one drastically conscious of criteria of livability' (1981: 35).

Antagonisms exist in a variety of areas of everyday life and social movements are a response to these; but the environmental movement may be sparked particularly by the increased application of rationalization to the natural world, and the effects felt by that increase. Ecological activists, then, initiate a kind of 'reflective process' that can 'demystify, decode, and repossess' the products of this rationalization (Luke and White 1985: 49). The point here is that, beyond either values or political alienation, increasing modernization and rationalization leads to a variety of social alienations. These alienations in turn spawn resistance, resulting in the articulation of various areas of concern in the existing environmental movement.[8]

Alienation, whether political or more broadly social, is a very general explanation for motivation. Both forms of the alienation argument posit that the feeling is a response to pervasive structural conditions. Another explanation for environmental action is a more specific one, that of deprivation. The deprivation perspective holds that people are most likely to protest when their expectations regarding a specific good or value are denied.[9] A large portion of the grassroots anti-toxics movement, for example, is made up of those directly affected by a perceived health threat. Some organizations are begun by victims or the families of victims (Freudenberg 1984). Others become involved when the home, farm, or business they worked hard to build becomes worthless due to contamination. The mobilization of African-American communities is seen, in large part, as a response to the deprivation of civil rights and social justice illustrated by the disproportionate dumping in their communities (Bullard 1990, 1993*a*; Hofrichter, 1993*a*).

Beyond values, alienations, and deprivations, some approach the study of social movements, including the environmental movement, not from the perspective of *why* people organize, but of *how* people

[8] Even here, however, there are differences within the movement. Some see the problem as modernization *per se*, and preach either a return to some premodern state or a move beyond modernism. Others see the problem in *particular* applications of modernism or instrumental/technical reason.

[9] This argument can be traced back to Davies (1963). In an interesting parallel, both Inglehart and Davies use Maslow's hierarchy of needs as the psychological underpinning of their different explanations for social protest.

are able to put grievances in motion. Resource-mobilization theorists argue that citizens will not protest unless a certain set of resources are available to them. The resource-mobilization model emphasizes the importance of pre-existing organizations and the availability of resources like money, professional expertise, and recruitment networks (McCarthy and Zald 1977; Zald and McCarthy 1987).

The resource-mobilization model also concerns itself with the influence of élites or patrons in stimulating a movement. Caulfield's (1989) analysis of the history of the environmental movement emphasizes the role of political leaders and other élites. Leaders relate ideology, proposals, and actions to an area of concern—in this case the environment—and convince people to join or identify with the movement. Political élites, academic and popular authors, and the media create the basis of the movement and forge a bandwagon effect.

This model could be used to explain how it is that some issues become central to the movement (such as the battle over various mammals and ancient forests that the Big Ten environmental groups are involved in) and others flounder until they are picked up and organized around by a pre-existing political organization (such as the inordinate amount of toxic dumping in minority communities, an issue which exploded in popularity after the civil-rights movement turned to it as a major concern). This model can also be expanded to include history and modes of action as resources, in addition to time, money, and expertise. Given this expansion, it can be argued that the skills and tactics of the 1960s and 1970s made the resurgence of direct action in the environmental movement more possible in the mid-to-late 1980s (Dunlap and Mertig 1992; Freudenberg 1984). Likewise, the history of the organization and practices of the civil-rights movement and American Indian Movement were invaluable for African-Americans and Native Americans organizing around issues of environmental racism (Bullard 1990; Truax 1990).

The Problem of Exclusivity

The problem with all of the above approaches to the movement, from histories to classification to hegemonic progressivism to the competing theories of environmental motivations, is their tendency to exclude examples, categories, or evidence that do not fit the proposed model. While all research needs to focus on particular areas, and sometimes categorize or simplify in order to aid in understanding empirical phenomena, the literature on environmentalism often does more than simply focus in this way. The study of the environmental movement to date has been made up of competing 'correct models' of the history, construction, direction, or motivation of the movement. In this competition, many examiners are willing, as are Paehlke and Kitschelt, to exclude other 'intelligent versions of reality' or dismiss common practices as 'aberrations'. Others may not intend such exclusions, yet the framing of their work leaves out much of empirical reality. Such is the case in many environmental histories and in many examinations of environmental motivations. My argument is that each of these studies may help to capture a portion of the movement; however, the idea of any singular model encompassing all of environmentalism is not only inaccurate, but also, in the end, undesirable and counterproductive.

A recent study surveyed the citizens involved in protesting a proposed nuclear waste dump in their New York community. The aim was to examine whether alienation, deprivation, or resource mobilization were factors in participation (Kowalewski and Porter 1992).[10] The findings, not surprisingly, were yes on all three counts, meaning that support for all three models was evident in the responses of citizens. Elsewhere, Inglehart continues his argument that post-material values have led to the increase in ecology-minded parties in Western Europe; but his data also demonstrates a significant amount of support for those parties from people who embody materialist values (1990: 378–80). Inglehart notes that situational or contextual factors—outside the materialist/post-materialist spectrum—are very important in determining the strength of support for such movements (pp. 378–80). These examinations of the movement suggest a variety of motivations for the people that mobilize on environmental issues. Just as classification systems or arguments for a particular environmental politics exclude and discriminate, singular motiva-

---

[10] The definitions of both alienation and deprivation were quite broad. While the former did not distinguish between political alienation (input or outcome) and general social alienation, the latter included 'deprivation of bioprotective values', which could include the realm of post-materialism (Kowalewski and Porter 1992: 531).

tional schemes deny the validity of the plurality of values and motivations that actually goes into constructing the environmental movement. The actors within the movement defy the singular assertions of the examiners on the outside.[11]

The point now is to examine what it is that exclusionary histories, classification, hegemony, and singular value systems have hidden about the environmental movement. Why is it that these ideas are, in the end, counterproductive? Each emphasizes a portion of the environmental movement at the expense of other parts and offers the movement up as a response to a particular condition or value. Standard histories focus on battles around resources and an external nature, rather than the everyday material environment. Classifications of ecocentric versus technocentric or of radicals versus reformers center on particularities of the movement—its aims, ideologies, positions on technology, or on political strategies. The emphases on motivations due to post-material values or a general social rationalization that leads to alienation are each, in themselves, crucial to understanding various aspects of the movement; but when put forth as a singular, 'correct' model for the movement as a whole, they work against one another, and against a more thorough understanding of the difference and diversity that is at the base of the movement.

So what is exposed when we take these examinations as complementary? What would it mean to take seriously the number of environmentalisms and motivations for environmentalists? The argument here is that plurality is not a phenomenon to be categorized, but rather needs to be the concept at the center of the analysis. Diversity is to be taken seriously, as it brings out the wide variety of areas of environmental problems and the numerous responses possible to each. Attention to these responses helps us understand how environmental degradation affects numerous people in different ways.

The point of all of this is not to focus on criticism of the work of any of the above theorists or examiners, but to deal with the existing

---

[11] The same type of conclusions are found in the demographic data on the environmental movement. The common assertion is that environmentalists are overwhelmingly younger and college-educated (see e.g. Eckersley 1989). The support for such arguments is quite weak. Van Liere and Dunlap (1980) found demographic variables of limited utility in explaining the variety of environmental concerns. In fact, the environmental movement in the past decade has seen most growth in the anti-toxics and environmental justice arenas, whose members are not overwhelmingly young or college-educated.

variety in the movement. An acceptance of variety brings forth an awareness of a richness in the movement and does not disqualify any part. A number of examiners of the environmental movement (e.g. Devall and Sessions 1985; Kitschelt 1986; Paehlke 1989; Shabecoff, 1993) acknowledge diversity, but attempt to move beyond it or subjugate part of it in order to push their platform or theory of motivation. The task argued for here is to extend these limited acknowledgements, to accept difference as the basic character of environmentalism in the US, and to examine what this acceptance of difference might mean for relations, structures, and political demands in the movement.

Conclusion

The object here has been to rethink, critically, approaches to the study of the environmental movement. The movement has evolved considerably since its early days of Muir and Hamilton. From species protection to municipal housekeeping to alternative technologies to incinerator resistance, environmentalists have focused on a variety of threats to their natural surroundings. From motivation by consumerism or post-materialism, frustration with political processes or outcomes, or alienation due to any number of political or social processes, the reasons for environmental action continue to expand. Classifying, offering hegemonic program, or arguing for a particular type of motivation as all-encompassing simply does the movement no justice. Plurality and diversity are the roots of modern environmentalism, and attention to these roots can illuminate the widespread nature of environmental damage as well as the diverse experiences of them.

The question we are left with at the end of this survey and critique is one that pluralism—at least in its origins and its recent resurgence—is designed to deal with: exactly how do we go about acknowledging difference? A return to some of the original themes of pluralism validates diverse positions, ideologies, and motivations for environmental concerns; it also requires that this difference be heard, recognized, and brought into the larger realm of environmental discourse and action. I turn now to a history of pluralist theory to explore the foundations for a recognition of multiplicity.

Part II

Critical Pluralism in Theory

3

Pluralism and Difference: A Genealogy of Multiplicity

Pluralism has seen a major revival in the recent theoretical literature. After years of thorough critique, a purge of sorts, and, finally, relative obscurity, political and social theorists have begun to return to the term 'pluralism'. Various notions of critical pluralism, radical pluralism, postmodern pluralism, cultural pluralism, reciprocal pluralism, pluralist democracy, and, my personal favorite, 'post-modern pluralism in a post-marxist form' (McClure 1992: 113) are flourishing. It is now possible to speak of a new critical and radical pluralism emerging in the realm of political theory. William Connolly, one of the earliest critics of the limits and 'bias' of pluralism, has returned to reclaim the meaning of pluralism—a more *critical* pluralism, he argues—and its focus on difference and multiplicity (1991). Chantal Mouffe has been cross-pollinating post-Marxism with a revived pluralism. And there has been a revised interest in the decision-making mechanisms necessary for these revived and revised pluralisms to function (see e.g. Bohman 1995; Cohen 1993).[1]

At the core of the revival of pluralist themes is the recognition and acceptance of difference and multiplicity. Defined generally as an antonym of singularity, consensus, or unity, and encompassing a

---

[1] I wish to emphasize the *critical* modifier here, rather than any of the other possible choices, in defining this new generation of pluralism. Critical theory is, in part, defined by the insistence on a dual focus on explanation and reconstruction (Benhabib 1986a: 226; Leonard 1990). As Fay (1987: 27) has argued, 'a critical theory wants to explain a social order in such a way that it becomes itself the catalyst which leads to the transformation of this social order'. The new pluralism is just such a dialectical theory, entailing both moments of critique and reconstruction. The very structures and practices of the new pluralism develop out of a critical understanding of the limitations of past liberal pluralist practices. While the *essence* of the new pluralism is critical in this sense, I would argue that this essence extends to new radical, democratic, and postmodern pluralisms as well—in addition to some theories that do not self-identify as pluralist.

recognition of the existence and value of diverse positions and views, multiplicity was celebrated early in the century by philosophers and political theorists as a concept, and a political reality, which could challenge both philosophical absolutism and the sovereignty of the state. The recognition of difference, against the insistence on singularity and unity, is at the core of the origins and revival of pluralism. Unfortunately, the post-war generation of political pluralists melted diversity down, and stirred differences away into a limited, inevitable consensus—what Robert Dahl called the democratic creed (1961: 309–25). But recently discussions of difference and multiplicity have re-emerged in a new generation of theorists and activists, and pluralist ideas have returned to the themes of early theorists like William James and Mary Parker Follett. The new pluralism thus revives many of the themes of an earlier generation of pluralism that were largely forgotten or obscured by the particularly homogeneous brand of pluralism that arose in the post-war period.

I want to examine some of this history of pluralism, specifically the development and treatment of the concept and practice of multiplicity, focusing on the similarities and differences of the approach of these three generations of pluralists.[2] The first two generations are quite explicitly self-identified as pluralists: William James, Mary Parker Follett, and Harold Laski early in the century; Dahl, Nelson Polsby, and David Truman, among others, later. But I want to argue that a number of recent theorists have returned to the themes of the earlier generation, while not necessarily identifying themselves explicitly as pluralist. Pluralist *concepts*—in a number of different forms and incarnations—have been resurrected much more than the *term* pluralism. It is often the case that the concepts of an earlier form of pluralism appear without an acknowledgment of either the term pluralism or the origins of the thought. As Gregor McLennan (1995: 78) notes in his examination of contemporary pluralism, pluralist themes are central to a number of critical discourses. Pluralism, for example, 'lies at the heart of much of what is tangible and valuable in postmodernist social theory' (p. 5). There is a greater discursive

---

[2] McClure (1992) is to be credited with the development of this notion of 'three generations' of pluralism, in a defense of the current generation's approach to subjects and subjectivity. My broader focus here is much more on the differences between the first and recent generations of pluralist thought on the one hand, and the post-war generation on the other.

continuity between the first generation of pluralism and recent theories than is acknowledged or realized by contemporary proponents—either those who explicitly call themselves pluralist or those that prefer terms like difference democrat, discursive democrat, cyborg feminist, or others. So the resurrection of pluralism that is occurring is as much unacknowledged parallel thinking as it is a consciously reclaimed term. In the following discussion of pluralism I am going to address those theorists who use the term openly and without shame, and others who use what I see as thoroughly pluralist language that dates back to the roots of pluralism early in this century.

My central argument is that much within the conscious and unconscious resurrection of pluralism owes something to an articulation and a form of pluralism that existed *before* the post-war, liberal variant that is so often taken to be the whole of political pluralism. The resurrection takes up and expands upon the themes of pluralists such as William James and Mary Parker Follett, who wrote early in the century of multiplicity, difference, group identities, the divided subject, and the political implications for all of this plurality. Much of what we witness in the contemporary resurrection of pluralism mirrors the arguments of this earlier generation, and continues the issues and themes that James, Follett, and others began before being interrupted (and ignored) by the post-war generation with which we are so much more familiar. Unfortunately, except for a few important exceptions,[3] there is very little awareness—or use—of this previous 'generation' of pluralism. Many theorists use the term, and assert they are doing something very different than post-war Dahlian

---

[3] In addition to McClure, Avigail Eisenberg's *Reconstructing Political Pluralism* (1995), Gregor McLennan's *Pluralism* (1995), and various works by John Gunnell (1993, 1995) address the earliest generation of pluralism. Gunnell discusses the first generation mostly to point out how far from the original arguments the second generation strayed, but does not acknowledge that the early issues are being revisited by a new generation of pluralist theorists. Eisenberg offers a thorough return to the first generation in an attempt to use them to bridge the chasm between contemporary notions of individualism and communitarianism. Her discussions of James, Follett, Laski, Cole, and Figgis are comprehensive, and she surveys the important differences among them. Oddly however, Eisenberg makes no use of the contemporary generation of pluralists in her argument about contemporary theoretical concerns. McLennan attempts to lay out a thorough map of the current state of theoretical pluralisms. This is quite comprehensive, but he misses the opportunity to make links with pluralism's past.

pluralism—which they are. Many more theorists continue to eschew the term, though they address issues key to early pluralist thinkers. Overall there is, for the most part, very little recognition of a relation to earlier, and quite rich and related, notions of pluralism.

McClure argues that the three generations of pluralism share four key characteristics. All identify themselves against unitary, mono-lithic, or singular conceptions of the philosophical or political do-main; all insist on the irreducible plurality of the social realm; all eschew ontological grounding for the political groupings that con-tinually emerge and evolve; and all view the social subject as a site of multiple and intersecting group memberships, of which state citizen-ship is but one (McClure 1992: 114). The first two of these, obviously, make up the central argument of pluralism.[4] The transformation is one from the regime of the state to that of groups (Follett 1918: 6, 9). For Laski, pluralism was based in the admission 'that the parts are as real and as self sufficient as the whole' (1917: 9). For the first genera-tion, this was an argument against the state as the center of political theory and political life, and what made pluralism such a radical and critical mode of thought.[5]

Pluralism, however, begins before the discussion of the move away from the state. The key to the pluralist universe is the *basis* of difference. It is true that one of the themes repeated across the generations of pluralism is the argument against a monolithic, uni-tary vision of the social. But there is a qualitative difference between how the first and recent generations approach this notion, and how the post-war theorists did. One of the key similarities between the first and most recent generations is not simply the argument for the plurality of the social realm, but the thorough philosophical *justifica-tion* of that acceptance.[6] While the second generation of pluralists focused on a limited notion of economic self-interest to justify and understand social groupings, the first and most recent generations examine *the grounds of difference itself*. In doing this, contemporary

[4] I disagree with McClure that the second generation argued against unitary notions of the political, and will return to this point later in this chapter.

[5] It should be noted that there was much resistance to this move from within the discipline of political science. Harsh critiques of pluralist authors in the *American Political Science Review* include those by Coker (1921), Elliot (1924), and Ellis (1920). This critical nature—and the harsh response of more disciplinary critics—is another link between the first and most recent generations.

[6] This is something missing from the post-war generation. Their emphasis was on the use of primarily empirical evidence to argue against the unitary élitist interpretation of political power.

theorists of plurality resurrect and mirror the important founding arguments of pluralism from the turn of the century.

I will review a pluralist genealogy, and construct from a number of different theorists what I consider to be a contemporary 'critical pluralist' account of the concept of difference. A new 'critical' pluralism, at its core, resurrects a central concern with difference, and focuses on the material experiences, situated knowledges, and contexts of these differences. I will explore the evolution of the concern with difference and multiplicity in three generations of pluralism, focusing on some of the similarities between early pluralists and more recent theorists. In concluding I shall address a key concern expressed by recent critics of the move to accept multiplicity: that the concern with difference and experience may be disempowering.

Pluralism: The First Generation

The acknowledgment of multiplicity and variety in political and social life was a key factor in the early works of pluralism in this century. Pluralists in the realms of both philosophy and politics used diversity to move beyond the limitations of what they saw as absolutism in thought and practice. The focus then, as it is now, was on the recognition and justification of difference. In the myriad areas discussed by contemporary pluralism—moral pluralism, identity/difference, group identification and differentiation, representing difference—the philosophical grounding is the recognition of the validity of difference in individual and group experience itself as the basis of discussion. Quite simply, this is how pluralism began.

The pluralist philosophy of William James was based in the validation of public diversity.[7] While his central philosophical concern was a critique of a monist absolutism, his interest in difference was influenced by involvement in public issues. Well-known as a defender of the varieties of religious experience (James 1985 [1902]), James was perennially open to the positions of psychics, mystics, and others with minority viewpoints. He testified against the licensing of

---

[7] My coverage of James's project is, of necessity, limited as I focus specifically on his construction of the epistemological foundation of pluralism. For overviews of James, see Perry (1948) and Cotkin (1990). For works which place James in a larger context of American pluralism and pragmatism, see Diggins (1994) and West (1989).

physicians, fearing such a system would eliminate alternative healing practices (Cotkin 1990: 124). He editorialized against the growing imperial role of the United States at the turn of the century, especially in its treatment of Philippine sovereignty.[8] All of these political positions come from an understanding of a universe that is diverse, unfinished, moving, and growing, rather than unified and static (James 1975 [1907]: 123–5). James's philosophy of pluralism was intentionally designed with an openness to diversity on a number of levels, and against the difference-denying results of philosophical absolutism, social discrimination, and political imperialism.

James's notion of pluralism began with a quite simple empirical observation—that 'all that we are required to admit as the constitution of reality is what we ourselves find empirically realized in every minimum of finite life' (James 1977 [1909]: 145). Diverse experience is the link between James's argument for radical empiricism as a method and his pluralist philosophy. As he explains in *Essays in Radical Empiricism*, there is not a clear separation between a thing and our consciousness of it, rather experience is 'double-barreled'. Experience defines what we know as real; it is made up of the *relation* between what we experience and how we experience it. As experience 'is an affair of relations, it falls outside, not inside, the single experience considered, and can always be particularized and defined' (James 1976 [1912]: 7). The central argument is that *'any kind of relation experienced must be accounted as "real" as anything else in the system'* (p. 22; emphasized in original). The point of James's radical empiricism is not just the recognition of difference, but its validation in the face of a monolithic unity.

Pluralism entails, as James explains, recognition of this radical empiricism, as opposed to an acceptance of the more singular, monist position of rational absolutists.[9] This is not just a validation of difference, but a recognition that difference may never come together into a coherent, single, social unity. James asserts that there is no *'general stuff of which experience at large is made. There are as many stuffs as there are "natures" in the things experienced . . . Experience is only a collective name for all these sensible natures . . .'* (James 1976 [1912]: 14–15). Everyday experience varies from person to person, in both

---

[8] See the various editorials in James (1987), as well as Cotkin's (1990) discussion of James's 'imperial imperative'.

[9] Here James addresses classic absolutists, such as Spinoza and Hegel, as well as contemporaries, such as Francis Herbert Bradley and Alfred Edward Taylor.

the 'stuff' experienced and the consciousness or nature of the experience, and so the absolutists' notion of a whole, rational, all-inclusive reality common to all becomes difficult to defend. According to James, the pluralistic view, based as it is in an understanding of radical empiricism,

. . . is willing to believe that there may ultimately never be an all-form at all, that the substance of reality may never get totally collected, that some of it may remain outside of the largest combination of it ever made, and that a distributive form of reality, the *each*-form, is logically as acceptable and empirically as probable as the all-form commonly acquiesced in as so obviously the self-evident thing. (James 1977 [1909]: 20)

James vindicated the diversity of human experiences and ideas from attempts to classify, to unify, to engulf. 'Reality, life, experience, concreteness, immediacy, use what word you will, exceeds our logic, overflows and surrounds it' (p. 96).

The absolutists, argued James, could not incorporate a reality defined as locatable and only partially possible of union in some areas. They insisted on an either/or: either there is a complete union of all things or a complete disunion; complete rationality or irrationality; pure universe or pure 'nulliverse'. The key for James was the acceptance of the notion of 'some' rather than all or none. 'Radical empiricism and pluralism stand out for the legitimacy of the notion of *some*: each part of the world is in some ways connected, in some other ways not connected with its other parts' (1977 [1909]: 40–1). Philosophical absolutists demand an all or nothing, and argue that a notion of some connections and some disconnections is ruinous to rationality. James simply wanted philosophy to recognize, embrace, and celebrate disunity (James 1975 [1907]: 53).

James brought another important component into his pluralist universe—that of time. Influenced by the evolutionary theories of Henri Bergson, James incorporated Bergson's notion that reality has a continuously creative nature. 'Knowledge of sensible realities . . . comes to life inside the tissue of experience. It is *made*; and made by relations that unroll themselves in time' (James 1976 [1912]: 29). Heterogeneity may have been at the center of James's pluralism, but the practice of radical empiricism also demanded inclusion of the shifting nature of experience, ideas, alliances, concerns, and reactions over time. 'What really *exists* is not things made but things in the making. . . . Philosophy should seek this kind of living understanding of the movement of reality' (James 1977 [1909]: 117–18). For James, the evolving nature of possible experiences became another defence for pluralism against the static and singular nature of absolutism.

While he remains in the realm of philosophy in *The Pluralistic Universe*, it is easy to see the link with James's own anti-imperial politics, and one can anticipate what the more *political* pluralists are to do with his empirical and philosophical foundation. As James was arguing that the production of diverse, local, and unstable truth claims in human experience and relations deny the possibility of philosophical absolutism, a generation of political pluralists was using similar arguments to deny the validity of forms of *political* absolutism. The reality of diversity and the concomitant acknowledgment of the variety and fluidity of experiences became the basis of the views of political pluralists such as Arthur Bentley (1908), Ernest Barker (1957 [1915]), Harold Laski (1917, 1921), and Mary Parker Follett (1918).

What united these writers was a critique of an absolutist concept of unity on both philosophical and political grounds. Their target was the overriding, singular concern of theorists with the sovereignty of the state; this came, they argued, at the expense of individual and group experiences. The pluralists of this generation took James's critique of absolutism and applied it to the state.[10] 'What the Absolute is to metaphysics, that is the State to political theory', insisted Laski (1917: 6). These pluralists argued for an understanding of the diversity of individual and group experiences as the center of political life. In the call for a singularity of definition and unity of beliefs, theories of the state were the political manifestation of the philosophy of absolutism. Pluralism used the diversity of group experiences to break the monopoly the state held on the focus of political theory.[11]

---

[10] For some, like Follett and Laski, the use of James's philosophical foundation was conscious and acknowledged. For others, such as Barker, there was no mention of James, though the target was still the unitary state and the aim a justification of the focus on differences in civil society.

[11] The context of many of these critiques of political absolutism would make for an interesting study. Laski's works are clearly anti-German in tone, written as they were during and after the First World War. He attributes the notion of unity to the Germans, specifically Bismarck on the political front and Hegel on the philosophical. Interestingly, Barker's 'The Discredited State' was written before the start of the war, yet he later wrote that the war 'brought back with a rush the claims of the State', and attempted to emphasize a concluding line in that work that seems to resurrect the sovereign authority of the state as an 'unconscious prophecy of what was about to be' (1957).

Laski argued that, without a focus on unity, including that of the singular, unified state, what is left is a 'plurality of reals', which, once acknowledged, destroys any prediction of, or attempt at, unity. For Follett, '[l]ife is a recognition of multitudinous multiplicity. Politics must be shaped for that' (1918: 291). Experience is plural, and any concept of a necessary unity discredits a range of experiences that fall outside its false boundaries. Follett and the pluralists of her generation attempted to redefine and expand the notion of sovereignty, to move it from the singular, absolutist point of reference of the state to multiple manifestations in individual and group experiences. Studies of sovereignty were no longer to focus solely on the state, but other political groupings and actors as well. It was a move towards what McClure (1992: 116) calls a more 'distributive sovereignty'. Pluralists pushed the study of politics from its emphasis on the state to multiple and varied regimes—in groups and the individuals that comprised them.[12]

Throughout these early pluralist writings, diversity is accepted as a given factor of social and political life. The primary identification of citizens is within any of a variety of groups based on identity, interest, or participation in diverse contexts. Diverse groups come from a wide variety of possible experiences and relationships; and each group, concrete and situated as it is, is given a valid and sovereign status. The focus of these early pluralists is on the various psychologies of group association, as opposed to and distinct from the unity of the state. The basic aim was to justify the authority, sovereignty, and moral authority of a variety of social groupings other than the state, and to justify the use of such political concepts—previously reserved only for discussion of states—in describing groups in civil society. The study of politics was to encompass political identities, agency, and relationships beyond the singular, institutional sphere of the state.

For Follett, this was not just a battle against the focus on the state in political theory. It was a call for the recognition of the diversity in civil society—a civil society she was deeply involved in. Follett began her public work in the Roxbury Neighborhood House of Boston, and was central in the development of the Boston School Centers, where the schoolhouses of Boston were opened after school hours for educational and social activities. She was at the center of progressive

---

[12] Many of this generation worked with other progressives and encouraged the active political formation and participation of various groups, such as neighborhood groups, unions, and trade associations.

social experiments in Boston early in the century, and it was this experience in the realm of civil society which she ultimately worked out theoretically in *The New State* (1918). As Follett's work moved from issues of the state to social administration to industrial organization, her focus remained on the place of the individual in human relations and on the importance of the recognition of individuals in organizations. While James argued against the new Hegelians, Follett attempted to reconcile James's radical empiricism with Hegelian unity. Her work, especially in *The New State*, should be seen as an expression of the tension between her desire to recognize a Jamesian plurality in civil society and her hope for dynamic, yet ultimately harmonious relations across that difference.[13]

Rather than seeing the individual and social life—civil society—as a construction moulded by the state, the pluralist focus was from the bottom up. Society itself is made up of the various 'feelings, faculties, ideas, and ideals' sprung from 'individual psychic content' (Bentley 1908: 165–6). Follett discussed society as a 'psychic process' and argued for a revision of the study of society from that of a single unit to that of a collection of units or as an organism (1918: 75).[14] It is this reversal that is at the core of her pluralism. Follett insisted on emphasizing the process of the group creating its *own* personality, as opposed to stopping with the satisfaction of the knowledge that the state does *not* create it. This change in emphasis, she argued, would 'unchain' pluralist thinking (p. 283).

But these pluralists also went beyond the general psychology of the group in their examinations of diversity and multiplicity. Some pluralists, such as Laski, focused on the more politically obvious differences of groups in various regions. He noted, for example, the different problems, thoughts, and desires of people in diverse locales, and argued that 'what are called the "interests of the Republic" in New York will probably be called "discrimination against the Middle West" in Kansas' (Laski 1917: 278).

---

[13] While I emphasize the important tension between difference and unity, or between James and Hegel, notable in Follett's work, others have focused more thoroughly on the danger of her interest in synthesis and unity (Kariel 1955) and her Hegelian idealism (see Kariel 1961: esp. pp. 161–2). I find this an incomplete, and unfair, characterization given Follett's own recognition of this tension. I will return to this point in Ch. 4.

[14] The fact that Follett could use an organic metaphor to refer to diversity rather than absolutism is itself an impressive break from past uses of naturalistic justifications. See Dryzek and Schlosberg 1995.

Diversity also went much further than these broad regional, or even group differences, into the very psyche of the individual. Follett argued that while group organization should be the methodological base of a new pluralist politics, the individual should remain the basic unit of politics. Individuals, she argued, have multiple natures, making it impossible for one, or even a number of groups, to enfold all of one's personality (1918: 295). James's notion that we are made up of a complex of experiences led to an understanding of many selves in each one (see James 1890). Laski put it more succinctly when he stated that 'we are bundles of hyphens' (1921: 170). These pluralists began to examine not only the divided nature of society as a whole, but the divided nature of the self, the myriad influences surrounding us, and our resultant multiple identities and interests.

The first generation of pluralists took James's discussions of experience and multiplicity seriously, and helped move the study of political relationships in the United States beyond sole concern with the state as the center of sovereignty, and into extra- and non-institutional relationships. But Follett, for one, was not satisfied with just this shift in concern. There was another step to be taken in the pluralist universe. 'The pluralists have pointed out diversity but no pluralist has yet answered satisfactorily the question to which we must find an answer—What is to be done with this diversity?' (Follett 1918: 10).

Retreat: Post-War Pluralism

Unfortunately, what the next generation of pluralists did with that diversity has given pluralism a bad reputation among those interested in a new democratic politics of difference. While the origins of the philosophy and politics of pluralism were based on the diverse and fluid nature of truth and the diversity of experiences that define political subjects, pluralism translated, after the Second World War, into a very limited realm of economically defined interest groups competing against one another before the authority of the state. While eloquently extolling the virtues of diversity on the one hand, Edward Banfield (1961), Robert Dahl (1961, 1967), Charles Lindblom (1965), Nelson Polsby (1963), and David Truman (1960) contributed to the development of a system of thought and political action that used the concept of heterogeneity in a constricted sense to defend and promote self-interested interest groups and their participation within a system defined by, unified under, and operating within a particular set of 'democratic' truths and processes. The overall aims of this pluralism were not the examination of political experiences, the recognition of diversity, or the devaluation of the sovereignty of the state. Gunnell (1995: 19) notes that Truman's work in this period mentions the earlier pluralist school, but does 'not explicitly employ the concept of pluralism'. The same can be said for others of Truman's generation. Rather than following James's radical empiricism of diverse experiences, these pluralists focused on empirical observation of decision-making and on the processes used to come to consensus on a system of both beliefs and benefits.[15]

It is not my task here to offer a full critique of this generation of pluralism, as this has been done from both outside and, later, within its ranks (see e.g. the collections edited by Connolly 1969, and Wolff *et al.* 1965; as well as Bachrach and Baratz 1962; Kariel 1961; Lindblom 1977, 1982; Lowi 1969; and Manley 1983). These authors have exposed the limitations of the vision of this stage of pluralism, both normatively and in political practice: its narrow notion of interest, the limited understanding of political action, the exclusion of some groups, the dismissal of the political power and economic resources of élites, and its flawed concept of tolerance. What is important to examine in this context, however, is how the promise of the first generation of pluralists was concealed due to the next generation's limited sense of political subjectivity and overemphasis on the need for unity.

The second generation of pluralists accepted the concept developed by their predecessors that the variety of social experiences would result in a multiplicity of framings or understandings of social and political issues. Explicit attention to difference continued to be at the core of pluralism. But this generation limited their attention to a particular type of experience—that in the economic realm. Their concept of interest groups was based originally on occupational category. Truman (1960: 60), for example, notes many times the diversity and overlapping nature of groups, but argues that most growth in

---

[15] I am not arguing here that this generation offered a single and homogeneous theory of pluralism. There are numerous differences—both theoretical and methodological—between the authors I note. Still, whether intended by its creators or not, pluralism came to be seen as a general theory of decision-making, power, and the American political way of life. See the discussion by Jordan 1990.

groups stems from economic/occupational institutions. The only part of individual or social life having a worthwhile defining characteristic, then, was an individual's labor or economic identity. As both Connolly (1969) and Wolff *et al.* (1965) note in their critical volumes, the encouragement to organize, politically, around existing occupational categories led to a quite limited, one-dimensional pluralism that excluded the whole range of issues outside the workplace.[16] Defining interests as subjective, every issue was to be articulated in the language of individual or group economic self-interest. Even the language of this generation exudes the economic focus, with discussion of 'resources', 'rewards', 'political profitability', and 'payoffs'. The range of varieties of political and social experience were forced through a filter which strained out all but particular economically based self-interest.[17]

Issues that could not be articulated in this manner were simply left out of the national conversation—remaining in the margins until they erupted into the social movements of the 1960s and after. Organized around a variety of experiences, including ethnic identity, race, gender, sexuality, and 'post-material' values, these movements exposed in practice the limitations of a focus on economic-based identity, and reopened the realm of political subjectivity that had been exposed by earlier pluralists and limited by the next generation.

In addition to their limited focus on a particular economic-based concept of political subjectivity, the second generation of pluralists also reoriented the focus of pluralism from an emphasis on the plurality of the social and the contingent nature of identity back to that of 'unity' or 'consensus'. Follett had asked what was to be done with the multiplicity that she and her contemporaries were exposing; Dahl and his generation answered her by accepting a number of notions of social unity that resembled aspects of the absolutist state earlier pluralists had critiqued. While McClure (1992) argues that all

---

[16] It is interesting that both generations of pluralism had defined themselves quite explicitly against a form of absolutism—for the first generation it was that of First World War Germany, for the second it was that of the cold war Soviet Union. In the latter case it is curious that the critiques of pluralism did not focus on the similarities between Soviet Marxism and American pluralism in their emphasis on the labor identity. Neither system seems to have had a care for their subjects beyond their role as producers.

[17] And even economic articulation was not a guarantee of entry into the political sphere. This generation of pluralists explicitly avoided the elevation of individual and group economic interests to *class* interests in their dismissals of élite power theory.

three generations of pluralism articulated an opposition to unitary, monolithic conceptions of the political sphere, I disagree; my point is that the second generation returned to such an emphasis. Dahl and others may have argued against the unitary notion of an economic élite as ruling class, but they returned to a notion of unity and consensus in terms of both political context and process.

As for context, the early Dahl discusses, in his history of power relations in New Haven, a certain 'vague political consensus' to which all the 'major' groups in the community subscribe (1961: 84). This is his general notion of a 'democratic creed'. He notes how this consensus limits the range of acceptable political strategies, to the point of offering a political axiom stating that '[i]n allocating rewards to individuals and groups, the existing socioeconomic structure must be taken as given, except for minor details' (p. 94). According to Truman, defiance of pre-existing norms will weaken a group's cohesion, reduce its status in the community, and expose it to the interest claims of other groups (Truman 1960: 513). Differences are inevitable even within the narrow band of economic interests this generation celebrates; but those differences must immediately be forged back into some sort of unity acceptable to all.

As for process, the rules of political engagement, as Lindblom (1965) lays out, involve the process of 'partisan mutual adjustment', aimed at moving toward the desired end of consensus. Similarly for Dahl, stability in both New Haven and the US are due to an agreement on the 'rules of the game' (1961: 315), and limits on strategies: 'In pluralistic, democratic political systems with wide political consensus the range of acceptable strategies is narrowed by beliefs and habits rooted in traditions of legality, constitutionality, and legitimacy that are constantly reinforced by a great variety of social processes for generating agreement on and adherence to political norms' (p. 225).[18] As with the general creed, any questioning or violation of these rules will lead to a loss of resources and a high risk of defeat. Difference is hampered by more than just the pre-existing context—

---

[18] Dahl, at the end of *Who Governs?*, begins to explore the 'indoctrination' and 'Americanization' at work in the construction of consensus (1961: 316–18), but he does not revise his conclusions about participation in the political system in light of these processes. Challenging power structures that create social norms is the aim of the 'third dimension' of power analysis, put forth by Lukes (1974) and Gaventa (1980). Dahl also makes no reference, as his critics later do, to the legitimating role of social science in the process of norm formation he describes.

a unifying creed; it is also limited by a very particular mode of political conversation aimed at keeping that consensus.

While these pluralists follow Follett and her contemporaries in the *acknowledgement* of difference, the *end* they pursue is a reconstruction of unity and consensus. The 'rules of the game' of this generation are tools used to deny the recognition and validity of multiplicity itself, and to forge even a limited diversity back into a vague singularity. The pluralist process of this generation worked against its very foundation in difference. Pluralism in practice, then, condemned itself to continued exclusions which led, inevitably, to conflicts. This is one key reason why, as we will see in Chapter 4, contemporary pluralist theory focuses on political processes designed to recognize, encompass, and include difference.

'Return to the Story of Multiplicity'

As noted, there have been numerous critiques of the pluralists of the last generation, focusing on issues of power, élitism, the exclusion of certain groups and types of political action, etc. But none of those critiques, aiming at the rejection rather than the redemption of pluralism, brought us back to the original theses and intents of the earlier pluralists; their promise was left unfulfilled. Yet much in recent social and political theory, from post-Marxism to postmodernism, reflects this promise—especially in the trend of bringing multiplicity to the forefront—as the base of a new generation of pluralism. Again, this resurrection of themes is not necessarily a conscious one; as I noted, few theorists refer explicitly to the earlier generation, and only a few more would consciously label themselves 'pluralist'.[19] What is important, however, is that a number of people are returning to some of the core issues of plurality raised by the first generation. At the base of the resurgence of pluralism now is the same type of argument James made in order to justify the validity of different ways of seeing and knowing the world. These ideas then help to form the foundation of a new generation of what might be termed a critical pluralism.

[19] In fact, of all the theorists cited in this chapter, only Laclau, Mouffe, and Connolly explicitly identify themselves as pluralists attempting to reclaim the term.

Donna Haraway's (1988) eloquent description of what she calls 'situated knowledges', or 'embodied objectivity', for example, returns us squarely into the realm of William James, though without a recognition of James's work. Haraway uses the metaphor of vision to examine the multiple ways things can be seen, depending on one's experience, context, or, more generally, the view from one's body. From varied experiences we see different things; the knowledge gained from these visions situates the subject. She argues for 'politics of epistemologies of location, positioning, and situating, where partiality and not universality is the condition of being heard to make rational knowledge claims' (1988: 589). Objectivity is not something accomplished by stepping back and taking it all in from above; rather, only partial perspectives can be considered objective. As James (1979 [1896]: 6) argued, 'there is no possible point of view from which the world can appear an absolutely single fact'. Since perspectives differ according to situation, objectivity is, then, always partial and multiple. Haraway here mirrors the earlier radical empiricism of James in three ways: the use of experience as opposed to universal concepts, the assertion of the situated nature of experience and knowledge, and the acceptance of multiple visions, and so experiences of truth. Haraway's target is the same singular notion of monolithic claims to unity in truth that James attacked in *The Pluralistic Universe*.

Gilles Deleuze and Felix Guattari (1987: 32) also, without mention of James, mirror his criticism of the search for the 'all-form' when they admonish us to

return to the story of *multiplicity*, for the creation of this substantive marks a very important moment. It was created precisely in order to escape the abstract opposition between the multiple and the one, to escape dialectics, to succeed in conceiving the multiple in the pure state, to cease treating it as a numerical fragment of a lost Unity or Totality or as the organic element of a Unity or Totality yet to come . . .

They argue that we live in an age of 'partial objects, bricks that have been shattered to bits, and leftovers' (1983: 42). We are those 'partial objects', and we are defined through the many states and situations through which we pass (p. 20). Deleuze and Guattari mirror the radical empiricism of James in their understanding of our differential make-up and knowledge, as well as the refusal of a singular unity or totality that comes with this acceptance of multiplicity.

McClure (1992) echoes and expands upon the generation of *political* pluralists who embodied James's philosophical pluralism; she is alone among contemporary pluralists in her acknowledgement of pluralist ties both in terms of an earlier generation, as well as in connecting her political pluralism with a contemporary pluralist epistemological foundation. The link between earlier pluralisms and her own is a central part of McClure's analysis, but she also argues that there is a radical pluralist political potential in the multiple subjectivities suggested by Haraway and other feminist epistemologists (McClure 1992: 122).[20] McClure's pluralism is based on a critique of the singular identity required by the citizen of the modern state; she argues for the political possibilities inherent in the recognition and validation of multiple subjectivities (ibid.).

While Ernesto Laclau and Chantal Mouffe (1985) do not acknowledge a link to the first generation of pluralists, or to recent philosophers who emphasize difference, they do attempt to reclaim the term pluralism, or at least 'plural democracy'.[21] Plurality, they argue, should be the starting-point of political analysis. The variety of contemporary social struggles has given rise to a theoretical crisis not just within their own Marxist tradition, but in standard notions of pluralism as well. Asserting the need to examine the profusion of different social responses or movements to various oppressions is Laclau and Mouffe's key break from past theories—unitary Marxist or liberal pluralist—based solely on the singular experience of labor or economic self-interest. More recently, Mouffe has argued that 'the type of pluralism that I am advocating gives a positive status to differences and . . . refuses the objective of unanimity and homogeneity which is always revealed as fictitious and based on acts of exclusion' (Mouffe 1996: 246).

But it is not just *admitted* pluralists such as McClure and Mouffe who have resurrected a concern with situated knowledges. In fact, the whole growing realm of literature on democracy and difference (see

---

[20] In addition to Haraway, McClure cites De Lauretis (1988), Harding (1986), and Spelman (1988).

[21] Radical empirical claims influence contemporary pluralists much as they did in the past—some directly and some indirectly. McClure uses Haraway and others as an epistemological base in an explicit recognition of that connection. Others, such as Laclau and Mouffe, and Connolly, base their arguments on the acceptance of multiplicity and difference while not explicitly referring to those who establish this ground. This is very similar to the practice of the authors in the first generation. See n. 9.

e.g. Benhabib 1996*a*) depends on the explication of radical empiricism. As Bonnie Honig suggests, 'difference is just another word for what used to be called pluralism' (1996: 251).[22] In this realm, difference is a resource and a status that is to be preserved and expressed; yet that cannot be done without the previous work of grounding and validating multiplicity. While *none* of these particular contemporary explorations of radical empiricism and plurality acknowledges any influence from, or similarities to, earlier pluralism, they certainly return us to many of the philosophical grounds and political positions of the first generation.[23]

A new generation—while not explicitly self-identified as pluralist— is stressing plurality. Accepting the partial and local, and moving beyond attempts toward unity and absolutism, brings political potential. Authors as diverse as Mouffe, Foucault, and Rorty argue that in the recognition of contingency and multiplicity lies the potential for freedom. Jane Flax, for example, has argued for the liberatory nature of multiplicity, and admonished feminist theories to 'encourage us to tolerate and interpret ambivalence, ambiguity, and multiplicity as well as to expose the roots of our needs for imposing order and structure no matter how arbitrary and oppressive these needs may be' (1987: 78).

Rather than attempt to forge a particular and exclusive conception of unity—as did the liberal middle generation of pluralists—an acceptance of ambiguity, contingency, and a diversity of experiences and truth claims forms the foundation for accepting and returning to multiplicity as the basis of political organization. As unity and singularity forge an image of stability, contingency and the 'plurality of reals' open up uncertainty and variability. The supposed safety of a commonality, a creed, or a singular set of rules of the game is being replaced with a need to be continually aware of the shifting nature of various experiences,[24] and the relations across these differences.

---

[22] In the index to the Benhabib-edited collection on *Democracy and Difference* (1996*a*), the term pluralism has few references but the section suggests that readers 'see also *difference*'.

[23] In addition to McClure, Eisenberg, and McLennan, Charlene Seigfried serves as an example of one who *does* make the connection between earlier pluralists/ pragmatists and the current resurrection of interest in difference. Seigfried argues that a pluralist/pragmatist recognition of difference is the key to the continuing vitality of feminism (1996: 260).

[24] It is important to keep in mind James's additional notion of time and evolution in the development of the pluralist universe. While lacking in Haraway's examination of situated knowledge, other contemporary theorists heed this addi-

Pluralism, finally, has returned to pluralism. The search now, as it was for James, is how to free ourselves from the confines of absolutism and singularity, or forms of unity and ultimate consensus. It was, and is, a search for a place beyond the false dichotomy of all or nothing, unity or disintegration. It is a search not for 'relativism'—a charge leveled against both James and contemporary theorists of multiplicity—but for a land, as Bernstein (1983) calls it, beyond objectivism and relativism.[25] James's recent descendants have attempted to demonstrate that theorists and activists can sail away from the land of Totality without falling off the ends of the Earth.

Exclusion, Context, and the Experience of Difference

Moving away from singularity and absolutism, a critical pluralism reintroduces an understanding of a world made up of diverse experience. Multiplicity based in experience is, in this view, thoroughly rational and empirical, as opposed to the utopia of unity. While there are key similarities between the first generation of pluralist thinkers on difference and more recent theorists, the *political* motivations of the latter differ in important ways from the former. The recent focus on difference comes out of a concern with both the exclusion of many people and groups from the political process and the construction of political identities themselves.

While James was arguing simply for a more realistic and commonsense notion of the diversity of human rationality, and Follett asserted the need for political theory to open itself to the variety of experiences in civil society, one focus now is a defense of difference in the face of the imposed injustices of exclusion enforced by various meta-narratives. Follett's concern was the exclusion of civil society

tional element in their own discussions of multiplicity. Deleuze and Guattari (1987: 249), for example, argue that 'a multiplicity is continually transforming itself into a string of other multiplicities, according to its thresholds and doors'. Experience and identity—even as used in cultural identity politics today—evolves. Stuart Hall offers the example that the identity of 'black' 'has always been an unstable identity . . . It too, is a narrative, a story, a history. Something constructed, told, spoken, not simply found' (1987: 45). The same can be said about the identities of 'gay' or 'environmentalist'—their meanings have changed, have signified a variety of things at different points of their evolution, and continue to be multiple. Objectivity, then, is both locatable in experience and fluid.

[25] It is interesting to note here that Bernstein provided the introduction for the reissue of James's *A Pluralistic Universe* (1977 [1909]).

from political *theory*; the contemporary concern is with the injustice of the exclusion of difference from political *practice*. The resurrection of notions of radical empiricism comes out of the political call for the legitimacy of subjugated knowledges, and the demand for the recognition of the validity of diverse local and culturally based knowledges. Hence radical empiricism and situated knowledge stand, for example, as the essence of the expanding fields of postmodern feminism and critical race theory, where social experience is examined in the context of the history of the experiences of women and people of color (Crenshaw 1995; Nicholson 1990; P. Williams 1991). Contemporary pluralism stands for an expansion of inclusion and participation of these, and other, varied experiences.

The argument of the environmental justice movement, for example, is that the homogeneity of the mainstream environmental movement excludes some experiences of the 'environment'—especially the urban environment—and this exclusion leads to inequality not just of *recognition*, but of the *distribution* of environmental risks.[26] This is a critique of interest-group pluralism in practice, as it illustrates how particular experiences may be organized off the political agenda.[27] It also illustrates where contemporary pluralist theory and action have gone beyond past generations, of necessity, into the central issue of how the exclusion of varied experiences is played out in political inequality.

In addition, many theorists have returned to first-generation pluralists' appreciation for the importance of context in assessing experience and consciousness, and the related acceptance of a historical construction of subjectivity. While the post-war generation of pluralists explored experiences defined by only a narrow concept of economic self-interest, a new generation has sailed a broader ocean in order to examine—and validate and critique—a whole range of grounded experiences, realities, and perspectives. But recent theories of difference have also taken another step second-generation pluralists did not, into the constructed nature of context. A contemporary shift in the nature of pluralistic theory is one away from concern solely with the *products* of social construction and their articulation of limited 'interests', toward an understanding of the *production* of a

---

[26] For discussions of the lack of attention to diversity in the mainstream environmental movement, see Dowie (1995) and D. Taylor (1992, 1993).

[27] The classic discussions of agenda-setting and exclusion are Bachrach and Baratz (1962) and Crenson (1971).

variety of identities and interests and responses to this production.[28] Both early and recent advocates for plurality argue that experience is constructed by situation—environment, locality, or view—as well as one's assimilation or internalization of that experience.[29] Situated knowledges, or an epistemology of location, call for an examination of both situation and assimilation in order to understand differences in experience and perception.

Individuals are defined by the states through which they pass (Deleuze and Guattari 1983: 20), and it is these states of experience which should be the primary focus. As Foucault argues, the change in emphasis from the political state to contextual states is based on discovering 'how it is that subjects are gradually, progressively, really and materially constituted through a multiplicity of organisms, forces, energies, materials, desires, thoughts, etc.' (1980: 97).

Thus we need to pay attention not just to the multiplicity and fluidity of experience, but to the context of assimilation. Hence, recent theorists express the need to examine the variety of processes—historical, political, social, cultural—that produce context and situate subjects in their experiences. As Kaufman-Osborn (1993: 131) has expressed it,

[w]e never eat experience raw. It is always already stewed in the juices of meaning, and it cannot speak either for or by itself. The relationship of meaning to experience is complexly mediated by the histories that enter into it, the bodies engaged in it, the languages employed to make sense of it, the shapes into which it is pounded by dominant institutions, the technologies that configure it, etc.

Attention to the broad context of experience is crucial, yet situated knowledge calls for an examination of both these various types of mediation as well as the felt experiences within them. To continue the metaphor, we examine not only the juicy ingredients, but also the *taste*, of the stew of experience. We do this through studies of general experiences largely shared (schools, mass culture, capital, government policy), more specific and multiple shared contexts, and the variety of interpretations of and reactions to these experiences.

---

[28] In this, I disagree with Joan Scott's call to look *outside* pluralism to theorize the production of identity (see Scott 1992). Rather than look outside, I am arguing for an expansion from within.

[29] See the discussion of Mead 1938, and the application to identity politics by Aronowitz 1992.

The critical pluralist transformation here is from an insistence on singularity and unity to an appreciation of the multiple, contextual, and evolutionary nature of experience. In the contemporary world, a variety of primary experiences shape the contexts and experiences, and so the knowledges and the objectivity of contemporary political subjects. We are constructed not just by a single position, but as a product of our place in each and all of them. We are still 'bundles of hyphens'. And while identity construction is a fluid process, these locations and contexts may be exposed to critical examination.

The Death of the Subject?

Recent concerns with multiplicity and experience have rearticulated and expanded upon the arguments of the earlier pluralists. They draw our attention, as James did, to the 'some' as well as the all, to the 'multitudinous multiplicity' that creates experience and rationality. But, as in the past, there are arguments against the acceptance of multiplicity, and I need to address some avenues of resistance.

As the nature of truth has become (re)centered around the subject, experiences, and context, and debate has increased on the processes of the construction of 'vision' or belief, questions have arisen around just how much individuals, or groups, are involved in that construction. How thorough are the hegemony and normalization processes of institutions, practices, or discourses, and what is our ability to resist? The last generation of pluralists was criticized for lack of attention to the power of the environment. Now, has a new version of pluralism gone too far in the other direction? Is the subject simply a dead receptacle for context, or can subjectivity be a mediating factor between context and experience?

As theorists of the postmodern condition began to examine the role of power in the construction of individual identity, some critics began to attack this focus as involving the 'death of the subject'. The argument is that a focus on structural constructions of identity limits the possibilities for the autonomy and sovereignty of individuals and groups. Feminist theorists, especially, have been suspicious of the move to critique the supposed autonomy of the subject at a time when women are finally being incrementally awarded a valid agency and subjectivity in the societal mainstream (see e.g. Di Stefano, 1990;

Hartsock 1987; as well as the excellent response of McClure 1992). But does an acceptance of the role of social forces in constituting the *subject* make impossible *subjectivity* and the possibility of agency (and feminism, or any movement)?

Some recent theorists do focus too myopically on the question of context alone—and do so at the expense of the validity of the experiences of those living in oppressive situations. Criticizing the construction of subjects, they dismiss any potential for subjectivity. Joan Scott, for example, examines the difficulties of using experience as evidence in writing history. She argues that using experience is problematic, as it 'leads us to take the existence of individuals for granted . . . rather than to ask how conceptions of selves . . . are produced' (1991: 782).[30]

Admittedly, a focus on experience might lead to ignoring the construction of situations, but this is not necessarily the case. I would argue, rather, that an understanding of experience as situated brings context into consideration. Scott makes the opposite error, focusing so much on context or discourse that she suggests that individuals cannot be considered 'reliable sources of knowledge' (1991: 783). Scott here mirrors Rorty, who argues that 'the job of putting [a subject's] situation into language is going to have to be done for them by someone else' (1989: 94). Both Rorty and Scott take the rather problematic position of claiming to understand a situation more than those living within it, as if those within a discriminatory, power-created, marginalized position could not recognize these aspects of their own context. I want to argue that attention to experience lets subjects speak about, and critically examine, their own situations themselves. Take the example of the polluted river I discussed in Chapter 1; the experience of that pollution differs according to context—proximity, uses of the river, cultural history, etc. Groups in the environmental justice movement attempt to bring out this context to more fully understand the meaning of that pollution in different communities.

Rather than deny the life and power of subjectivity, the acceptance of multiplicity and attention to the methods and contexts of constructing experience brings the existing variety of subjectivities to the forefront of a new pluralist politics. Examining experience as the

---

[30] Scott insists on focusing instead on language, as 'experience is a linguistic event' (1991: 793). Kaufman-Osborn's (1993) essay responds to this limited understanding of experience.

basis for knowledge and subjectivity allows a *critique* of alienating and oppressive situations, *organization* around those experiences or identities, and an understanding of the creation of *resistance* to unwanted aspects of those experiences.[31] Organization around identity allows previously constituted subjects to examine their own production, and to identify and resist certain conditions of that construction.

In the same regard, we can see some recent work in post-Marxism, feminism, and identity politics as examinations of the various experiences and contexts of subordination, oppression, and domination—from work, to urban situations, to constructions of gender and sexuality, to the relation of humans to the remainder of the natural world.[32] Political movements such as those organized around race, ethnicity, gender, and sexuality both assert their identities and critique the construction of their meaning and the experience of discrimination. Environmental justice groups, such as those organizing as victims of workplace toxics or environmental racism, do so not to continue that identity, but to examine its production and to resist and transform it. The subject may be at the center in each case: as the subject asserting identity, as the body enduring institutional or cultural discrimination, and as the body responding to those practices through organization and expressions of resistance. Identity is asserted, and interrogated, without reification.

Foucault has been the object of much of the 'death of the subject' criticism (see Hartsock 1987; Philp 1985). But just as Foucault argued that we are, in many ways, constructed by the various discourses that surround and penetrate us, he recognized reactions to those discourses. For Foucault, power is not generated from a single place, and it does not assert itself in another single place; both the generation (institutions, discourses) and the reception (experience, subjectivity) of power is multiple. But that power does not *limit* resistance—rather, it may actually *create* a response. Even the disciplined subject is capable of resistance. 'Where there is power, there is resistance . . . These points of resistance are present everywhere in the power network' (Foucault 1978: 95). The variety of contemporary

---

[31] Once again, we find traces of this argument in the first generation. Mary Parker Follett concludes her *Creative Experience* (1924: 302) with the note that '[w]e seek reality in experience . . . [And we] seek progressive advancement through the transformation of daily experience.'

[32] Examples here would include such diverse offerings as Hall 1987; Hofrichter 1993a; hooks 1984; and Laclau and Mouffe 1985.

social movements illuminates Foucault's point, as they respond to a variety of conditions and experiences and develop new identities out of that resistance (see e.g. Epstein 1991; Laclau and Mouffe 1985; Melucci 1989; Quinby 1990).

There can be little doubt that some manifestations of power result in alienation and oppression, and stifle the production of individuality and subjectivity. But rather than killing the subject, the practice of examining those structures of meaning-production allows subjectivity to flourish. Connolly (1991: 84) argues that 'individuality secures space to be through resistance and opposition to bureaucratic pressures'. Haraway (1988: 580) pleads that '[w]e need the power of modern critical theories of how meanings and bodies get made, not in order to deny meanings and bodies, but in order to build meanings and bodies that have a chance for life'. Deleuze and Guattari (1987) argue that there is a difference between seeing the world as a repository of meaning in a static sense, and understanding the world as a 'cauldron of becoming'. And even Judith Butler, an advocate of what Seyla Benhabib calls a 'strong version of the Death of the Subject thesis' seems to open a space for the subject by noting a difference between being 'constituted' by discourse and being 'determined' by it (Butler 1990: 143). There is room to argue, as Benhabib does (1992: 214), that 'we are not merely extensions of our histories, that vis-a-vis our own stories we are in the position of author and character at once'. Social movements that begin as resistance to the existing systems of repositories of meaning—on issues from race to gender to the environment—can quickly evolve to movements of meaning and identity creation. Resistance to the products of social construction, resistance to the real attempts to kill the subject, is the practice of autonomy—a new life for subjects, rather than their demise.

Again, what can be seen in the new generation of theorists of plurality is a return to key concerns of the first generation. Bentley, Laski, and Follett attempted to bring about a shift in the understanding of sovereignty from the state to various groups. They assumed that a shift from unity to multiplicity was accompanied by a shift in sovereignty from the central unified power of the state to the sovereignty of multiple power centers of individuals and groups. The *real* death of the subject was in the economically interested/occupationally defined subjectivity of the last generation of pluralism. *That* concept of the subject filtered out much of the life of individuals and reconstituted any identity as interest. If any subject is now dead, it is the singular, limited, filtered, one-dimensional subject of post-war pluralism; the death of that subject is the rebirth of the multiplicity of subjectivity.

Pluralism has expanded from an assertion of a variety of identities in the first generation to a reassertion of that diversity in the third generation. What has been added is a critical examination of the construction of political subjects—not in order to kill the subject, but in order to understand the context of subjugation and the possibilities for subjectivity. This move embraces multiplicity in the recognition of varied visions or identities created both by, and as a response to existing political, social, economic, and cultural practices. As such, subjectivity is not only kept alive, but expanded into multiple directions of assertion, examination, and reconstruction.

Conclusion

The first, and basic, component of a critical pluralism is the recognition and acceptance of difference. This is the core of pluralist thought, both in its origins and in its recent resurgence. The first generation of pluralists began the push to recognize difference and bring it into both political theory and practice, and a recent wave of theorists—some explicitly 'pluralist', others not—are also formulating a politics based in the potential of acknowledged diversity. This acceptance includes a basic recognition of the different ways people experience political life, and is based on an acknowledgement of the plurality of the social realm. In this basic component of pluralist thought, the diverse, contingent, and evolutionary nature of identity is asserted, rather than one singular, predetermined, and permanent. These aspects of a recognition of difference form the basis of a politics that can enable agents to act from a variety of situations against multiple social problems—a politics of difference, resistance, and reconstruction. With this key element of pluralism in place, the focus, then, returns once again to Mary Follett's question of 1918: what is to be done with this diversity? I now turn to some of the political practices and relations necessitated by the recognition of difference.

4

Components of a Critical Pluralism: Ethics and Processes

Mary Follett's question has never been answered directly by those calling themselves pluralists, but there is much in contemporary theory that attempts to respond to the issue. What is to be done with diversity? With difference and multiplicity at the base of a resurrection of pluralism, what follows? How does the acceptance of contextualized rationality, situated knowledges, and diversity play out in political relations? How are diverse identities and subjects to relate to one another? What difference does difference make? What ethics and processes should a new critical pluralism adopt that work with the resurgence and insistence on multiplicity?

With the real recognition and acceptance of difference, the possibility develops for a series of new pluralist relations. This chapter will lay out what I see as key aspects of a newly developing generation of pluralism. Numerous contemporary authors have approached notions of pluralism anew, with discussions of the necessity of agonistic respect across differences, processes of intersubjective understanding and open discourse, a redefinition of 'unity', and the construction of solidarity and diverse political networks—each components of a growing realm of critical pluralism.

As I noted in the previous chapter, I am not arguing that all of the theorists I cite are explicitly pluralist—in fact very few actively seek to take on that label. I draw from numerous sources with far different aims and conclusions than my own, but each, I believe, has at (or near) the center of their concerns the key theme of difference and pluralization. My use of the term *critical* pluralism comes primarily from the desire to see pluralism as a form of critical theory, with both critical/deconstructive and reconstructive components.[1] I purposefully engage both critical modernism and constructive postmodern theory in my effort to distill a variety of theories into a workable definition of a contemporary pluralism that is both theoretically sound and practically implementable.

Taking at their root the multiplicity that James and Follett explicated, and that recent theorists have returned to, the proposed ethics, relations, and processes of a critical pluralism are quite different from those familiar notions of conventional pluralist behavior, centered around competitive self-interest, that were constructed and defended by many of the generation of pluralists in the middle of the century.

A Critical Pluralist Ethic: Agonistic Respect

As with the first generation, the basis of a re-emerging pluralism is an acknowledgement of multiplicity, an openness to ambiguity and the differences it spawns. This openness applies to both our own identities and those of others, as ambiguity and multiplicity are acknowledged as a basis of human agency. A number of contemporary theorists, such as Benhabib (1992), Connolly (1991, 1995), and Honneth (1992) argue for an ethic built around a respect for and acceptance of ambiguity and difference in ourselves and others. Agonistic respect is at the core of relations in a critical pluralism.

As Connolly argues, uncomfortable with difference, with multiplicity, with ambiguity, and uncomfortable with our own identities, we have tended to construct our own images of Others. These constructions serve to both bolster our own security and secure it against the incursions of other possibilities. And in the process, the Other is degraded and demonized.[2]

---

[1] There are two authors, as I have found, that use the term 'critical pluralism' in their work: Schumaker (1991) and Connolly (1991, 1995). As will be plainly seen, I am partial to Connolly's understanding of pluralization, though I expand upon the pluralist *ethics* he proposes, and include elements of critical pluralist *processes* and *practices*.

[2] Connolly has discussed this process as consisting of two faces of evil (1991: pp. ix, 3–8). (1) Attempts are made to protect a particular identity by defining as evil all the threats to the integrity of that identity. The purity of a religious identity, for example, is defended against the evil of sin and sinners. (2) The problem of uncertain identity is solved with the construction of the Other, against which an identity may more completely define itself. 'Identity required difference in order to

The question Connolly raises is why our own ambiguity and our differences with others necessarily entail building and demonizing generalized Others? Why, instead, could we not have a civil contestation of positions and an admiration of differences? A recognition and respect for identity and difference may entail a curiosity and interest in the position of the other, and the ability to view positions from a variety of standpoints and views. Affirmed ambiguity and reciprocal respect can only enhance political debate; it makes positions contestable and open to a form of critical responsiveness unavailable where otherness is demonized.

An ethic of agonistic respect exceeds the bounds of past pluralist notions of tolerance, as it moves to include an aspect of recognition. Classical notions of tolerance are usually grounded in one of two types of reasoning—a pragmatic skepticism that allowed for varying moral or political views, or a moral of respect, which was granted as a right to citizens as autonomous agents (Mendus 1988: 2). Toleration, however grounded, is simply the moral of allowing otherness, and difference, to be. Authors of the canonical tracts extolling the virtues of toleration differed on the relationship between toleration and diversity. Locke's defense of toleration in the *Letter Concerning Toleration* simply calls for the neutrality of the state, remaining neutral on the value of diversity (Waldron 1988). Mill's discussion of toleration in *On Liberty*, on the other hand, focuses on the value of diversity itself for the vitality of public life (Edwards 1988). Toleration in practice, then, can be manifest either in the blindness and indifference of the state to diversity, or in a more equalizing respect for the representatives of varied positions. While post-war pluralists focused on the former, both first-generation pluralists and recent theorists of plurality, democracy, and difference focus on the latter.[3]

Critics of the tolerance espoused by pluralists after the Second World War, and adopted in post-war political practice, are numerous.

be, and it converts difference into otherness in order to secure its own self-certainty' (p. 64). For an enlightening history of demonology in US political culture, see Rogin 1987.

[3] An example of indifference on the part of the state might be color-blind hiring policies at educational institutions, where the focus is on the process rather than the end. An example of equalizing respect would be a conscious effort at constructing a diverse workforce—not just to include tokens, but in order to validate the value of difference itself and the varieties of experience which would be brought to the institution.

Some focus on which positions, or identities, were consistently decided against; and how meaningless and 'repressive' the concept of tolerance became without real political recognition (see, especially, Wolff *et al.* 1965). Others argue that the toleration exemplified in this era results in conservatism. Even when tolerance has allowed a variety of evolving identities and issues into the political sphere, recognition continues to be limited. As conventional pluralism admitted new positions into the political discourse, it further marginalized those left out. The admission of some forms of racial criticism and environmental discourse, for example, served to further marginalize others, and this marginalization has allowed them to be dismissed. For example, the acceptance of civil-rights arguments allowed for the marginalization of black nationalist discourse; the ascendancy of mainstream environmental concerns with compromise and appeasement of industry has led to a state disdain of more radical and grassroots positions. Dryzek (1996*b*) argues that this inclusion has been a way to co-opt and disempower the radical potential of possible challenges to the state; this 'mere tolerance' is seen by others as the 'grossest reformism' (Lorde 1984: 111).

Finally, some theorists and activists have come to argue that a toleration based either in blindness or respect is too limited. As Lorde (1984: 115) argues, 'we have no patterns for relating across our human differences as equals'. An equal blindness is not equalizing recognition (W. Brown 1993: 392). Contemporary toleration is, as Connolly (1995: p. xvii) argues, 'an underdeveloped form of critical responsiveness grounded in misrecognition'. The contemporary logic of toleration, these theorists argue, is simply inadequate to deal with contemporary diversity.[4] A focus on expanding toleration into agonistic respect and critical responsiveness—a recognition and acceptance of the validity of a variety of positions and standpoints—revives the possibility for pluralistic relations. The ethic of agonistic respect serves the facilitation of differences; it is, as Connolly (1995: p. xvii) argues, 'an indispensable lubricant of political pluralization'.[5]

[4] For a thorough discussion of the way the grounds of toleration have changed, and an argument for toleration's inadequacy in the face of contemporary diversity, see McClure 1990.

[5] Connolly began a move in the evolution from mere tolerance with the concept of 'slack' proposed in *Politics and Ambiguity*. The introduction of slack in a political system is the opening of space for otherness to be (Connolly 1987: pp. xi, 11). Connolly continued this evolution in *Identity/Difference* (1991) with the move

A critical pluralism moves beyond the notion of tolerance and opens a space for the recognition of others. The evolution from toleration to agonistic respect includes both expanding respect to a wider range of others than toleration ever claimed, as well as attempting to move beyond the dogmatism of particular positions, towards a 'cultivation of care for the ways opponents respond to the mysteries of existence' (Connolly 1991: 33–4). In this way, Connolly follows William James, who argued that an important component of pluralist philosophy was an attempt to understand the other, to see alternatives, and to imagine foreign states of mind (1978: 4). James's discursive ideal was a sort of diverse banquet, 'where all the qualities of being respect one another's personal sacredness, yet sit at the common table of space and time' (1979 [1896]: 201). Connolly's notion of agonistic respect, in a way, helps finally to set the table for James's banquet in the current generation of pluralism—though, for Connolly, the assemblage resembles a potluck rather than a formal dinner (1995: 95).

Respect, and a cultivation of care, becomes the necessary relationship between self and other, away from the detachment, isolation, and demonization of conventional notions of competitive pluralism. An acceptance of ambiguity and others requires a refusal to repress difference whether we are in a hegemonic position or are marginalized. And this acceptance and refusal apply both internally and in regard to others. Connolly brings up the importance of a 'care of the self' as a basis for the ethic of agonistic respect. Here it is that a critical pluralism can develop an ethic to tie together two crucial pluralist themes: a care for ambiguity in the self, and a concomitant care for the same in the other.

Connolly's discussion mirrors that of Foucault in the final volume of the *History of Sexuality* (1988*a*). Here, Foucault focused on the cultivation of the self, and how this self-care 'came to constitute a social practice, giving rise to relationships between individuals, to exchanges and communications, and at times even to institutions' (p. 45). The care of the self, then, is linked to relations with others.[6]

---

towards a theory of agonistic respect, and in *The Ethos of Pluralization* (1995) with the discussion of critical responsiveness. With the avoidance of universalism and its accompanying exclusions, argues Connolly, and with the introduction, through slack, of ambiguity and multiplicity, the need for an agonistic ethic emerges.

[6] Both Foucault and Connolly see care as being evoked by a sense of curiosity, and the readiness for the unknown that accompanies it. See Foucault 1988*c*.

At one point, Foucault takes this link a bit further, when he posits that a care of the self 'includes the possibility of a round of exchanges with the other and a system of reciprocal obligations' (1988*a*: 54). He continued this link between the care of oneself and the care for others in an interview shortly before his death, where he argued that '[c]are for self is ethical in itself, but it implies complex relations with others, in the measure where this *ethos* of freedom is also a way of caring for others' (Foucault 1988*b*: 7). Once we include recognition or validation as part of the care of *oneself*, then mutual or reciprocal recognition becomes part of the relationship with others. On the other side, implicit in Foucault and argued by Connolly (1991: 76), if one lacks care for oneself, one will surely lack the ability to care for the identity and diversity in others.[7]

By bringing Connolly and Foucault together here, what emerges is a reciprocal, and self-perpetuating, ethic of care. Individuals cannot maintain identity in isolation. One's own identity depends on care for oneself, but it also depends on the existence of, and recognition from, the other. We are ethically implicated with others; we depend on differences with the other for our own identities (Connolly 1991: 166; C. Taylor 1994: 32–3). One needs both one's own care, and recognition from others, to strengthen one's own identity. Self-care is also the prerequisite of care for and recognition of *others*, which they, likewise, need in order to strengthen their own identity. The reciprocal ethic is one of recognition of, and care for, the identities of both self and other.[8]

This reciprocal respect for the other works in a variety of ways—all, again, beyond simple tolerance. As Connolly discusses (1991: 179), 'Sometimes one shows respect for another by confronting him with alternative interpretations of himself, sometimes by just letting him be, sometimes by pursuing latent possibilities of commonality, some-

---

[7] Foucault and Connolly are not alone on this track. The notion of care, both in regard to others and oneself, appears in other areas of contemporary theory. Difference feminism (Gilligan 1982; Ruddick 1980) and critical theory (Benhabib 1992; White 1991) serve as examples here. See also Tronto (1993).

[8] Reciprocal recognition by itself is not a novel concept. Hegel discussed it in his dialectic of master and slave; Adorno spoke of a reciprocal recognition in which one would no longer 'annex' the other, but remain 'distant and different . . . beyond that which is one's own' (Adorno 1973 [1966]: 191). But neither spoke of the additional need for a reciprocal *care* along with recognition. Both focus, ultimately, on a self- (and other-) destructive process. The reverse, however, is just as possible and self-perpetuating: reciprocal recognition and a self-perpetuating ethic of care of self and other—a more positive dialectic.

times by respecting her as the indispensable adversary whose contending identity gives definition to contingencies in one's own way
of being.' Each form includes a recognition, a respect, and a care for
the other; and each form expects reciprocity. The ethic and the
practices perpetuate themselves.[9] Again, critical responsiveness is a
'lubricant' for political pluralization.

Reciprocity is key here. We need not suffer fools, fascists, nor those
who refuse to grant us recognition, gladly. Agonistic respect is
an ethic of choice—it cannot be forced on the unwilling. There are
those for whom difference and pluralization is a threat. Fascisms and
fundamentalisms cannot be reciprocally appreciated.[10] But we cannot
dismiss particular identities out of hand without an attempt at recognition. It may be possible that the hateful and violent beliefs of
a young skinhead, for example, will preclude conversation, and, so,
individual or societal care. But it is also possible that an attempt at
understanding, and care, for them—a validation of their agency—
may garner a like response. Lack of care, and the concomitant alienation it breeds, may have led them towards their identification
with hate and violence. This destructive cycle may, possibly, be
reversed.

It is also crucial to make explicit that the relations of care and
respect do not dilute difference. Connolly's admittedly idealistic picture affirms identity without a need for dogmatization; but it remains
an *agonistic* democracy, matching care for the diversity of human life
with the real strife of political practice. It affirms human dignity and
respectful relations with others without recourse to communitarian
consensus, and opens the political space for difference to emerge
and flourish at the level of both the individual and in contending
constituencies (Connolly 1991: p. x).

For Laclau and Mouffe, it is continued antagonisms that keep

---

[9] This process may also offer a dialectical resolution of the dichotomy between
negative and positive liberty. The basis of negative liberty, or non-interference, is
not simply toleration, but an intersubjective recognition of the validity of others.
This, in turn, justifies and strengthens the positive liberty of self-definition. Others
do more than let me be; they offer a recognition and validation of my creation of
myself. My positive liberty, in turn, is limited, by the agonistic ethic, to the extent
that it does not interfere with the valid self-expression of others. Intersubjective
agonistic respect does not put one form of liberty over the other; rather, it incorp-
orates each to produce simultaneously both forms of liberty. See also Habermas's
discussion of the relationship between justice and solidarity (1990*b*).

[10] Habermas (1994) takes on this issue in a discussion of recognition issues in the
united Germany.

society from 'finally' constituting itself. Antagonisms keep the contingency of identity, and so the recognition of the validity of difference, alive (Laclau 1990: 17; Laclau and Mouffe 1985: 125). At times, however, Laclau and Mouffe come dangerously close to demonization, insisting on the necessity of others as *enemies*. These enemies, they argue, are the key to politics, always out there challenging identities and various alternative hegemonic projects (Mouffe 1990: 64; 1992*a*: 234). A word of caution is necessary here. True, others may use their power to attempt to negate or marginalize certain positions; but authentic democratic exchanges between competing visions can only occur when others are not demonized. Antagonisms can help to define, explore, and attempt to explain differences, but only if we keep the process of exploration open and not succumb to a demonization of others.

Intersubjectivity

An ongoing ethic of agonistic respect depends on the next component of critical pluralist relations—the practice of intersubjective communication. Intersubjectivity, as defined here, involves three different processes: the ability to recognize and accept concrete others, the ability to understand the position and view of the other, and the ability to communicate across differences with others. Intersubjectivity offers an understanding of, and a method for, each of these processes.

For Habermas, intersubjectivity is the precursor to and necessary process for communication among diverse subjects.[11] Language, simply put, is based on intersubjectivity—the ability of people to come to an understanding. The foundation for communication, argues Habermas, is the capacity of each to recognize the other as a subject. This basic footing for communication involves a key recognition of the other as a like, but separate, being. In this process of reciprocal recognition, each subject will recognize the other as both distinct and like oneself (Habermas 1970*a*: 211). Ironically, then, the first step in

---

[11] While I argue that much in Habermas's exploration of communicative action is of use to the practice of critical pluralism, I must emphasize again that the label could not apply to him. While his discussion of process deals explicitly with the limits of discourse within conventional pluralism, as I will argue, Habermas places some severe limits of his own on pluralization.

doing something with diversity is the recognition of similarities. Whatever our differences in terms of vision, situated knowledge, or position, the beginning of relations with others is a recognition of likeness, of subjectivity.

Intersubjectivity guarantees the recognition, the autonomy, and the identity of each subject who participates in conversation. It is a symmetrical process; relations of recognition travel both ways in communication. The process includes both asserting one's self and simultaneously recognizing the other. For Habermas, this mutual recognition establishes what he calls a 'democratic equivalence' among subjects. Benhabib describes this 'complementary reciprocity' as a relation where 'each is entitled to expect and to assume from the other forms of behavior through which the other feels recognized and confirmed as a concrete, individual being with specific needs, talents and capacities' (1992: 159). The first step into relations based in multiplicity, then, is our ability to see a concrete other who, while different, deserves the same recognition as a worthy subject that we expect from them.

In addition to this simple recognition of the other, however, intersubjectivity also calls for one to be able to see, in a sense, from the perspective of another. Habermas, at times, distinguishes between relations that are based on simply taking positions and responding to others' positions, and a more thorough intersubjectivity, where each participating subject will actually step into and internalize the understandings, attitudes, and expectations of the other (Habermas 1987a: 10). While intersubjectivity demands the recognition of each participant, it also calls for each to examine the subjective world of the other.

A recognition of the validity of multiplicity helps justify this process. If we accept situated knowledges (Haraway 1988) or radical empiricism (James 1976 [1912]) as the basis for multiplicity, there is a need, as discussed in Chapter 3, to examine the contexts of subjects in order to attempt to understand their perspective. To reach understanding, we attempt to communicate not just our positions, but where and how those positions come to be; simultaneously, we react not just to the position of the other, but the construction of their situation. In order to accomplish this, 'the capacity to reverse perspectives, that is, the willingness to reason from the others' point of view, and the sensitivity to hear their voice is paramount' (Benhabib 1992: 8). Benhabib (following Arendt) describes this as an 'enlarged mentality', where one develops the ability to reverse perspectives and take on the standpoint of the other (p. 145).

As I have noted, William James saw an understanding of the other, the ability to see and imagine others' states of mind—what we would now call intersubjectivity—as part of pluralist philosophy (1978: 4). G. H. Mead, who examined notions of intersubjectivity as a contemporary of James and Follett, borrowed a metaphor from the relativity theory of physics—that of passing trains—to discuss this capacity to hold onto one's own standpoint while understanding the other. Mead asks us to imagine ourselves sitting by the window in one train, watching another pass by. Then, visualize yourself in the passing train. In essence, we can occupy passage in both trains at once, holding two different positions by seeing the same occurrence, or the view, from two different standpoints. The two standpoints are both legitimate, as we are able to imagine ourselves in either one (see Mead 1932: 80–1). We are able, in other words, to take on the standpoint of another, understanding it as grounded and valid, while simultaneously remaining within our own world.

There is, however, a hesitance around intersubjectivity, especially around Habermas's model and the universalist ends he pursues. For all of Habermas's discussion of intersubjectivity and communication across differences, the end of the process is, for him, universal agreement on universalizable norms (Habermas 1990*a*: 67). Habermas attempts to portray positively the diversity and locality of positions and 'validity claims' by stressing the importance of local context. Reasoned argument and agreement, he asserts, depends on a diversity of voices. But Habermas argues that diversity is important solely in its role of bringing about singular consensus. For Habermas, the acceptance of contextuality ends when 'the transcendent moment of *universal* validity bursts every provinciality asunder' (1987*b*: 322). In this view, diversity necessarily converges on unity. All the trains of reason have a single destination; all views will eventually be identical.[12]

Critics have picked up on this insistence on a singular end in order to dismiss the entire intersubjective *process* as inherently universalizing. Iris Young (1986), for example, ties the process of intersubjectivity in with a critique of the normalizing and difference-denying end of communitarianism (which she sees in Benhabib

---

[12] Habermas continues this treatment of particularity in the discussion aptly titled 'The Unity of Reason in the Diversity of its Voices' (Habermas 1992).

1986*b*; C. Gould 1978; Sandel 1982; M. Taylor 1982). Young argues that theorists and activists alike should distrust attempts at reciprocal recognition 'because it denies difference in the concrete sense of making it difficult for people to respect those with whom they do not identify' (1986: 12). So those who are different from us will be left out of the intersubjective process and be denied validity. Moreover, she argues, for those within the process the sharing of subjectivities inevitably leads to unification and fusion, denying the reality of difference. 'The striving for mutual identification and shared understanding among those who seek to foster a radical and progressive politics, moreover, can and has led to denying or suppressing differences within political groups or movements' (p. 13). Bursting provinciality asunder leads to some real political problems.

While the move towards unification may be a possibility, especially if one insists on Habermas's model, I want to argue that it is in no way a necessary outcome of the intersubjective process. There are three ways of responding to the insistence on this necessity: there is a difference between *recognition of* and *unity with*, the *process* of understanding does not necessarily have to culminate in agreement, and our own ongoing ambiguity requires that intersubjectivity be an ongoing process.

First, Young obscures the difference between a *recognition* of the other and a *unity* with that other. In her view, to recognize the other is to become the other. Young sees this process as one that ultimately results in 'shared subjectivity' and the denial of difference. But recognition does not necessarily produce or demand unification. We can see a recognition of the like *capacities* of subjectivity—the series of experiences that create or construct our subjectivity, and the process of expressing that subjectivity—rather than the recognition of the like *content* of other subjects. Intersubjectivity entails the capacity to both see similarities and understand differences. With the recognition of the like process and capacities of subjectivity, we can have both a unity with others as subjects and agents as well as an understanding and appreciation for the differences our experiences create: agonistic respect. Agency is the commonality or the universal; difference is the inevitable result of that agency placed in a variety of contexts. Recognizing this likeness in others' agency is wholly different from denying all difference; in fact, it is the agency and the process of intersubjectivity which allows us fully to understand difference. Agency is the bridge between 'us' and 'them'; it is also the bridge between the universalistic place rightly feared by Young and a world of difference with no way of communicating—pure relativism (see Mohanty 1989).

Young, in her critique, also confuses the important difference between the *process* of reaching understanding with another with the universalistic *end* of agreeing with the other. The process of attempting understanding is equated with an attempt at 'common consciousness' (Young 1990: 231). But one can use the inter-subjective process in order to recognize the position of the other without taking on that position yourself. You can *understand* the other without becoming one with them. As Benhabib argues (1992: 197), Young does not heed the distinction between consensus and simply reaching an understanding. In this view, intersubjectivity does not call for a state of perfect understanding, or even basic agreement; it is simply a process of conversation which includes both understanding and misunderstanding, agreement and disagreement. As a method, it 'suggests the infinite revisability and indeterminacy of meaning' (Benhabib 1992: 198). The process of reaching under-standing is the only thing necessary to agree to—not any particular content or end that may come out of it. Intersubjectivity, then, does not end at consensus; it is a continual process of attempting to come to an understanding of the other. And as contexts and others change, as do we, the process allows that attempt at understanding others to continue.

Finally, it is also this continual change of ourselves and others that makes intersubjectivity impossible for Young (1986: 11). If we acknowledge that our own selves are multiple, ambiguous, and evolving, she argues, then it is not possible for us ever to have a set knowledge of ourselves—and, therefore, simply impossible for others to know us. Young here uses a critique of a unified self to argue against the possibility of any external unification. But again, what is important within intersubjective relations is the recognition of agency and the process of attempting to understand others. If we are multiple and ambiguous—as pluralists have believed from James and Follett to the present—then that is an aspect of agency. And if we focus on intersubjectivity as an ongoing process rather than as a means to a unified, set, and final end, then ambiguity and evolution, whether internal or external, will always give us something to do. Rather than ambiguity and change making intersubjectivity impossible, as Young argues, it makes it that much more necessary as an ongoing relation.

Intersubjectivity is a process, a method that enables the exchange of an understanding of otherness among subjects. And it can be used without any attempt to universalize the particular position, or any particular content, being discussed. Intersubjectivity, in this sense, is a tool for the recognition and communication of diversity. It is a process for attempting an understanding of the position of the other, a process by which multiple visions come to make sense to us. The question to ask is what diversity would be *without* the possibility of intersubjectivity. Would we prefer a continued growth of the atomization of individuals? An ever-expanding world of warring factions? Rather than either of these, and rather than the just as distasteful subordination of all differences to a universalistic singularity, the intersubjective process is a method for understanding and living within a wide range of diversity. Young laments that '[w]hatever the label, the concept of social relations that embody openness to unassimilated otherness with justice and appreciation needs to be developed' (1986: 23). The concept, and practice, *has* been developed.[13] Intersubjectivity can meet these desires of Young, and others, without necessarily falling into the dangers they presume foretold. It calls for an understanding of others without isolation or unification. It is the basis for communication in the pluralist universe.

Discourse and Pluralist Process

What, then, is the model of conversation for the agonistically respectful, intersubjectively attuned participants of a critical pluralism? The practices of agonistic respect and intersubjectivity call for one to communicate, and sustain a discourse, across the divide of differences. They enable a conversation across differences by setting the standards for a communicative process. This makes the discursive and decision-making process of a critical pluralism quite distinct from past pluralist notions. Once again, in discussing this process, I draw on a number of contemporary theorists who may or may not embrace the 'pluralist' label. But all of these theorists, taken together, represent a move to incorporate recognition and agonistic respect into new forms of pluralistic and democratic discourse.

The history of pluralism offers both interesting suggestions and

---

[13] For a discussion of models of intersubjectivity in practice in social movements, see Schlosberg 1995.

numerous problems around decision-making. The most common image we have of conventional pluralism's method involves interest groups competing against one another for scarce resources. For David Truman, pluralism meant interest groups which were, in essence, *pressure* groups. Groups within a pluralist system were defined as collections of people with shared attitudes that make claims against other groups, ostensibly with the state as a neutral arbiter (Truman 1960: 37). The inherent conflict between groups was both expected and understandable, to Truman, in view of the doctrine of competitive individualism infused within American culture. Truman harkened back to James Madison's Federalist #10 to make his case that state regulation of factional conflict is the principal task of government (Hamilton, Madison, and Jay, 1961). It is, then, the competing claims of groups that spark the conflict and controversy that make the essence of politics. Interest and pressure are central, rather than any discourse across differences.

The focus in other second-generation pluralist writings centered on the winners and losers of this competitive process. Both Dahl's study (1961) of New Haven and Edward Banfield's of Chicago (1961) examined the power and influence of various groups. For these authors, pluralism became the simple tenet that there will be different victors in various issue areas. The core question for each was what qualities add up to victory in group competition. The measure of Dahl's 'influence test' was which individual or group was able to pass or reject specific policy initiatives, and he examined the qualities of the successful 'homo politicus'. The whole focus of Dahl's pluralism at this point was on the power that some individuals and groups have *over* others in particular issue areas. Dahl argued that systems were open to a variety of groups; but the real center of the study was what it took to secure a win for a particular position.

The exception to these conventional pluralist considerations of competition and victory was Lindblom's (1965) attempt to reveal the intelligence and existing practice of 'partisan mutual adjustment'. Lindblom's discussion offers a good example of both some of the promise and problems of the pluralist thought of his generation. His focus was on a decision-making process that stood in contrast to centralized state decisions. He argued that a form of 'mutual adjustment' could already be found in a variety of forums, and was the fundamental form of political decision-making, in opposition to that by any centrality or state (p. 11).

Within this realm of partisan mutual adjustment, however, lay some of the aspects of pluralism many came to criticize. Lindblom acknowledged the inclusion of a variety of forms of direct and indirect manipulation, authoritative prescriptions, prior decisions, and reciprocal exchanges within the practice of mutual adjustment. Decision-making may have moved away from the centrality of the state, but much of it simply mirrored the larger, state-centered, play of competing, winning and losing, factions.

Lindblom did, on the other hand, offer an *ideal* form of mutual adjustment which mirrors the discussions of both earlier and later generations of pluralists. Lindblom saw the value in a process of decision-making that occurs when the parties at hand do not share a set of common values (1965: 132). It is exactly at such points of difference that partisan mutual adjustment can come into play. Lindblom was interested in how conflicting values were to be weighed against one another and reconciled in the process. Rather than sacrificing one value to another in the usual win-lose battle, Lindblom argued that 'partisan mutual adjustment sometimes stimulates a reconsideration of values that moves decision makers toward agreement. It is not only a process for resolving conflict among given values, but it also forms values' (p. 206).

Earlier in the century, Mary Follett picked up on the need for a discursive model for communication across differences. She eschewed a simple notion of compromise, which she considered dysfunctional, and called for something more inclusive, and respectful, of difference. 'When two desires are integrated, that means a solution has been found in which both desires have a place, that neither side has had to sacrifice anything' (Follett 1942: 32). Follett here is not simply arguing that all desires can be integrated into a compromise, but that inclusive solutions can be developed. Agreement was to be brought about 'by the reciprocal adaptings of the reactions of individuals, and this reciprocal adapting is based on both agreement and difference' (1918: 35). She was concerned that difference not lead to conflict, but was equally concerned that addressing conflict did not lead to the dismissal of diversity:

What people often mean by getting rid of conflict is getting rid of diversity, and it is of the utmost importance that these should not be considered the same. We may wish to abolish conflict but we cannot get rid of diversity. We must face life as it is and understand that diversity is its most essential feature. . . . Fear of difference is dread of life itself. (1924: 300–1)

Difference should not be confused, she argued, with antagonism, and should not arouse hostility (1918: 40). Discourse, then, should not be seen as contest.

[A]s long as we think of discussion as a struggle, as an opportunity for 'argument,' there will be all the usual evil consequences of the struggle theory. . . . We must learn to think of discussion not as a struggle but as an experiment in cooperation. We must learn cooperative thinking, intellectual teamwork. There is a secret here which is going to revolutionize the world. (1918: 97)

The key to Follett here is the focus on a communicative process open to difference. While she discusses notions of compromise and agree-ment, her central concern was with the nature of the process itself, and not just its conclusion.

There are certainly similarities in the goals held by Follett and Lindblom, as they both see understanding and modification replac-ing the standard practice of victory of one and sacrifice of the other. Their ideal also replaces the demonization of the other that goes with the competition of conventional pluralism. Unfortunately, Follett was largely ignored by the post-war pluralists, and Lindblom's ideal of partisan mutual adjustment did not become a major concern for others of his generation. This focus on difference and communica-tion, however, is a central part of the recent pluralist resurrection.

A return to a focus on alternatives to instrumental and alienating discursive processes is at the core of an emerging critical pluralism. Much of the literature on the inclusion of difference in public dis-course focuses on the *process* of deliberation that the recognition of, and respect for, difference engenders. Again, while not always explic-itly identifying themselves as pluralist, many theorists in the growing realm of deliberative democracy root their arguments in pluralistic assumptions of radical empiricism and situated knowledges. As Joshua Cohen (1996: 96) argues, deliberation is based in difference, and a

reasonable pluralism leads to a procedural conception of democracy. Accord-ing to such a conception, the democratic pedigree that lies at the source of legitimacy can be settled by looking exclusively to the processes through which collective decisions are made and to values associated with fair proc-esses: for example, values of openness, equal chances to present alternatives, full and impartial consideration of those alternatives.

Deliberative democracy is the procedure of a revived pluralism. As such, I read much of the literature of deliberative democracy as designs for the intersubjective banquet that both James and Connolly imagine.

While Habermas would eschew a number of the components of the critical pluralism I am attempting to lay out here and, for various reasons could not be considered a critical pluralist, we can see part of his project as following the discursive desires of Follett and Lindblom. Habermas's discussions of the 'ideal speech situation' are the most well known example of critical theory's foray into discursive decision models. The various rules Habermas (1970a, 1970b) lays out for communicative exchanges directly address issues of power and distortions of discursive processes that the second generation of pluralists were criticized for; they allow for a diversity of voices in open conversation. Moving towards the implementation of Habermas's communicative rationality in practice would, arguably, resolve a major concern of the critics of the post-war generation, removing the impediments to open participation.

Habermas lays out the conditions in which conversation across differences could flourish. Rather than the 'systematically distorted communication' of more instrumental relations, Habermas suggests a practice of 'communicative competence' within an 'ideal speech situation'. This ideal realization of intersubjectivity in decision-making would involve a situation free from domination and strategic motivations on the part of any participant. Anyone capable and interested would be included in the conversation; each could offer their own proposals and question those of others; and anyone could freely voice opinions, attitudes, and/or needs without any fear of reprisal. This ideal situation would be the perfect space for intersubjectivity to thrive and discussion to produce decisions mutually and freely agreed upon by all. As an ideal, this situation is unattainable; still, it is not unapproachable, and should be held up as a desirable counterfactual.

Habermas's model, however, is problematic in a number of its aspects, most obviously in his emphasis on universal ends. He calls for a revision of the Kantian categorical imperative, substituting the discourse of a group for the isolated individual in developing moral norms (1990a). But the end remains the development of universal norms (remember the effort to burst every provinciality asunder: Habermas 1987b: 322). Whatever Habermas's attempts to address issues of power and participation in discourse, the end remains the formation of universal norms, seemingly without concern for the disciplinary role of those norms—the importance of context in forming experience—even when more explicit manifestations of power are addressed. It is difficult to argue simultaneously for openness to difference within the process and an end that will burst these differences asunder.[14]

While Habermas offers much in the move towards more open and intersubjective communicative structures, his universalistic aims contradict the ideals of agonistic respect and intersubjectivity. Fortunately, a number of recent theorists offer more useful models, expanding the theory of discursive processes in directions beyond Habermas and developing deliberative models more thoroughly based on inclusion of and respect for difference.

While still focusing on a type of universalist end, Seyla Benhabib emphasizes the open nature of discourse toward a 'postenlightenment project of interactive universalism' which is continually open to difference (1992: 3). Multiplicity, locality, and identity construction are all taken into account, yet Benhabib insists that this diversity does not rule out a common process or end. Benhabib argues (1992: 153) that ' "universality" is a regulative ideal that does not deny our embodied and embedded identity, but aims at developing moral attitudes and encouraging political transformations that can yield a point of view acceptable to all'. The deliberative model she envisions embodies 'a *plurality of modes of association* in which all affected can have the right to articulate their point of view' (1996*b*: 73). Benhabib is clearly interested in the critical pluralist project of a validation of the contextual origins of identity and diversity and an extension of agonistic respect to others in open-ended conversation. The 'enlarged thinking' of intersubjectivity, or the ability to take the standpoint of others, necessarily includes the validation of multiplicity in any notion of communicative action. The ideal becomes not simply an open communication process, but the ability to reverse perspectives and take on the position of the other for the sake of

[14] Another problem is Habermas's focus on the inherent nature of this process in language. In order to give the theory of communicative action a solid, rational ground, Habermas argues that the communicative rules he describes are inherent and universal to all language. This essentialist grounding, however, is much less important to other theorists (see e.g. Lyotard 1984; Rorty 1986*a*). and those participating in actual discursive relations. There is no problem, for many looking for improved communication, in adopting processes that are new, different, or alien. In numerous examples of political practice, the main concern is the intersubjective value in a discussion—the recognition, validation of difference, and respect given each side—rather than an attempt at a rational and universal grounding of the theory (see Schlosberg 1995).

argument. Benhabib's interactive universalism does not *supersede* difference, but instead attempts to keep difference at the center of continued consensual agreements.

James Bohman, in a discussion of 'Public Reason and Cultural Pluralism' (1995), argues that the deep conflicts that are aroused when we take cultural diversity seriously cannot be solved by attempting to forge a public consensus based in a singular public reason. These conflicts can only hope to be solved if justice is made more inclusive, dynamic, and plural. Basically, Bohman argues for the acceptance of tenuous agreements that may be based on numerous types of reasoning: 'Political unity does not require that there be one public reason' (p. 263). This allows for an acceptance of political agreement without requiring that those agreements be reached for identical reasons (as both Habermas and Rawls demand). Bohman's model also calls for a type of compromise referred to by both James and Follett. Compromise is not simply 'splitting the difference' or finding some third and impartial position. Instead, the moral compromise Bohman sees as necessary with the recognition of pluralism is one in which parties establish a framework for discussion that includes the positions of each. In this process, parties 'modify their conflicting interpretations of the framework, so that each can recognize the other's moral values and standards as part of it' (p. 269). The very nature of the discussion is modified to be respectful, and inclusive, of difference. Bohman's discursive pluralism—his attempt to set a stage for the working through of 'deep disagreements'—represents another move away from toleration as impartiality towards a form of reasoning based on agonistic respect.

John Dryzek notes the distance in critical theory from discussions of political and social applications, and concentrates on the possibilities of a discursive process in the design of real-world political and social practices (1990a). Like Benhabib, his focus is on the process, rather than the universalist origins and ends of Habermas's discursive theory. Dryzek draws a picture of non-hierarchical spaces where citizens—from either similar or different backgrounds—discursively design political organization and policy. He offers examples of the process in practice—mediation, some forms of regulatory negotiation, and the internal practices of new social and political movements—and argues for the expansion of these practices in policy design.

Iris Young attempts to take pluralist discourse further than these examples of deliberative democracy. For Young (1996), the notion of deliberation itself limits and excludes many forms of communication. The norms of deliberation, she argues, privilege assertive, confrontational, formal, dispassionate, and disembodied speech. Those same norms disregard and disempower tentative or conciliatory speech, as well as other forms of communication, including forms of greeting, rhetoric, and storytelling. All of this, asserts Young, silences individuals or groups who are less confident in their speaking style, or who communicate in a manner that differs from the ideal of rational argument. To be truly inclusive, Young insists on what she calls 'communicative' democracy, rather than deliberative democracy. While Young has a valid argument with Habermas, who does insist on the force of the 'better argument', she overstates her case against discursive democrats like Dryzek and Bohman. As I read them, there is nothing in Dryzek (1990*a*), Bohman (1995), or for that matter Benhabib (1992, 1996*b*), which would lead to the exclusion of the types of communication that Young defends.[15] Young illustrates that there are certainly differences—at least of emphasis—in the attempts to expand democratic discourse. But she also illustrates the length to which pluralist democratic discourse must go if it is truly to embody the epistemological and methodological pluralism on which it is based.

Crucial to *all* of these extensions of communicative action is an emphasis on the ongoing nature of the process. The point here is that decision-making for a resurrected pluralist universe focuses not on the *substance* of decisions, but on the *process* for making communication across diversity both possible and fruitful.[16] The openness to difference and the emphasis on process helps show the impossibility of finally fixing a consensus on identity, truth, or a social order. Rather, relations are continually evolving. The ongoing generation of different antagonisms, and the discourses among them, keep us from finally constituting ourselves. This focus on process brings with it a suspicion of completion. A critical pluralism eschews a permanent

---

[15] Numerous theorists, such as Dryzek and Benhabib, begin within a Habermasian framework of open discourse and expand what it is that is valid within that realm. Storytelling, for example, is explicitly included in Patsy Healy's Habermasian rules for public planning (Healy 1993).

[16] See Bickford (1996) for an argument on the central role of *listening* in this process.

consensus. The final consensus, or 'generalized norms', that have been emphasized in both past notions of pluralism (e.g. Dahl) and in much critical theory (especially Habermas), are regarded as inhibitions to the further and continuing interplay of differences. Conscious of the normalizing tendencies of unity, the emphasis on process simultaneously combats normalization while emphasizing the continuation of, and the communication between, difference.

Dryzek, for example, emphasizes that a 'a succession of discursive exercises held up to critical scrutiny could create and reinforce norms of free discourse. . . . In so doing, such exercises would . . . help constitute a world increasingly hospitable to truly discursive designs and to the participatory *process* of discursive design' (1990*a*: 87). Bohman argues that, rather than focus on like reasons, moral decision-making demands only that parties cooperate within a certain process of public deliberation. Likewise, Benhabib argues that the 'emphasis now is less on *rational agreement*, but more on sustaining those normative practices and moral relationships within which reasoned agreement *as a way of life* can flourish and continue' (1992: 38). Young (1996) also emphasizes the importance of process rather than substance in searching for unity; she argues the only unity necessary is that around the open deliberative process and the respect that allows it to proceed.

Connolly notes the benefits of what he calls 'democratic turbulence' (1987: 15; 1991: 200). Expanding on the desire for the openness to 'slack', he suggests a practice based on periodic, or ongoing, renegotiations. Likewise, Laclau and Mouffe argue that notions of social orders are precarious and ultimately failed attempts to domesticate differences, and suggest an openness like that of Connolly (Laclau and Mouffe 1985: 96 and 142). Similarly, Rorty (1989: p. xvi) argues the end is not one of utopia, but of a continual process of envisioning further utopias. The focus on process and continual openness to difference is consistent with a focus on freedom rather than truth, process rather than end. The openness to difference and the emphasis on process helps show the impossibility of finally fixing a consensus on identity, truth, or a social order. Rather, relations are continually evolving. The ongoing generation of different antagonisms, and the discourses among them, keep us from finally constituting ourselves.

Within a critical pluralist world of multiplicity, the concern is not primarily with the creation of the content of consensus, ends, or truth, but rather on this ongoing process. The ethics of attempts at intersubjectivity, agonistic respect, and discursive practices are all *processual* ethics. The critical pluralist project emphasizes these processes over content, allowing for an institution of discursive practices among a plurality of positions, knowledges, and understandings.[17]

The emphasis on the benefits of process has become a focus in social movements that have moved towards open discursive processes, and critical pluralists can heed lessons learned in the theory of these movements. Melucci (1985, 1989, 1996), for example, argues that one of the most important and unique features of new social movements is their concern with the very *form*, or organizational structure, of the movement as a sign or message for the rest of society. The focus is on the present, on form, and on process, rather than the sole vision of some all-embracing form of order which was a focus of past movements. 'The new organizational form of contemporary movements is not just "instrumental" for their goals. It is a goal in itself. Since the action is focused on cultural codes, the *form* of the movement is a message, a symbolic challenge to the dominant patterns' (Melucci 1985: 801). In Habermas's terms, these movements and their forms show a key concern for the 'grammar of forms of life' (1981: 33).

Finally, this realm of discursive process expands beyond, and opens possibilities outside, the sphere of the state. From Lindblom's discussions of partisan mutual adjustment, to Dryzek's advocacy of discursive competency, to Melucci's descriptions of new social movements, this aspect of critical pluralism extends the process of political discussion beyond the boundaries of the state. In a focus on the development of discursive processes, critical pluralism revitalizes the emphasis of the first generation of pluralism on the importance of political relations in the spaces *between* individuals and the state. New social movements, being a key example of the emergence of critical pluralism in practice, are interested in form and process specifically because of the manipulation, instrumentalization, alienation, and

---

[17] This emphasis on process, however, does not make the outcome of debate irrelevant. No outcome would be acceptable that put limitations on discourse in any way; an overriding concern would be enhancing the conditions for broadening participation.

normalization created by existing political processes of the state. What is truly new about new social movements, and critical pluralism, is a *dual* concern with a critique of existing institutions of the state and civil society *and* the creation of new forms and spaces for their political and social practices. These movements, focusing on process, form, lifeworld, etc., proliferate new and different political spaces. They create and emphasize free spaces between the state and individual. These free spaces are not only where more instrumental forms of organization and communication are criticized, but they also become the training grounds for new forms of communication and new activism (see Evans and Boyte 1986).

Here we are able to come back to a realm more familiar with the first generation of pluralists, that of group life. Social movements are a living example that have helped to reinvigorate the discussion of civil society (see esp. Cohen and Arato 1992: ch. 10). A focus of critical pluralism is on the creation of and practices of these free spaces and liberated areas of civil society, whereas the form and process of voluntary associations were of little interest to the last generation of pluralists. As Laski argued early in the century, decentralization is key to pluralism, 'because it is realized that where administrative organization is made responsive to the actual associations of men, there is a greater chance not merely of efficiency but of freedom also' (Laski 1921: 247). The first generation heavily emphasized moving the understanding and practice of political processes from the state to civil society, and the next generation ignored this plea. A critical pluralism restates that key concern, focusing on political processes within and among individuals and groups in the social realm.

The discursive process of a revised pluralism envisions conversations based on a recognition and acceptance of multiplicity, agonistic respect, and intersubjectivity. Moving away from the partisan and competitive nature of communication in the last generation of pluralism, as well as the universalism of the origins and ends in Habermas's communicative action, a critical pluralist process focuses on the ongoing nature of communication across differences. The discursive process, as the communicative form a critical pluralism takes in practice, is simultaneously a means and an end. And it returns the pluralist's attention away from its conventional and sole

focus on state-centered decisions, back into the various levels of civil
society where crucial political discourse takes place.

Unity Without Uniformity: Pluralist Solidarity

Discourse, however, is only a part of pluralist process, focusing on
communication across difference. But the other crucial part of a
critical pluralist process is the construction of political *solidarity* and
action. The question is not simply how we are to communicate across
differences, but how we are to build relations, movements, and political structures that have an ethic of agonistic respect at their base. The
structure of pluralist action is as central to process as discourse. As
we saw in Chapter 3, the basic recognition, acknowledgement, and
philosophical justification of difference, and the defense of difference
against unitary tendencies, is certainly the core of the pluralist universe. But a pluralism based on this recognition of difference and
ongoing discourse is subject to the charge that it will never allow the
possibility of unity, in either theory or political practice. The fact is
that pluralists have, from the beginning of the century, had difficulties reconciling the recognition of multiplicity with the necessity of
political action on a scale larger than the individual or small group.
Here is one area where recent theorists are not only resurrecting the
concerns of pluralists such as James and Follett, but are expanding
on and building from those concerns. From these explorations, and,
as we will see in Chapter 5, from the practice of new social movements like the environmental justice movement, the structures of a
critical pluralism become apparent.

In her lament about what to do about diversity, Follett (1918: 10)
was looking for 'a new conception of modes of association', a model
for building political action both within and across diverse groups.
While critical of the normalization associated with more singular and
absolutist visions of the state, Follett and others saw that *some* elements of unity must emerge if disparate ideas, people, and/or groups
are to relate and work together. In both the first and recent generations of pluralist thought, some sort of unity or solidarity—the necessity of relations across differences—have been as central as eschewing
a unitary, homogeneous uniformity.

James argued that his concept of radical empiricism represents
order as always in the making. The notion of evolution in James's
pluralism keeps unity forever over the horizon—moved towards but

never arrived at. But James did not dismiss the possibility of some level or form of unity. Pluralism, he argued,

has no need of... dogmatic rigoristic temper. Provided you grant *some* separation among things, some tremor of independence, some free play of parts on one another, some real novelty or chance, however minute, she is amply satisfied, and will allow you any amount, however great, of real union.... This leaves us with the common-sense world, in which we find things partly joined and partly disjoined. (James 1975 [1907]: 78–9)

It was crucial for James that things could remain both independent and, at times, connected. The pluralist universe was a place that emphasized both plurality and unity—but a particular, tenuous, and non-dominating type of unity. Pluralism 'means only that the sundry parts of reality *may be externally related*... Things are "with" one another in many ways, but nothing includes everything, or dominates over everything. The word "and" trails along after every sentence. Something always escapes' (1977 [1909]: 145). Connections can be made in the pluralist universe without recourse to an insistence on uniformity or monism; the result is a 'multiverse' rather than a universe.

Unity, then, is still possible, but of a very different sort. James pondered a number of representations of how difference could come together:

Our 'multiverse' still makes a 'universe'; for every part, tho it may not be in actual or immediate connexion, is nevertheless in some possible or mediated connexion, with every other part however remote, through the fact that each part hangs together.... The type of union, it is true, is different here from the monistic type.... It is not a universal co-implication, or integration of all things.... It is what I call the strung-along type, the type of continuity, contiguity, or concatenation. (1977 [1909]: 146–7)

James's ideal reaches for the possibility of unity, but continues to contain the reality and necessity of a remaining disunity. In constructing a picture of unity, James not only insists on the possibility of parts remaining outside, but also on the tenuous nature of the unity itself. In both of these, James refers to the metaphor of a mosaic. 'My description of things, accordingly, starts with the parts and makes of the whole a being of the second order. It is essentially a mosaic philosophy' (1976 [1912]: 22). But James differentiates his own use of the metaphor from the standard image of a mosaic: 'In radical empiricism there is no bedding; it is as if the pieces clung together by their edges, the transitions experienced between them forming their cement' (p. 42). Elsewhere he argues that '[t]hings cohere, but the act of cohesion itself implies but few conditions, and leaves the rest of their qualifications indeterminate' (1979 [1896]: 201). The point here is that unity does not require a singular unifying commonality, glue, or mortar. Instead, the mosaic James wants to construct from pluralist foundations holds itself together along the common edges of the pieces, and the mosaic itself becomes the only commonality.

Again, this struggle with the need for a revised definition of unity was not uncommon in this generation. Mary Follett also advocated a very particular type of 'unity', and her concerns of 1918 resonate loudly in an era in which 'unity in diversity' has become a rather undefined slogan. Evolution, instability, and diversity play central roles in her definition. Unity, she argued, is an essential characteristic of social and political relations, but it is 'always in unstable equilibrium, always shifting, varying, and thereby changing the individual at every moment . . . [Society] can be understood only by the study of its flux of relations, of all the intricate reciprocities which go to make the unifying' (Follett 1918: 76). Follett differentiated quite clearly the terms 'unity' and 'uniformity' by arguing that '[u]nity, not uniformity, must be our aim. We attain unity only through variety. Differences must be integrated, not annihilated, nor absorbed.' Inclusion is key, as opposed to incorporation. She argued for building relations across differences, but understood the difficulties the process could bring: 'Good words: integrate, interpenetrate, . . . compound, harmonize, . . . coordinate, interweave, reciprocally relate . . . Bad words: fuse, melt, amalgamate, assimilate, weld, dissolve, absorb, reconcile' (Follett 1918: 35 n. 1). In the end, it is heterogeneity, and not homogeneity, which makes a unity without uniformity (p. 40). Unity, for Follett, is a concept of entirety; its meaning is made out of continually shifting differences and the understanding of those differences by participants. The problem of universals was for Follett, as it was also for Barker (1957 [1915]: 160), the problem of identity/ difference.

The metaphors may differ, but the central concerns of James and Follett on the nature of pluralist unity have been resurrected in some illuminating approaches of recent pluralist theory. The key continues to be the separation of unity and totality, and an acceptance of a range of possible, and shifting, unities. As with James, contemporary authors who defend radical empiricism address the concern with reconceptualizing unity.

Richard Rorty (1989) has focused on solidarity across differences, and offers a (somewhat limited) glimpse at a conscious construction of relations of solidarity.[18] Rorty centers on the similarity we might have with others in the experience of pain and suffering. Solidarity is a goal that 'is created by increasing our sensitivity to the particular details of the pain and humiliation of other, unfamiliar sorts of people. Such increased sensitivity makes it more difficult to marginalize people different from ourselves' (Rorty 1989: p. xvi). Solidarity comes when the range of differences we have with people around religion, race, customs, etc., are seen as 'unimportant when compared with similarities with respect to pain and humiliation' (1989: 192). We consider different people as part of the range of 'us' when we recognize this similarity of singular importance.

But solidarity ends, in Rorty's scheme, solely with a recognition of pain and humiliation. We are not to include any other emotions or aspects of human agency or experience in the range of 'us'. In addition, as solidarity ends with the *recognition* of pain and suffering, we are not to explore, in Rorty's 'post-modernist bourgeois liberalism' (Rorty 1983, 1986*b*), what might be the various *causes* or *origins* of this pain in either our own social situations or that of others. An emphasis on 'private perfection' in his pragmatic liberalism precludes furthering solidarity beyond either pain or recognition (see the discussion in Bernstein 1990). Rorty takes pragmatism and radical empiricism from Dewey and James, but ignores the radical pluralism of the same generation, leaving us with a private life of contingency within existing liberal public institutions. There is no sense of the

---

[18] According to Rorty, we believe things are true either because they are *absolutely* true, or because they are what our *community* has developed as truth. Rorty himself favors the later view of the world, and cites James's pragmatism in his reasoning. It is what we experience and believe that is, in fact, truth, as opposed to some objective basis away from human experience. What James argued against as absolutism, Rorty labels objectivist. James emphasized the impossibility of a singular end, Rorty the illusionary methodology of a 'god's eye view'. Unfortunately, Rorty's first foray into the notion of solidarity (Rorty 1985) is contaminated with an insistence on 'ethnocentrism'. To be in solidarity, in this view, is necessarily to privilege one's own group. With 'others' who do not share our beliefs, Rorty argues, it is not possible to have fruitful conversation (1985: 13). This ethnocentrism, and necessary exclusion, obviously opens the door to both the universalization Young (1986) warns against, as well as the demonization of others Connolly (1991) so thoroughly fears.

importance of groups, of civil society, as there was in the first generation of pluralists, and which has become central to a revived pluralism as well. While others have criticized Rorty for a lack of the
radicalism that informed Dewey's pragmatism (see Bernstein 1987;
McCarthy 1990), the same can be said for his disregard for James's
pluralism. For James, radical empiricism 'harmonizes best with a
radical pluralism' (1976 [1912]). Rorty refuses to follow through on
the radical political possibilities, and reality, of the building of real
solidarity.[19]

Other recent theorists offer more expansive notions of pluralist
structure and processes. Foucault, for example, offers an exposition
of this concern in principles derived from Deleuze and Guattari's
Anti-Oedipus (1983: p. xiii): 'Free political action from all unitary and
totalizing paranoia. Develop action, thought, and desires by proliferation, juxtaposition, and disjunction, and not by subdivision and
pyramidal hierarchization. . . . Prefer what is positive and multiple,
difference over uniformity, flows over unities, mobile arrangements
over systems.' Foucault here mirrors—certainly without intent—
James's validation of multiverse, and Follett's call for heterogeneity
over uniformity. The difference is that Foucault eschews the word
'unity' while arguing for the same multiplicity, flows, and mobile
arrangements these early pluralists advocated. While Foucault calls
for 'flows over unities', mobile arrangements can be seen as flows *of*
unities, allowing for both the possibility of unity, or alliance, and the
reality of ever-changing experiences and positions.[20]

Deleuze and Guattari themselves use the metaphor of the rhizome
to express this type of unity. Rhizomes are a type of root system that
do not send up just one sprout or stalk; rather, they spread under-
ground, emerge in a variety of locations, and connect in ways that are

---

[19] The limitations of Rorty's solidarity are numerous, but aspects of it are redeem-
able. It is important to Rorty to note that any solidarity must be *created*, rather than
simply found. It takes effort to bring those previously considered 'other' into the
fold of 'us'. It is also important that solidarity focuses on something we are to
recognize in the other as similar to ourselves. Fortunately, we have more in common
with others than pain and humiliation—though those are crucial, and quite common, bases for the formation of real political movements. Solidarity can, however,
be more expansive. If the previously discussed practices of intersubjectivity,
agonistic respect, and open discursive process are brought to bear in the relationship between 'us' and 'them', the realm of solidarity can develop beyond the
singular, painful, plane of human experience that Rorty emphasizes.
[20] Foucault has often been branded a nihilist by his critics, but he offers a lesson
on keeping the tension between multiplicity and unity alive. 'My point', he argues,
'is not that everything is bad, but that everything is dangerous, which is not exactly
the same as bad. If everything is dangerous, then we always have something to do'

not always visible. The first three characteristics of a rhizome are connection, heterogeneity, and multiplicity (1987: 7–8). Deleuze and Guattari's assertion of these characteristics as principles mirrors the desire of James and Follett for both difference *and* connection. While the decentering that Deleuze and Guattari argue for is what is usually focused on, it is crucial that they see *connection* as a central—in fact, the *first*—principle. The metaphor specifically illustrates a particular form of unity; they insist that 'the rhizome is alliance, uniquely alliance' (p. 25).

While neither Foucault nor Deleuze and Guattari use the term pluralism, William Connolly uses this rhizome metaphor in constructing his version of a radical, critical, or in this case rhizomatic, pluralism: 'A rhizome might be varieties of plant life without deep roots, connected by multiple nodes. Or it might be a variety of human constituencies, each touched in what it is by the dense, multifarious networks, human and nonhuman, in which it participates (1995: 94). The recognition and acknowledgment of this diversity is the key to rhizomatic linkages; for Connolly, a contemporary democratic pluralism is based on the contingency and evolving nature of both one's own identity and one's links with others. 'In rhizomatic pluralism the possibilities of collaboration around a particular issue increase as each constituency enhances the experience of contingency and social implication in its own formation' (ibid.). The rhizome metaphor is about alliance, but an alliance that is distinguished from singular, set (and, to Connolly, 'arboreal') notions of conventional pluralism.

Haraway has also addressed the issue of unity in her general discussion of the 'cyborg' (1991 [1985]). One of the many notions of cyborg that Haraway emphasizes is that of a 'cyborg community'—a community that is artificially constructed. For Haraway, solidarity is made up of elective affinities. She follows up on the reality of contingency and situated knowledge, making for a sense of solidarity that is congruent with radical empiricism and multiplicity. Haraway sees solidarity, based in a mutual intersubjective understanding of other viewpoints, forming around a large realm of possibilities: '[A] cyborg world might be about lived social and bodily realities in which people are not afraid . . . of permanently partial identities and contradictory

(1983: 231–2). The something to do is not an imposition of conceptions, discourses, or systems, but a vigilance against that imposition. It requires a continued openness toward difference, the situated and mobile nature of meaning, and the continued tension between multiplicity and unity.

standpoints. The political struggle is to see from both perspectives at once because each reveals both dominations and possibilities unimaginable from the other vantage point' (1991 [1985]: 154). Haraway pushes the reality of contingency and situated knowledge further than Rorty does, making for a sense of solidarity that is much more congruent with radical empiricism and multiplicity.[21] Expanding on the concept of cyborg politics, Gray and Mentor discuss 'building new political bodies and bodies of bodies across the nets . . . Field, system, network, web—these "inhuman" metaphors, these apparent antitheses to an organic "bodily knowledge" and scale—are the new geopolitical territories to be inhabited and contested' (1995: 459–60).

These cyborg constructions, these solidarities, are, importantly, partial. The making of connections is not total, but based on areas of partial overlap. Partial, locatable knowledges sustain 'the possibility of webs of connections called solidarity in politics and shared conversations in epistemology' (Haraway 1988: 584). For Haraway, there is nothing in assertions against objectivity—and for partiality, local knowledge, and differentiated experience—that rules out the construction of a solid collective in the realm between individuals and the state. As the first generation of pluralists discovered, it is that partiality that makes the construction of localized solidarity possible.

Iris Young has invoked Sartre's concept of a 'seriality' to explore the reality of shared experience creating unity without uniformity. A serial collectivity is used to identify a collective without insistence on a common identity—to note both connection and disconnection. 'A series is a collective whose members are unified passively by the relation their actions have to material objects and practico-inert histories' (1994: 727–8). Sartre's examples include people waiting for

---

[21] It is quite interesting that Haraway uses the case of the anti-nuclear Livermore Action Group (LAG) as an example of her notion of solidarity. 'I like to imagine LAG . . . as a kind of cyborg society, dedicated to realistically converting the laboratories that most fiercely embody and spew out the tools of technological apocalypse, and committed to building a political form that actually manages to hold together witches, engineers, elders, perverts, Christians, mothers, and Leninists long enough to disarm the state' (Haraway 1991: 154–5). They held together long enough to attempt it, anyway, and get thousands of themselves arrested (the present author included). But what is crucial to this example is that LAG actually practiced many of the components of the critical pluralism that I am laying out here, in addition to solidarity. Their discursive, or consensus, process was based on attempts at agonistic respect and intersubjective understanding—the only way to build solidarity from the quite varied subjective positions that made up the organization. For more on LAG, and the practices of the direct-action movement in general, see Epstein (1985, 1991).

a bus or listening to the radio—collectives brought together by their relation to a material object, the bus or the radio station. But their collective ends there—they do not necessarily identify with each other in other ways, and their membership in these serial collectives does not define their identity. Young argues for the use of seriality in feminism; it would, she argues, allow for some conception of women as a collective without insisting on a common identity, and allow for a notion of commonality while simultaneously problematizing 'women' and 'gender' as social constructions. Self-conscious groups may form out of serial collectives—as when a bus is late and riders talk of past problems or alternative modes of transport, when radio listeners band together to protest when an offensive song is played, when mothers form a group to protest toxins in their neighborhood, or when women band together along any of the lines that connect them as a serial collective. One of the key points for Young, however, is that identification with others does not necessitate a singular, monolithic identity. Difference abounds, even in instances of serial recognition. This notion begins to differentiate contemporary pluralists (though Young prefers 'difference democrat') from more conventional notions.

In addition, Young insists upon the partial and fluid nature of any of the groupings that come out of seriality. She agrees with Sartre that all groups arise and fall back into serial groupings, and with Butler that the question of solidarity should never be settled, but continually shift. This is not just the nature of series and groups, but larger coalitions of groups as well. In discussing women as seriality in particular, 'groupings of women will always be partial in relation to the series . . . because a group will have particular objectives or purposes that cannot encompass or even refer to the totality of the condition of women as a series. This is why feminist politics must be coalition politics' (Young 1994: 737). At the core, of course, is the construction of James's mosaic and Follett's unity without uniformity. And at the end is an ever-evolving and permutating seriality—again, certainly a form that distinguishes a new critical pluralism from past conventional notions.

The attempt to redefine the notion of unity is also mirrored in some respects in Laclau and Mouffe's attempt to develop a pluralistic linkage across diverse social movements. Like James, they believe that all experience cannot logically be explained by one logic or 'all-form'. The universalism which was the aim of past Marxist *and* pluralist accounts is decisively dismissed (1985: 191–2). In the political realm, their conception of a radical pluralism emerges from a foundation of multiple social movements and calls for an acceptance of the multiplicity and autonomy among resistances, rather than attempting a new unification of these movements under a single founding principle (p. 167). Laclau and Mouffe argue for an understanding of 'equivalence' among various movements, and the possibility of shared democratic discourse—the articulation of similarities across differences. Like Follett, they stress a unity that is based on a proliferation of differences and the possible relations among them.[22]

Young and Laclau and Mouffe illustrate how these pluralistic conceptions of unity have been brought into recent political practice in the increasingly popular use of alliances and networks in grassroots organizing. Political theorists, of course, were not the first to recognize the significant nature of this organizational form. African-American artist and activist Bernice Johnson Reagon (1983) has written of the importance of the incorporation of difference in the development of coalition politics. Coalitions, necessary because experiences are diverse, are not comfortable sites of homogeneity. They are instead places where differences meet—places made up of the hard work of constructing unity without insisting on sameness. As Susan Bickford argues (1996: 137) in discussing Reagon, 'working and speaking together do not require unitary conceptions of community and identity'. Bickford quotes Audre Lorde (1984: 142): 'You do not have to be me in order for us to fight alongside each other.' The ideal of the coalition here is one that builds unity from heterogeneity—not by subsuming difference into a singular new group identity, but by keeping the tension of difference palpable as part of a constructed unity.

Multiplicity, and the validation and examination of diverse experiences, does not make unity—either ideological or political—impos-

---

[22] Acting from a revised conception of unity is not easy. There is a tension both inherent and necessary in a unity created by difference rather than similarity, but it is not difficult for this tension to break down. Laclau and Mouffe's redefinition of hegemony is based on a unity of different and disparate struggles, but at times their new hegemony breaks down into the worst type of the old hegemony: a singular vanguardism. At a symposium on identity and diversity, Mouffe's talk emphasized an anti-essentialist position. But in audience discussion regarding the role of the left, Mouffe exclaimed that '[w]e've got to impose our conception; that is absolutely central in the struggle for democratic politics' (1992b: 39). Imposition of conceptions quite obviously runs counter to a continued tension between unity and diversity (not to mention democracy).

sible. Rather, a new construct of unity is produced through recognition and inclusion of multiplicity and particularity. Finally, it is important to note that in addition to constructing solidarity and community around possibilities *other* than pain, there is the possibility of solidarity being built around an *analysis* of pain, or domination—a more thorough solidarity than Rorty, for example, would desire. Many political groups focus not just on the similar experience of pain, but on the similar symptoms of specific experiences. In other words, solidarity is often formed out of similar critiques of social conditions and agreement on methods and tactics for alleviating the pain and humiliation of those conditions. Groups organizing around any of numerous identities or positions do so not only to identify themselves as part of a particular population, but also to *change* their position. In essence, they organize not just to acknowledge pain and humiliation and share in the experience, as Rorty would have, but to analyze their situations and actually do something to alleviate them.

As I will argue in Chapter 5, the political strategy of networks as practiced in the environmental justice movement embodies the definition of unity and the structure of solidarity or coalition that is the heart of critical pluralist action. The movement really has no center; rather, there are a number of identity- and issue-based organizations and networks, as well as regional networks working on a variety of issues. The movement serves as a model of Follett's notion of unity without uniformity, and represents all the contemporary pluralist metaphors: mosaic, rhizome, cyborg, and serial community. Recognition of diversity need not be followed by a classification, a hierarchization, or a filtering into a normalizing unification, as we have seen in much of the literature surrounding environmentalisms. Rather, a critical pluralism demands a conception of unity which does not deny the basis of 'mobile arrangements' or alliances among the differing experiences of those that construct them. Difference, and the proliferation and juxtaposition of diversity, may spawn a plethora of possible unities. And this unity is, by the very nature of the subjects who construct it, situated, evolutionary, and of course critical of the social conditions that spur the need for their action.

It is crucial to close with a note on the tensions within pluralist theory on the concept of unity. James's 'multiverse' and Follett's 'unity without uniformity' still retain the possibility and the necessity of solidarity and the making of connections. And both held open the hope for a sense of unity that was not as destructive or exclusive as the monism they were arguing against. James even expected unity to increase over time, as 'trains of experience, once separate, run into one another' (1976 [1912]: 43). While his understanding of experience should have led James to see these trains running *away* from unity as well as towards it, he had a religious or spiritual attraction to the possibility of some form of unblemished unity. Follett's attraction was to a Hegelian sense of unity; while other pluralists singled Hegel out as one of the monist problems, she argued a very particular interpretation of his unified ends.[23]

Similarly, there is a tension now, and an attraction towards both plurality and a new type of unity. Some theorists, such as Mouffe, focus on the reconstruction, a counter-hegemonic project that holds out the possibility of unity. Others, such as Deleuze and Guattari, see the promise embodied in a radical decentering. This remains an unresolved tension, as it was for James and Follett. This tension is in social movements as well, torn between the importance of locality and the necessity of addressing more broad issues.

Conclusion

In the emerging theory and practice of critical pluralism, the political expression of multiplicity harkens back to the first generation, with serious attention to difference and the expansion of authority, sovereignty, and organization in civil society. But recent theory can also be used to address the specific relations of heterogeneous subjects, finally offering a response to Follett's question as to what to *do* with diversity. A practice of agonistic respect calls on us to recognize and validate the agency and otherness of a variety of subjects, eschewing the all-too-easy process of stereotyping and demonization. Communication is central, and notions of intersubjective understanding and the discursive process offer methods for communicating across differences *without* the necessity to forge singular identities or consensus.

---

[23] As discussed in Ch. 3, Follett's struggle over the meaning of unity is palpable throughout *The New State*. While she has a Hegelian attraction to 'the unification of feeling, affection, emotion, desire, aspiration—all that we are' (1918: 44), she remains very particular and insistent about the basis of this unification in heterogeneity.

Solidarity, then, can be constructed into real political networks at the place where various subjectivities, or understandings, intersect. All of these processes work together, as a base of solidarity is created through an open discursive process, in the mutual recognition, and respect, of the autonomous subjectivity of others.

Throughout these interrelated aspects of critical pluralist relations run some common themes. Multiplicity—recognized in one form or another—forms the base of all pluralist relations; but a critical pluralism, for the first time, embodies relations not just among those similar to yourself or your primary groups, but among others different from you as well. Relations across differences are key to the emerging generation of pluralist theory. Secondly, an aura of partiality pervades these relations. We attempt to understand and relate to others different from ourselves, but in that we recognize difference as a key aspect of human agency, we acknowledge that understanding will never be complete. We may construct solidarity with others in some area—form a bond or affinity around a particular issue—but we accept that though we may be alike in this, there are other portions of that individual or group that we are not allied with. Our ties will be partial ties.

In addition, each of the components covered here embodies an understanding of relations as an ongoing process. Once we give up on the necessity of universalism and embrace relations with others, ends, convergence, and finality remain forever distant. The focus is on the means, on a practice of relating with others, and on the continuing evolution of those relations. Agonistic respect calls for a constant cultivation of care for self and others, intersubjectivity is ongoing, discourse is never-ending, and solidarity is forever creating new networks and mosaics.

Part III

Environmental Justice:
Critical Pluralism in Practice

5

The Politics of Networking in the Grassroots Environmental Justice Movement

While theorists have focused on issues surrounding the theoretical evolution of pluralism, many in the environmental movement have addressed and tackled some of the perceived problems of conventional pluralist organization and practice. Over the last decade or so in the US, many grassroots environmental groups have become increasingly alienated from the major environmental groups and the mainstream environmental lobby. Criticisms have increased of a number of aspects of the major organizations, both in their everyday actions and their organizational form. There has been anger at the lackluster and ineffective campaigns of the larger groups, disappointment at the lack of attention to the diversity of the grassroots, distrust of the professional atmosphere of organizations, frustration with control by the major funding organizations rather than memberships, and criticism of the centralized, hierarchical, professionalized organizations that are not accountable to memberships or local communities.[1]

In addition, and more specifically, the environmental justice community has been critical of the larger organizations for what they claim is their disregard of the wide variety of environmental hazards faced by people of color, a paternalistic attitude toward low-income and minority communities and grassroots groups, and the lack of

---

[1] Examples here are numerous. See Dowie (1991, 1995) and Gottlieb (1990, 1993) for discussions of these complaints. From within the movement, see Bullard (1994b, 1994c), Montague (1995), Cockburn and St. Clair (1994). For a fascinating account of the limits funding organizations put on the movement, see Rozek (1994).

attention to diversity in the memberships, staffs, and boards of the Big Ten groups.[2]

Increasingly, the grassroots movements—around both wilderness and resource issues and environmental justice—have developed an entirely different *form* of organizing. The environmental justice community, for example, has responded by organizing a movement quite distinct from the mainstream—in its model, its structure, and its tactics. Rather than create large, Washington-based, bureaucratic organizations exemplified by the Big Ten, concerned and active citizens have created a number of grassroots environmental networks. The environmental justice movement has been networking and making connections, creating solidarity out of an understanding and a respect for both similarities and differences, and working from a variety of places with a wide array of tactics.

It has become quite popular to talk about networks in both social movements generally and the environmental justice movement specifically. Sociologist Mario Diani argues (1995: p. xiii) that it has become the rule rather than the exception to talk about social movements as networks in recent years.[3] This trend began, one could argue, with the seminal work of Gerlach and Hine (1970) on the loose, dispersed networks of social movements in the 1960s. More recently, environmental justice academic and activist Robert Bullard describes the environmental justice movement as a network of civil-rights, social-justice, and environmental groups.

My question in this chapter is twofold, and attempts to delve a bit further into the concept of networks—beyond the obvious and into some specifics. First, the task is to examine thoroughly the processes that make up the network that is the environmental justice movement. What does it mean, and what does it look like, to be a social movement that is structured as a network? Second, the task is to examine this model as an alternative to the one used by the

---

[2] The Big Ten consists of Natural Resources Defense Council, Environmental Policy Institute, National Wildlife Federation, Environmental Defense Fund, Izaak Walton League, Sierra Club, National Audubon Society, National Parks and Conservation Association, Wilderness Society, and Friends of the Earth. For criticisms from an environmental justice perspective, see various essays in the collections edited by Bryant (1995), Bullard (1993*a*), and Hofrichter (1993*a*). Numerous environmental justice organizations and activists signed two key letters to the mainstream leaders listing these complaints. They were reported by Shabecoff (1990), and published in Friends of the Earth (1990).

[3] Diani's own work, especially his definition of social movements as networks (1992), has certainly aided this trend in the sociological literature.

larger, major environmental groups in the US, which are structured more like the interest groups of conventional pluralist thinking and design.

The argument here is that, just as theorists have begun to re-examine pluralism, and move away from the conventional post-war model, activists in parts of the environmental movement have done the same. The contention is not that social movements, like the environmental justice movement, take concepts from recent political theory and implement them like a blueprint. If anything, much recent theory takes its cue from the criticisms and practices of the social movements of the past three decades. Nor am I going to argue that the environmental justice movement is the ideal embodiment, or perfect reflection, of all of the components of critical pluralism that I have laid out in the previous chapters. The task here is to explore the development of a new and more critical form of pluralism in another realm, that of political practice. The thesis of the book as a whole is that a new form of pluralism has been developed in both theory and in practice; just as theorists have responded to the normative lapses and political problems of the post-war generation of conventional pluralism, the environmental justice movement embodies another reaction, and another articulation of a new form of political ethics, structure, practice, and demands. At the base of the structures and processes developed by the broad environmental justice movement lies an acknowledgment of plurality, varied experiences, and diverse understandings of environmental problems. The focus of this chapter is on the building, from this base in the acknowledgement of plurality, of the solidarity and networks that make up the movement.

I begin by exploring the value of difference in the movement, as the base of the newly developed network structures and processes lies in an acknowledgement of plurality, varied experiences, and diverse understandings of environmental problems. I continue by examining the bases of the environmental justice movement in a number of pre-existing social and political networks. I then turn to how networks link issues and establish alliances among diverse groups, and how networks form in order to deal with environmental issues of varying dimensions. I will also examine some of the reasons why this form of organizing is a tactical strength, as it mirrors and maps itself onto changing practices in capital movement and political oversight. Finally, in an initial attempt to evaluate the network form, I examine some of the difficulties in, and criticisms of, networking as a social-movement strategy.

It is important here to note that the emphasis of this chapter is on the structure and process of the movement, rather than on the specific environmental demands made by the groups and networks within it. As discussed in Chapter 1, the *justice* in the environmental justice movement begins with two central issues: the inequity in the distribution of environmental risks, and the recognition of the diversity of the participants and experiences in the environmental justice movement. These issues of justice, I argued, are addressed in the *processes* that the environmental justice movement both embodies and demands. This chapter examines the attention paid to recognition within the movement, and the processes it has developed; the following chapter continues this exploration, focusing on the communicative and participatory processes within the movement, and the demands made on corporations and government agencies. In these examinations of the process of the movement, I do not aim to take away from the central concern of the inequitable distribution of environmental ills to communities of color and the poor. Rather, the aim is to emphasize the other realm of justice in environmental justice—recognition—and the particular processes and methods the movement has developed in order to seek justice in the realms of distribution and recognition.

The Value of Plurality

As discussed in Chapter 3, the basis of a critical pluralism is the acceptance of difference. From William James's (1976 [1912]) understanding of radical empiricism to Donna Haraway's (1988) situated knowledges, a variety of theorists have insisted on acknowledging that diverse understandings are bred by varied experience. Such an acknowledgement, however, has had trouble making the crossover from theory to political action; numerous examiners of past social movements and attempts at democratic process have pointed this out.[4] But environmental justice takes difference seriously, and the recognition of diversity is really at the center of the movement.

While Capek (1993) writes of a singular environmental justice

---

[4] Pertinent examples that address this issue directly include Breines (1989) and Miller (1987) on the new left, and Freeman (1975) and Sirianni (1993) on the feminist movement.

'frame', she acknowledges that many environmental justice groups and networks incorporate ideas and themes outside of the frame she defines. This inability to frame the movement completely is crucial. In the various organizations and networks that make up the environmental justice movement, there is no insistence on one singular point of view, one policy that will solve all problems, or one tactic to be used in all battles. The movement is constructed from difference, revels in that fact, and negates the importance of a singular history, experience, or ideology. There is no one 'environmental justice', 'minority', or 'grassroots' view of the environment. The Environmental Careers Organization survey of social and environmental justice organizations found diverse organizational structures, varied motivations for organizing, and a basic belief in the heterogeneous nature of the movement: 'The views and voices are as varied as the issues that drive them. There is no single vision about how the issues are defined and what methods best address them' (1992: 35, 39). While there are obvious themes repeated throughout the movement—for example around health, equity, survival, subjugation, and the inattention of governmental agencies and representatives—the particular experiences of these issues, and the formulation of understandings and responses, differ according to place. Rather than one particular frame or ideology, there is a coexistence of multiple political beliefs as to the causes, situation of, and possible solutions for issues of environmental justice. Rather than insistence on a system of beliefs, the movement is constructed of an eclectic pluralism.

The environmental justice movement has an understanding of perspective and culture as grounded in the experiences of individuals and their communities. The epistemological base of the movement is the situated knowledge of a critical pluralism. Knowledge is seen as grounded in place, and hence the diversity of perspectives that emerge are seen as points of view located solidly in the context of the lives of participants and their communities. The challenge of the movement is to validate this diversity in order to bring it into a network and add to its strength. This understanding of difference, and its importance in adding to the movement, is a basic project of environmental justice. As Barbara Deutsch Lynch argues (1993: 110)

If environmental discourses are culturally grounded, they will differ in content along class and ethnic lines. Where power in society is unequally distributed, not all environmental discourses will be heard equally. Thus, questions of environmental justice must address not only the effects of particular land uses or environmental policies on diverse groups in society, but the likelihood that alternative environmental discourses will be heard and valued.

Lynch's words demonstrate how environmental justice links a critique of inequity with a need to validate and recognize difference. Environmental *justice* requires an understanding of the existence and importance of multiple perspectives and the need to validate that variety. The cultural pluralism that forms the base of the movement, once recognized, opens opportunities for collaboration and the innovations of common action.

The processes that led up to, and that were present in, the First National People of Color Environmental Leadership Summit of October 1991 serve as an example of the importance placed on plurality. Resisting a political process that many saw as built on keeping people of color divided, participants emphasized that all those coming to the table would be respected, that there would be equity in participation across race, ethnicity, gender, and region. Numerous participants noted the openness to difference, the listening to others, the mutual respect, solidarity, and trust that were both expressed and affirmed at the conference (see e.g. Grossman 1994; Lee 1992; V. D. Miller 1993). Organizers worked to make the experience, at its base, inclusive.

Participants affirmed that difference and plurality, forged with mutual respect into solidarity, add a strength to the movement. There were differences around race, gender, age, culture (especially indigenous culture), and the urban/rural split, among others.[5] Dana Alston argued that the Summit brought a spirit of solidarity, and that the most important thing was the bonding that occurred across the differences (Di Chiro 1992: 104). Charles Lee notes that the openness and inclusivity of the process showed that 'difference can be cooperative instead of competitive, that diversity can lead to higher harmony rather than deeper hostility' (Lee 1992: 52). What appeared through a respect for the many different stories, perspectives, and cultures, were some common themes. 'The diverse representation contributed to a clearer perspective of the commonalities of the problems' (Moore

[5] Paul Ruffins's account of the Summit includes a discussion of the effect of bringing together Native American and Hawaiian activists with more urban-based African-American activists. After years of bitter feeling about the white environmental community's focus on wilderness and animals rather than the urban environment, indigenous activists helped him to experience, for the first time, 'the moral imperative of protecting animals and trees and land' (1992: 11).

and Head 1994: 205). Difference was forged into unity, but a unity that kept diversity, rather than uniformity, at its base. Participants entered diverse; they left both diverse and unified.[6]

The point here is that diversity is more than a slogan for environmental justice. There is attention paid to the many different experiences people have in their environments, the cultures that inform those experiences, and the various evaluations and reactions that emerge from them. Recognizing and validating these differences is at the heart of environmental justice.

The Social Bases of Networks

The networks that make up the environmental justice movement differ radically from the organizations of the Big Ten. The political expression of a critical solidarity contrasts with the interest-group liberalism that is both the standard model of pluralism and the mode of operation of mainstream environmentalism. One of the key differences between the major organizations and grassroots networks is where participants actually come from. Big Ten groups grew tremendously in the 1980s with the growth of mass-mailing technology. These organizations have become increasingly dependent on recruiting people from mailing lists—people that have no previous connections to the groups, but share basic interests.

The dominant pluralist paradigm of the second generation underplays—and some would say denies—people's roots in their own communities (Ackelsberg 1988). But while the major environmental organizations consist of members who exist almost exclusively on lists, local environmental justice and anti-toxics groups most often begin with people as members of community networks. Solidarity originates in community relationships—pre-existing social networks around where people live, work, play, and worship. A number of sociologists (e.g. C. S. Fischer 1977; Wellman *et al.* 1988) have written about the importance of social and civic networks in creating community, and social-movement theorists have picked up on the relationship between these networks and social action. As Sidney Tarrow (1994: 6) has argued, the magnitude and duration of much collective

---

[6] I will return to a discussion of the communicative practices at the Summit in the following chapter.

action 'depend[s] on mobilizing people through social networks and around identifiable symbols that are drawn from cultural frames of meaning'. Organization emerges out of shared experiences and existing social networks around family, neighborhood, school, work, religion, and racial and ethnic identity. Examples here abound. Much has been written of the importance of extended families and community networks in the activism of working-class and African-American women (see e.g. Haywood 1990; Krauss 1994; Naples 1992). The emergence of individuals in social networks also played a key role in determining participation in the civil-rights movement (McAdam 1988). Churches, obviously, have also been a source of activism around civil-rights issues in African-American and Latino communities. One progressive organization, the Pacific Institute for Community Organization (PICO), relies specifically on these pre-existing church relations, organizing in communities only after being invited by a sponsoring congregation (O'Brien 1993).

Pre-existing relations and social networks have been crucial in the organization of the environmental justice movement. Churches have played a major role: the United Church of Christ's Commission for Racial Justice did the first major study of the relationship between toxic wastes and race (United Church of Christ 1987) and was the major organizer of the First National People of Color Environmental Leadership Summit. The United Methodist Church's Department of Environmental Justice and Survival and the National Council of Churches Eco-Justice Working Group have also helped to bring religious networks into the development of the movement.

The Mothers of East Los Angeles (MELA) serve as an apt example here. MELA is a closely knit group of Mexican American women who organized in opposition to the siting of a prison, oil pipeline, and toxic waste incinerator in their neighborhood; it illustrates how pre-existing networks are translated into political assets, organization, and resistance (Pardo 1990). The mothers already had some contact with one another through traditional roles as the caretakers of the health and schooling of their children, and it was through these networks that they disseminated information about the numerous unfortunate plans for the neighborhood. They also used the common experience of the church: as the group began their organizing, they informed the community through the most visible network available in the neighborhood—people coming out of Sunday mass. Weekly Monday marches would be organized through these Sunday contacts

(Schwab 1994: 56). Likewise, the organization of African-American families in the contaminated community of Carver Terrace, Texarcana, used pre-existing social networks based in family, neighborhood, and worship in their organization of what has become known as the 'Black Love Canal' (Capek 1993). Kerr and Lee (1993: 13) note the transition in the Newtown Florist Club, in Gainesville, Georgia, from a group that began by collecting money to buy flowers for ill residents to one organizing to learn about toxics released in the community and fighting for clean-up.

Other pre-existing social networks have also played a part in the development of the environmental justice movement. Numerous established social-justice organizations, community organizing centers, and historically black colleges have added to the movement. In the Southwest, the establishment of the Southwest Network for Environmental and Economic Justice (SNEEJ), came out of an original meeting and 'dialogue' that built on a decade of previous organizing of groups working in issues such as police repression, immigration, food and nutrition, health care, campus issues, land and water rights, and worker/community issues of plant sitings (Moore and Head 1994: 192). Recruiting for this movement is not through national mailing lists, but from the already existing variety of support systems.

People get to build support, friendship, camaraderie, goodwill, and fellowship with people they already know. If they have to form a coalition with others, it is not one person going cold turkey to deal with a group of unfamiliar people; it is a group of people who have already established some relationships with others whose interests might be similar, interfacing with another group. (D. Taylor 1992: 43)

New networks build not only on community relationships, but also on the relations established by past networks. At the base of networks are not simply shared interests, but more broadly shared experiences. Their origins demonstrate a politics of relations rather than a politics of isolated bodies of interest.

Linking Issues, Creating Networks

The environmental justice movement expands the notion of environment by defining it not just as external nature or the 'big outside', but as the places where people live, work, and play. Environment is community (Di Chiro 1995). The movement makes connections among various environmental experiences in the everyday lives of people. As Charles Lee (1993*a*: 40) describes, the environmental justice movement sees the ecosystem as made up of three overlapping subsystems: the natural or biophysical environment, the manufactured or built environment, and the social environment. The movement address 'environmental' issues as they relate to a broader agenda which includes employment, education, housing, health care, the workplace, and other issues of social, racial, and economic justice (Austin and Schill 1991). All of these issues are linked together and defined as broadly environmental. Grassroots environmental justice, encompassing diverse anti-toxics groups and environmental justice organizations of people of color, reflect, by their very make-up, the interrelationship between various forms of power and subordination.

This sentiment is echoed throughout the environmental justice community. A survey of seventy-six social and environmental justice organizations by the Environmental Careers Organization (1992: 35) found the holistic approach a key characteristic of these groups. This linkage of issues is evident in much of the literature of the movement itself (see e.g. Alston 1990: 13; Cole 1992: 641; Lee 1993*b*: 50; Moore and Head 1993: 118). Lois Gibbs, of the Citizen's Clearinghouse for Hazardous Waste,[7] argues that the new

> Grassroots Environmental Justice Movement seeks common ground with low-income and minority communities, with organized workers, with churches and with all others who stand for freedom and equality . . . Environmental justice is broader than just preserving the environment. When we fight for environmental justice we fight for our homes and families and struggle to end economic, social and political domination by the strong and greedy. (CCHW 1990: 2)

As Richard Moore, co-ordinator of SNEEJ, argues, 'we see the interconnectedness between environmental issues and economic justice issues' (quoted in Almeida 1994: 22). Scott Douglas, a past community organizer with the Sierra Club's Southeast office, argues that

---

[7] The Citizen's Clearinghouse for Hazardous Waste (CCHW) has recently changed its name to The Center for Health, Environment, and Justice (CHEJ). As the following research is based on practices and publications before the name change, I will continue to refer to them as CCHW throughout the following chapters.

[t]hese problems are all wrapped up together, and it teaches us a very important lesson: oppressed people do not have compartmentalized problems. Very seldom do you go to a low-income black community, and the only problem is the incinerator: 'Man, if we got rid of the incinerator, we'd be fine!' The incinerator is merely the external reflection of a whole host of problems. (Quoted in Anthony *et al.* 1993: 58)

Robin Cannon, a resident of South Central Los Angeles who battled against LANCER, the city's plan to locate an incinerator in the neighborhood, expresses the sentiment: 'This fight has really turned me around, things are intertwined in ways I hadn't realized . . . all these social issues as well as political and economic issues are really intertwined' (quoted in Hamilton 1990: 13). As a result, environmental justice networks such as SNEEJ and CCHW address the links between community poisoning, racism, environmentalism, housing, and the lack of public participation in community decisions (Wright *et al.* 1994: 121). As Laura Pulido has argued (1996: 192–3) environmental justice struggles are not strictly environmental. Instead, they challenge multiple lines of domination, and 'it is difficult to discern where the environmental part of the struggle begins and where it ends'.

This understanding of an environmentalism with diverse issues and an assertion of linkage calls for a broader movement—one that must necessarily forge a solidarity among a range of groups and movements. This type of networking across issues and groups is a key defining characteristic, and a crucial organizing strategy, of the growing environmental justice movement.

Examples of these issue linkages, and the concomitant networking, are numerable. Individual member organizations of SNEEJ often deal with the interrelationship of issues of race, class, and gender. Activists battling computer chip plants often have to deal not only with issues of contamination, but also with the politics of public subsidies of private corporations. Organizers working on health problems of strawberry pickers in California are inevitably brought into the contested terrain of immigration law. Lois Gibbs notes that organizers of the CCHW national convention in 1989 were fearful of their decision to join a march for increased low-income housing:

[W]e weren't really sure whether our people were willing to cross that, to say, 'What does this housing march have to do with environment?' . . . [P]eople participated in that march and actually not only saw the crossover but went and talked to folks who were at the march about their common ground . . . So they were able to . . . understand, again, the power structure, and how people are oppressed, all different types of people, all different types of issues. (Quoted in Szasz 1994: 159)

While individual groups begin by working on specific issues, they often come to see not only the theoretical links between diverse problems, but usually begin to take on some of the other issues that affect them. The linkage of issues leads to the creation of alliances. During the course of a specific campaign, people are exposed to others with problems that relate to their own. In addition, as time goes on, groups that developed around one particular issue will broaden their scope and take on other issues that impact on their membership. As Peggy Newman, a past field organizer for CCHW, explains, '[i]nstead of seeing differences in our work for environmental justice and homelessness, health advocacy, worker rights, immigrant rights, community economic development, gay and lesbian rights, we must look for the common ground among the issues and be willing to assist in each others' efforts and coordinate our work' (Newman 1994: 94). Some see the issue of environment as a broad, 'powerful unifying phenomenon that can link seemingly separate issues and peoples' (Hofrichter 1993*b*: 89).

But it is important here to note that this type of unity does not emphasize uniformity. Networks and alliances in the environmental justice movement depend as much on their differences—and their autonomy—as they do on unity. It is crucial to note that networks do not necessarily form around one single unifying commonality. Instead, networks form and hold themselves together around numerous issues where there are similarities or solidarities across groups. The resulting mosaic itself—the movement—becomes the major commonality. Within a network, there remains both multiplicity and commonality.

Some networks or alliances are very conscious of this issue. Groups that share environmental concerns may still have radical differences. Yet the commonality of environmental experience serves as the mortar, even when there are differences in culture, style, ideology, or tactics. One of the most impressive examples of such an alliance was built between Latinos and Hasidim in the Williamsburg section of

Brooklyn, New York (Greider 1993).[8] While organizing around the unifying symbol of the local environment, leaders of this Community Alliance for the Environment (CAFE) have taken pains not to offend, ignore or marginalize anyone involved in CAFE activities. Respect for differences goes hand in hand with the building of an alliance.

In another example, when the women of South Central Los Angeles began the battle against the LANCER incinerator, they were not alone. They were joined by a variety of groups, including white, middle-class women from two slow-growth groups across the city (Not Yet New York and the California Alliance in Defense of Residential Environments, CADRE). Cynthia Hamilton, of the Los Angeles-based Labor/Community Strategy Center, notes that '[t]hese two groups of women, together, have created something previously unknown to the City of Los Angeles—unity of purpose across neighborhood and racial lines' (Hamilton 1990: 11). Add Greenpeace, the Center for Law in the Public Interest, and Citizens for a Better Environment to the mix, and the differences in the battle became as distinct as the common ground.

El Puente, one of the founding members of CAFE in Williamsburg, literally translates as 'the bridge', and it sees as its basic mission the creation of links among various individuals and groups (Greider 1993: 37). Numerous organizations have come to see part of their task as the building of bridges between diverse communities and organizations (see Anthony and Cole 1990: 16; Schwab 1994: 415; Williams 1993). Part of the crucial task of building networks is developing cooperation across numerous gaps—geographic, cultural, gender, social, ideological. The core of networking is 'the work of overcoming divisions by constructing links' (Brecher and Costello 1994*a*: 107). The resulting alliances and networks span diverse issues, individuals, and groups, connecting them while continuing to recognize the numerous foundations on which those bridges are based.

[8] Luis Acosta, chief executive officer of the Latino organization El Puente, invited Rabbi David Niederman of the Hasidic social service agency United Jewish Organizations to an El Puente meeting on the environment in 1991. Their two organizations worked together against a nearby storage facility of low-level radioactive waste and a massive garbage incinerator the city planned for the neighborhood. In 1992, they organized the first environmental town meeting in Williamsburg; it included not only Latinos and Hasidim, but also the African-Americans, Polish-Americans, and Italian-Americans from the neighborhood. Out of that meeting, the Community Alliance for the Environment (CAFE) was formed. By January 1993 CAFE was able to organize a multi-ethnic march of 1,500 local residents across the Williamsburg Bridge to promote unity and protest the incinerator.

Rhizomes, Locality, and the Breadth of Networks

Networks have grown beyond the bounds of these examples of working together solely on the local level. Environmental problems do not limit themselves to the imposed boundaries of neighborhood, city, state, or nation. Neither nature on its own nor the environmental problems we construct through our interaction with it are confined to a single level. Networks have developed along a number of lines spread by environmental problems and issues themselves. Some have stayed local, others have grown regionally, others along rivers, watersheds, and the flow of the wind. And still others have developed, simultaneously, both locally and across great distances.

Environmental problems are often defined with spherical or linear frameworks. Air pollution may begin at a plant located in a particular city, but affects those in outlying areas. Toxins leaking from an industrial site spread outward with the rains, or enter groundwater systems. Carbon monoxide emissions and the release of ozone-destructive chemicals have global consequences. In a more linear example, polluted waterways may flow through a variety of administrative boundaries: city, county, state, reservation, nation. Environmental problems may confine themselves to a local dimension, but are just as likely to take on larger regional, national, or global proportions. These spherical and linear images, however, limit the understanding of another way environmental problems may be shared.

The metaphor of the rhizome is, once again, useful here. As discussed in Chapter 4, rhizomes are a type of root system that spreads in numerous directions, emerging and sending up sprouts in a variety of locations. Rhizomes connect in a way that is not always visible— they cross borders and reappear in distant places without necessarily showing themselves in between.[9] The rhizome metaphor may be helpful in discussing situations that may be localized, but still shared by people in different places. The conditions outside an oil refinery, municipal incinerator, or silicon chip manufacturer will be similar no matter where they are located, and so those communities will share environmental problems. These problems do not occupy all of the space in between the communities—their ties are less visible than that.

[9] Deleuze and Guattari (1987) spawned the use of the rhizome metaphor. For other discussions of the metaphor in environmental politics, see LaChapelle (1994), and Kuehls (1995).

Foucault argued for an understanding of power as localized—that it is held and exercised in innumerable points. Power's locality should be considered not simply a physical place, but also as an experience of a particular form of power which may arise in numerous places. Locality is similarity of experiences, traditions, and understandings; it is not necessarily limited to physical location. The same notion is applicable to environmental problems. People may share environmental experiences over distances, as particular practices or conditions arise in their communities.

Networks, then, may be built not only by people and organizations with differences coalescing around a particular local or regional problem, but also as people in distant areas respond to similar circumstances—toxic waste sites, types of manufacturing, particular toxins, shared health problems. As Deleuze and Guattari (1987: 7–8) explain, the rhizome represents alliance; its first three characteristics are connection, heterogeneity, and multiplicity. Networks, in the practice of a critical pluralism, embody each. Rhizomatic organizing is based in making the connections, recognizing patterns across both distance and difference. The metaphor of the rhizome, and an expanded notion of locality, can help us understand how environmental networks can form around similarities experienced over great distances. Experience can be shared in the workplace or across the neighborhood, but it can also be shared across distant workplaces and communities.

The growing anti-toxics and environmental justice movement organizes in just such a manner. Local groups rarely remain isolated and unconnected. What makes environmental justice a *movement* are the linkages formed beyond the local. Most groups make links to other groups in their own locale, but, increasingly, groups make contact with outside organizations, other local groups, and existing networks which can provide resources, information, and solidarity. This 'translocality', as Di Chiro (1997) calls it, brings together groups and communities that would not otherwise have identified or developed a sense of commonality.

Examples of networking that expand on the notion of locality, and create connections and solidarity where none existed before, are numerous in the environmental justice movement. Networks have formed at every level from the local to the international to the virtual, while building the connections between them. The first key large-scale network to develop came directly out of Love Canal and the Love Canal Homeowners Association (LCHA). Lois Gibbs and the LCHA were inundated with requests for information as the story of Love Canal and their fight with the local, state, and federal governments grew. Gibbs and other volunteers began the Citizen's Clearinghouse for Hazardous Waste with the idea of helping other communities organize for environmental justice. By 1993, they reported having assisted over 8,000 groups (CCHW 1993: 3).

Networking at the CCHW happens in a number of ways. As a resource center, the CCHW funnels information about key toxics, issues, industries, and companies to communities who are faced with these particular environmental problems. Communities share their experiences with the CCHW, enriching the resource base for other communities. The CCHW also distributes information about specific problems and issues in organizing, such as fund-raising, research, leadership, running meetings, legal issues, and the problems faced by women as they become increasingly involved in a political battle. The CCHW has also regularly sent organizers out into the field to work with citizen groups on environmental and organizational issues.

The organization sponsors regional leadership development conferences, where local leaders from various communities come together to share knowledge, experiences, and tactics. On a larger level, the CCHW holds a national gathering every year, which in addition to enabling networking, gives people the sense that their local battle is part of a larger, diverse movement. In addition, the CCHW helps to bring individuals and communities together in a number of ways. Often, individuals or groups that call with a specific toxic issue, or company are put directly in touch with nearby groups that have had similar experiences and have had assistance from the CCHW. One of the unwritten rules of the CCHW is that if you get help, you are also expected to give it to others (CCHW 1989: 1). Networking is suggested as a method of thwarting industry tactics. The CCHW notes that a company looking for a site will choose a half-dozen or so communities that would be potentially suitable; they then sit back and watch how the communities react, moving into the one that is least resistant. In these cases, the CCHW suggests a meeting of groups from each target site to form a 'non-aggression pact' and unite around the principle of not in anyone's backyard (Collette 1993: 5). In other instances, a local group that has been victorious, keeping a facility out of their community, will be encouraged to follow the story and see where a company is likely to try again. They then contact grassroots groups in these communities, warning them of the impending issue and offering assistance in organizing.[10]

The CCHW also focuses on the space between the local and the national, with an emphasis on 'larger than locals'. As local grassroots groups continually spring up, they need someone or some group to turn to. The national group is there, but they cannot be continually everywhere and all-knowing. The 'larger than locals' occupy the middle space. They are often state-wide organizations who know specific state laws and related battles, and are more accessible for help on a daily basis (S. Lynch 1993: 48–9).

'Larger than locals' may develop and stay focused around specific issues, offering networking and assistance to groups dealing with these issues. Or they may expand either on the issues they deal with or on the tactics used. They may move from resistance to proactive attempts to change the law. 'For example, they have beaten the local cement kiln incinerator but now focused on changing rules and regulations that may keep future cement kilns all across the country from doing the same thing' (S. Lynch 1993: 48). Groups that focus on multiple issues can assist by getting local groups to understand and possibly help work on the different problems of other community groups. They help develop areas of common ground that different groups can work on. As Joe Szakos of Kentuckians for the Commonwealth (KFTC) notes, urban African-Americans working on utility rate reform and rural whites pushing for landowners' rights discover they have a lot in common when the bills they favor are killed in closed-door sessions. They can work together for a more open and democratic legislative process, and at the same time deal with issues of racism and their differences (Szakos 1993: 51). Solidarity, again, does not necessarily mean similarity. Networks may evolve towards agreement in terms of the understanding of a problem and the development of singular solutions and political tactics.

One of the other most well-organized environmental justice

---

[10] Marty Chestnutt, an organizer with CCHW, gives an illustration: 'They tried to put a hazardous waste incinerator in [Marion County, Tennessee] and they defeated it; they ran them out. And when they called me and told me they had won, I said, "You haven't won until you find out where they're planning to put that incinerator and you help the next group," and within about a week they called me back, said, "We found out where it's going. We've already been in contact with the people over there and we're helping them organize."' (Quoted in Szasz 1994: 160.)

organizations is the Southwest Network for Environmental and Economic Justice. SNEEJ began as a dialogue of Latino, Asian-American, African-American, and Native American activists from over thirty community organizations in Oklahoma, Texas, New Mexico, Colorado, Arizona, Utah, Nevada, and California. The Network is involved in campaigns around environmental justice in the EPA, the impact of high-tech industries on communities, justice on the US–Mexico border, sovereignty and toxic dumping on Native lands, and farmworker pesticide exposure.

SNEEJ focuses on the development of linkages across distances, and has used networking to make a variety of connections. Richard Moore gives one example:

Many of the pesticides and chemicals are being produced in urban communities of color that later contaminate the groundwater and workers in rural communities of color. This is another example of the necessity of merging urban and rural struggles together in the environmental justice movement . . . This will help people see the environmental and economic linkages that are impacting their lives. (Quoted in Almeida 1994: 30)

Member groups of SNEEJ include those involved in struggles in both types of communities, such as those fighting contamination from oil refineries in Richmond, California, and those who live near the waste site in Kettleman City, California, where toxic materials from the refinery are dumped.

SNEEJ's border justice campaign has reached out across the border and involved Mexican organizations. The attempt has been to internationalize, at the grassroots, the fight for environmental and economic justice. Richard Moore argues that '[w]e need to have in place our contacts in other parts of the world so that there are other campaigns ready to address the possibility of relocation' (Almeida 1994: 25). The border project network is built around the similarity of environmental and labor experiences in distant areas and the desire to halt the free movement of these problems from one community to another.

SNEEJ also has developed a network of communities that have dealt specifically with issues raised by the location of particular industries, such as the microelectronics industry. SNEEJ expanded this work in developing, with the Campaign for Responsible Technology (CRT), the Electronics Industry Good Neighbor Campaign. In its origins it tied together communities in Albuquerque, Austin,

Phoenix, and San Jose; it has expanded to include groups in Portland and Eugene, Oregon, as well as groups across the border in Mexico.

The growing concern with networking and alliances, and the development of a rhizomatic movement, works against the NIMBY (Not In My Backyard) misnomer and the claim that local protests against environmental problems and undesirable land use comes from an 'enclave consciousness'. Plotkin (1990: 226, 229) argues that 'the place-bound confines of neighborhood constituted the relevant "environment" of community land-use protest . . . Clearly the end result of the enclave consciousness is a policy of "beggar thy neighbor" as community groups regularly seek to export or exclude the perceived "bads" of urban life while fencing in the goods.' The only aims of these groups, he claims, are to avoid domination and be left alone (p. 227). But the development of networks and alliances expands the understanding of community and locality. Numerous neighborhoods need protection, and the way to get that is not to be left alone, but to develop solidarity with others facing the same dangers in their neighborhoods. Activists celebrate the grassroots links forged with other communities and insist on NIABY ('Not in Anyone's Backyard'), not NIMBY. As they argue, environmental justice is not about NIMBY, but rather the critical invention of new forms of coalition politics (Avila 1992).

The anti-toxics movement may have begun isolated, with communities fighting companies and local governments on their own, lacking contact with others, but events at Love Canal changed that. After Love Canal, hundreds of citizen groups began to form, and they reached out to others. Some groups that formed in isolation before Love Canal, without help from other groups, began to go to community after community helping other groups get started.[11] The EPA's own study on public opposition to the siting of hazardous waste facilities (USEPA 1979) notes that siting opposition before 1978 was done almost exclusively by groups on their own, while after 1978 more than half of the groups were networking in some way. Just as Love Canal became a focal point in 1978, resistance to PCB dumping in the majority African-American Warren County, North Carolina, in 1982 became a focal point for further organizing around environ-

---

[11] Sue Greer of People Against Hazardous Landfill Sites (PAHLS) notes this about her own group in Szasz 1994: 71.

mental racism and environmental justice. Community groups no longer need be isolated. And far from NIMBY and enclave consciousness, connections are being made among communities with an understanding that, with networking and solidarity, the concern is with 'Everyone's Backyard'.[12]

Network as Organizational Structure

The concept and practice of networks apply not only to pre-existing structures that evolve into political organizations, or the formation of groups around interrelated issues in various localities, but also to the very organizational structure of many of these groups. The informal networks that have been tapped into by grassroots environmental justice groups have been formalized into movement organizations. Previous ties in the neighborhood, such as those that aided in the development of MELA, or previous social-justice networks, which came together to form SNEEJ, become the basis of more formal organization. The environmental justice movement has come to depend much more on these networks than on a centralized, hierarchical, formal social-movement organization—what Zald and McCarthy (1987: 20) call an 'SMO'. Diani (1995: 6) uses the concept of network to distinguish between social movements and more rigid SMOs. This same distinction can be drawn between the environmental justice movement and the structure of the major environmental groups in the US.

In fact, it is a critique of the SMOs, or major environmental organizations, that has driven the environmental justice movement to a more decentralized structure. The top-down, centralized managerial style and structure of the major groups has been criticized as disempowering, paternalistic, and exclusive. Organizers of the environmental justice movement, mindful of both these structures and the similarly centralizing organizing mistakes of the past, have been conscious of the need to keep ownership of the movement in the hands of everyday participants, rather than in centralized organizations.[13] The key for organizers has been to create organizational models that are sufficient for networking purposes and strong

---

[12] Appropriately, this is the name of the newsletter of the CCHW/CHEJ.
[13] See e.g. the discussion by SNEEJ co-ordinator Richard Moore in Almeida (1994).

enough to confront issues, but yet are both flexible and diverse enough to respond to changing circumstances at the local level.

Documents and discussions within the movement repeatedly stress the importance of decentralization, diversification, and democratization, as opposed to the centralized organization with a singular leadership. When activists gathered for the regional dialogue that eventually led to the development of SNEEJ, there were some that wanted a national organization, but most argued for the importance of developing the network at the grassroots and regional levels (Almeida 1994: 30). On the occasion of the ten-year anniversary of the CCHW, that organizational network expressed the same sentiment. 'Should our movement become centralized with a single spokesperson? No . . . it is empowered communities and local group autonomy that makes us strongest' (CCHW 1993: 3).

Those gathering at the First National People of Color Leadership Summit also declined the temptation to develop a centralized organization, and emphasized the importance of organizing networks. Many activists noted that one of the most promising achievements of the summit was its commitment to an organizational model that stressed diversity, as well as egalitarian and non-hierarchical principles, in contrast to the technocratic, top-down managerial style of the major environmental groups (Di Chiro 1992: 105). As Pam Tau Lee, of the Labor and Occupational Health Program at UC Berkeley, notes: 'What I see is a wonderful phenomenon . . . the development of networks. Those networks are based on actual work that is coming out of the grassroots . . . [S]o the approach is, I feel, one that's going to win. It's a winning strategy, the top-down strategy is not a winning strategy' (quoted in Di Chiro 1992: 106–7). Richard Moore argued that the Summit was not about building an organization, but rather 'building a movement. As a movement gets built, it starts from the bottom up. And those movements that we have seen develop from the top down are no longer there. So what we are about here is building a network, or building a net that works' (Lee 1992: 19).

Recognizing, drawing on, and formalizing the loose links among activists and other neighborhood, familial, or occupational ties of solidarity, recent networks have developed a unique relationship between their center and base. As Tarrow (1994: 146) argues, 'the strategy of drawing on existing structures of solidarity may weaken the ties between center and base, but, when it succeeds, the resulting heterogeneity and interdependence produce more dynamic movements than the homogeneity and discipline that were aimed at in the old social-democratic model'. Brecher and Costello (1990: 333) note these differences between new networks and old forms of organizing in their study of emerging labor-community coalitions: 'What is emerging differs from several common approaches to unifying social movements . . . It does not take the form of a single unified organization, but rather involves multiple organizations and many levels of coordination. Rather than being controlled and perpetuated by a distinct central leadership group, it is continually reconstructed by coordinating initiatives from below.' The heterogeneity and dynamism discussed by Tarrow, and multiplicity and co-ordination noted by Brecher and Costello, are apparent throughout the grassroots environmental justice movement. Rather than a singular, centralized, and formal organization, the movement has stressed a network structure: bottom-up, informal, spontaneous, and multiple. All of the qualities that supposedly destroy organization have served, in fact, to build and sustain a movement.

Both SNEEJ and the CCHW have developed organizational and decision-making structures that take these lessons and principles seriously.[14] In SNEEJ, guidelines lay out the right of member organizations to be heard, respected, and involved in all aspects of the network, including participation in committees and the co-ordinating council, in the decision-making process, and in resolutions for the annual gathering. SNEEJ guidelines (1993) insist that each individual and organization that is part of the network also has the right to self-control, autonomy, and self-determination. The ideals of the network are based on the combination of decentralization and solidarity.[15]

The CCHW has recently changed their organizing model to emphasize even more community networking than in the past. The 'New Deal' replaced field offices with an 'Alliance of Citizen Organizers' (Brody 1994). On a two-year contractual basis, the CCHW will

[14] Neither the environmental justice movement nor CCHW and SNEEJ hold a monopoly on this type of organizing in the environmental movement. Bron Taylor (1995) discusses this type of 'solidarity activism' in both Earth First! and the Rainforest Action Network (RAN). For a thorough picture of networked solidarity in Earth First!, see Ingalsbee (1995).

[15] This is not to assert that relations in the network actually work this way all of the time. The point here is the attention to principles in the establishment of a grassroots network. I will return to a discussion of some of the limitations of the network form.

train local groups who will volunteer to help other groups and leaders in their area. The CCHW will provide reimbursement for expenses, an intensive training program, computer linkages, assistance with local fund-raising, a structure for meeting with and learning from other groups, and scientific and corporate research (p. 12). But the individual Alliance groups will be responsible for following up on organizing and specific technical assistance to groups in their region. Alliance members will also participate as strategists for the CCHW, meeting in roundtable format on specific issues such as dioxin, sludge, and economic development. This new model puts primary emphasis on direct networking between groups, further strengthening the network rather than the central CCHW office or staff.[16]

A network, then, is not simply the connection between issues and groups, but is a particular method and practice of that connection as well. Function, in this case, follows form.

Diversifying Tactics and Resources

One of the other key strengths of networking is the use of numerous, yet interlinked, strategies and tactics. Networking allows for two types of strategic diversity in the realm of tactics. First is the use of various points at which the movement addresses an issue, from the local level up through the national and international. Local groups have been involved in front-line struggles at plant sites and waste dumps. Groups have coalesced regionally and statewide, bringing a number of groups into a focused attack. And the movement has addressed national issues, including government and industrial policy, as well as the practices and policies of the national environ-mental groups.

In addition, at each of these levels the movement has used a variety of tactics and strategies, both legal and extralegal. People have circulated petitions and talked to neighbors; they have attended local government meetings and organized their own accountability sessions for local officials, candidates, agencies, and companies. There have been innumerable legal demonstrations, rallies, marches; a few picketed shareholder meetings and creative street theater actions;

---

[16] The model also, not coincidentally, conserves scarce resources.

and a variety of organized illegal sit-ins and blockades.[17] There have also been numerous administrative complaints, citizen suits, and tort actions (Cole 1994*a*, 1994*b*, 1994*c*, 1995). Finally, environmental justice groups and networks have pushed for changes in public policy, again from the local level up to the international.

All of these tactics are seen as useful to the progress and growth of the movement, and none are seen as ends in themselves. Even those that focus on changing environmental policy and laws see the limitations of a focus on that singular strategy. Mililani Trask, an attorney active in environmental justice and sovereignty issues in Hawaii, argues that the legal realm is a valid one, but warns against a singular faith in the image of legal justice: '[D]o not put your eggs in the basket of the blind white lady. We must try other approaches' (Lee 1992: 38). And Luke Cole, one of the leading attorneys in the movement, has argued the importance of focusing on the building of a movement, rather than on specific court victories (Cole 1992).

The key to the success of the networking strategy is the simultaneous use of a wide range of tactics. A movement organized as a network has an inherent organizational flexibility. Groups can use the types of tactics suited to their own local situation while coordinating these actions with others. And individual groups can themselves try a variety of tactics as their struggle continues. As a CCHW activist has noted, '[t]ogether we have learned the meaning of flexibility. We evaluate our positions and try new approaches when old ones quit working' (CCHW 1993: 36).

It is the respect for the importance of cultural and ideological diversity in the CCHW's network which leads to a respect for diverse tactical approaches.

Instead of trying to walk, talk and look the same we should celebrate how different cultures, ways of acting and approaches to fighting the issues have involved many more people in our struggle and brought about change . . . Some communities protest in the streets and take over public meetings, while others hold prayer vigils outside public buildings and walks of concerns led by their religious leaders. It is allowing people to act in a manner in which they are comfortable, and retaining their cultural ways and values that keeps us moving forward. This diversity of people and cultures also keeps those in power from knowing what to expect and from controlling us. We

[17] For specific examples, see various issues of some of the newsletters of the movement, such as *Everyone's Backyard*, *Race, Poverty and the Environment*, *Crossroads*, *New Solutions*, and *Voces Unidas*.

should embrace our diversity as it is one of our most powerful tools. (CCHW 1993: 3)

The CCHW welcomes a variety of types of community participation in the movement, and encourages local groups to design an action plan or strategy that fits in any way a group feels is appropriate (Williams 1993: 18). Once again, inclusivity builds strength.

Networking also allows for a thorough and efficient pooling and mobilization of resources. Local groups involved in a project, campaign, or action require a variety of resources. Groups need technical information, advice on, and analysis of specific issues. They need support for their own research. Assistance will be needed on organizational issues—structure, leadership, participation. Most will need either advice on finding funding or direct monetary support. More than likely groups will eventually have a need for legal advice and services. And there is always the issue of how to approach, use, and deal with the media. Networking makes for the possibility of the mobilization of resources—both internally, by the sharing of the existing resources of the network, and externally, by linking with other groups or networks who can provide various resources.

The internal sharing of resources is one of the basic reasons for organizing networks. The CCHW, for example, is seen as a 'support mechanism' that assists thousands of grassroots groups around the country (Newman 1993). SNEEJ notes that part of its task is the provision of a broad base of support for local, state, and regional work. Both organizations provide education, technical assistance, training in leadership, assistance in obtaining funding from various sources, and help in attending and participating in actions and events from local to international.

Resources flow not only from the center of the network outward, for example from the main offices of CCHW or SNEEJ, but from group to group within networks as well. Leah Wise, of Southerners for Economic Justice in Durham, North Carolina, argues that the point of networking 'is that we can teach each other. And that is how you begin to pool resources, monetary, intellectual and strategy' (quoted in Lee 1992: 45). Within networks, individuals and groups share work and learn from the work of others. Kim Philips, of Save Lake Waco, near Waco, Texas, notes that her group networks with groups all across the country. 'I cannot imagine not sharing all the knowledge we have now' (quoted in CCHW 1993: 36). Groups use networks to build on local knowledge of a particular issue, and then pass that information along to other groups. This networking greatly increases the resources available to any single, isolated, group.

Networks also help in the exchange of ideas and the pooling of resources by helping local groups get in touch with other networks or groups who may specialize in a particular issue area. They may help locals get in touch with experts in law, government processes, or particular areas of environmental research. Groups which contact CCHW or SNEEJ, for example, may be put in touch with the Environmental Research Foundation, which publishes the *RACHEL's Environment and Health Weekly* and assists groups on both particular toxins and governmental and industry use of risk assessment and cost-benefit analysis. Groups may also be directed to the Environmental Health Network, which provides a link with the medical profession, Work on Waste (WOW), which specializes in issues surrounding solid waste disposal, or the Good Neighbor Project, which has assisted community groups in negotiating agreements with problematic industries (Lewis 1995).[18]

This practice of linking up with larger, more issue- or tactic-specific groups is a common one in the movement. In the two incinerator battles in Los Angeles in the 1980s, for example, both the Concerned Citizens of South Central Los Angeles and the Mothers of East Los Angeles (MELA) were assisted by a variety of other organizations and networks. Large environmental groups such as Greenpeace and the National Resources Defense Council (NRDC), and organizations such as the National Health Law Program, the Center for Law in the Public

---

[18] An increasing amount of the pooling, sharing, and communicating of resources has been done over the internet. Technical, legal, and legislative information is available from a variety of cyberspace sites. CCHW has its own website, which includes information on its dioxin campaign. *RACHEL's Hazardous Waste News* is available on-line. The Right-to-Know Computer Network (RTK NET) aims to make government information more accessible to citizens, and claims that its data 'opens up possibilities that have not been seized of linking the toxics information with other data in order to obtain broader community and company profiles in order to address persistent problems'. The most comprehensive environmental justice sites include the Econet Environmental Justice Project website (http://www.igc.apc.org/envjustice/), and the Environmental Justice Resource Center headed by Bob Bullard at Clark Atlanta University (http://www.ejrc.cau.edu/). Both offer thorough information of their own, and provide links to numerous other sites and organizations. This is not the place to describe at length the variety of environmental resources available over the internet, but it is important to note how this evolving medium helps to foster communication among various groups and networks.

Interest, and the Western Center on Law and Poverty offered much technical advice, expert testimony, research, lobbying, and legal help (Bullard 1993*b*: 32). People United for a Better Oakland (PUEBLO) has argued that their campaign against lead in the community would not have been possible without the resources of several national organizations. One of the key lessons learned, and passed on, by the organization is to '[a]ctively make links with other organizations, whether they are on the next block or across the country' (Calpotura and Sen 1994: 255). Patsy Ruth Oliver, a resident of what has come to be known as the Black Love Canal, the Carver Terrace neighborhood in Texarkana, reflects on one of the key lessons of her decade-long battle:

You cannot fight a fight like this by yourself. You need help . . . [Friends] helped us organize and plugged us into a larger environmental and political network out there in this big world, and once we were started, there was no stopping us. So the first lesson is to start out the best way you can—and look for friends. Through allies, plug into other networks . . . Join hands with other environmentalists, social justice activists, and concerned citizens far and wide. Make contact with the national environmental groups that have expertise you feel will be useful to your struggle . . . They are out there, and they *want* to help you. At the same time, *always* help other grass-roots environmental organizations. You will need to keep building the network. (Oliver 1994: 90–1)

Other organizations are a resource; as each local group develops, it becomes an aid for others as well.

Here it is important, and interesting, to note that even with the grassroots critique of the major environmental organizations many local environmental justice groups network with, and use the resources of, those same organizations. There is a long history of this type of synergy and cooperation, going back to the Environmental Defense Fund's work with the United Farm Workers and California Rural Legal Assistance on the issue of DDT in the late 1960s. More recently, a number of national groups have assisted in the development of the national environmental justice networks even as they have been criticized for policies, or their presence in local communities has created problems. EDF, for example, has been thoroughly criticized for its well-known hijacking of the McDonald's styrofoam campaign (see Dowie 1995: 139–40), and has been specifically accused of environmental racism in their support of pollution trading rights (which gives permission, say critics, to older facilities in poor neighborhoods and communities of color to pollute over otherwise legal limits). Yet recently EDF has been of assistance to the National Oil Refinery Action Network (NORAN), which has filed an environmental racism suit against the California Air Resources Board for an emission trading scheme in Los Angeles (Cone 1997). Greenpeace has also been criticized by local groups in the past for being outsiders who hijack issues and campaigns, but the organization has been active in key environmental justice battles from the founding protest of the movement in Warren County, North Carolina, to key victories in both Kettleman City and Los Angeles, California.[19]

The central issue in relationships such as these is *how* the groups are to work together. Again, it is the *process* that is crucial to grassroots groups, and it is not surprising that issues of process are central to grassroots criticisms of the major organizations. Grassroots groups in the environmental justice network have been willing to work with the major groups (especially given their resources), but the emphasis is on the *with*. The movement has welcomed tactical alliances and meaningful partnerships, but has insisted on retaining local control over issues and campaigns. The national organizations are respected parts of a network as long as they *assist* in an issue rather than attempt to *direct* local groups. I will return to this discussion of the relation between environmental justice groups and networks and the larger environmental movement in my evaluation of the network form and in the following chapters.

Confronting Changes in Capital and Politics

As discussed in Chapter 2, there are many who argue that the environmental movement must continue its liberal organizational strategy—that differences in the movement must be smoothed over in order to present a united front as an interest group pushing for plausible legislation (e.g. Norton 1991). And there is no shortage of environmental pundits attempting to push the movement in one direction or another, with one singular ideology or another. The argument here, on the other hand, is that a political strategy of

---

[19] Greenpeace has recently imploded in the US, closing field offices, firing canvassers, and shutting down most of its active projects, including environmental justice.

networking strengthens the movement with a mobilization of diversity. Networking gives a movement many points of attack, positions from which to argue, and tactics to use, while helping to pool resources efficiently.

Networks are also a countermeasure against changes in power, capital, and politics. There are three interrelated issues here: changes in the understanding of power, changes in political oversight, and, most importantly, changes in the nature of production and political economy.

First, many theorists have discussed the relationship among various forms of power or control and the value of a diverse, and linked response. Foucault (1978, 1979, 1980) has argued that power itself is a network that needs to be examined in its extremities, the everyday experiences of those subject to its reach. Laclau and Mouffe (1985) have also asserted that there is a litany of forms of power and antagonisms in the social realm, and networks can develop in response. Haraway (1991: 170) argues that an understanding of the web-like structure of power may lead to new couplings, new coalitions. Networks develop, then, not just out of pre-existing social relations and responses to environmental problems, but also out of an understanding of, and alliance around, how power links issues. Shared experiences are once again at the base, but these experiences are often ones of subjection. This is illustrated most forcefully by the fact that most local environmental justice organizations may begin with a single issue in mind, but most often begin to relate issues and various forms of domination.

Second, and perhaps most obviously, capital itself has taken on a more rhizomatic form, which poses a problem for previous interest-group strategies. Capital's expanding strategy includes flexibility in production systems, a geographical division of labor, a geographical dispersal of production, and an ethic of mobility which enables companies to take advantage of capital and employment conditions they judge to be most advantageous (Harvey, 1991). In response, a number of recent works on grassroots environmentalism (e.g. Brecher and Costello 1994*b*; Gould *et al.* 1996; Karliner 1997) have focused on the need to revise and update the political strategy of the environmental movement in the face of the transnationalization of political economy. On one level, individual localities and states have less control (in terms of environmental and labor laws) over such mobile capital—and the trend is increasingly to *lower* such controls in order to attract industry (Gould 1991). On another level, neither national nor local organizations working alone can produce the pressure necessary to implement such controls. National environmental organizations simply do not have the political clout to impose restrictions on capital, and local groups working in isolation are up against the corporate promises of economic development (and political contributions). As Gould *et al.* (1996) describe, environmental protection is sacrificed in the face of the 'treadmill of production'. Increasing regimes of 'free trade' will continue this transition.

The necessary response to this treadmill, however, is the network. In that network organizing makes it possible to respond in numerous areas simultaneously, it is a more formidable opponent to such structures and strategies. The response to transnational capital (and the translocal mobility of that capital) must, of necessity, be co-ordinated networks and coalitions.

Finally, though obviously related, the third type of change that networks are suited for is the evolving nature of the political sphere, especially when it comes to environmental oversight. Political decisions are made on more than just the national level. At the state, county, and local level, decisions on issues of growth, environmental regulation, and corporate incentive packages are crucial to both industry and citizens. On the other hand, however, the globalization of capital also minimizes the decision-making realm of the nation-state as the market seeks to take its place. If traditional organizations continue a strategy that focuses on the national government, then they can address only a small portion of the issues, and miss a host of relevant political decisions. Citizen action is necessary on the regional and local level, because that is where much of the control remains lodged; it is necessary on the global level because the institutions of governance there are so limited (and undemocratic). And it is necessary to network across each of these levels, as political power flows through them simultaneously.

In his analysis of what he calls 'ecopopulism', Szasz (1994: 164) notes that 'political activities that are confined to a single zone tend to yield disappointing results; in contrast, when political events occur simultaneously in several different zones, the interactions that ensue among them tend to generate real forward motion'. Similarly, Gould, Schnaiberg, and Weinberg (1996: 176) conclude that 'resistance to the transnational treadmill of production must be carried out in novel ways, through new local, national, and, perhaps most important, transnational coalitions'.

Brecher and Costello (1994*a*, 1994*b*) have used the metaphor of Jonathan Swift's Lilliputians to describe the networking strategy. The little people used a web of hundreds of threads to capture Gulliver. 'Similarly, facing powerful global forces and institutions, people need to combine their relatively modest sources of power with often very different sources of power available to participants in other movements and locations' (1994*b*: 758). A variety of local actions, woven together, creates a network strong enough to harness problems larger than any of the localities might be able to on their own. At the core of the Lilliput Strategy is this process of linking together a net out of the variety of otherwise isolated groups, communities, and issues, and putting that net to work.

In the Lilliputian metaphor, the various threads of the powerful network come from numerous positions. The basis of network organizing is to recognize, validate, and forge solidarity with these various positions. The emphasis is on both the importance of each and the strength in numbers of the numerous strands. The argument here is that the environmental justice movement represents just such a Lilliputian, transnational, translocal, rhizomatic movement. It is a 'large' movement, but it is large because of the sheer number of local and small-scale groups that have interacted and intertwined as local concern with toxics, environmental inequity, and environmental racism has grown. Both the movement, and its political success, have come with this linking.

The Southwest Network illustrates the Lilliputian strategy. In attempting to construct 'a net that works', organizers at SNEEJ have been quite explicit about the benefits of the networking strategy. SNEEJ has long used the power of the network to address specific community issues, such as lead clean-up in West Dallas, Texas, as well as more general toxics issues facing communities of color and low-income peoples across the South and West. Central to their efforts has been the application of pressure, from a variety of places, on the EPA. Following the initial pressure by SNEEJ, the EPA released a statement on environmental equity,[20] instituted an Office of

---

[20] There has been debate about whether the EPA's initial response was genuine or not. A confidential memo released by the office of Congressman Henry Waxman reveals that some in the EPA were less interested in specific policy changes than in using the media and contacts with mainstream environmental groups to 'win recognition' for the efforts of the EPA before 'long-simmering resentment in the minority and native American communities about environmental fairness [becomes] one of the most politically explosive environmental issues yet to emerge'. See the press release from Congressman Waxman, 24 Feb. 1992. I will revisit this

Environmental Justice, established the National Environmental Justice Advisory Council (NEJAC), and began a grant program for community groups working on environmental justice issues. Regional EPA offices have also begun environmental justice projects and have established relations with local environmental justice organizations. Moore and Head (1993: 122) argue that SNEEJ's work to make the EPA more accountable to environmental justice issues has shown that grassroots organizations of poor people can win against a powerful US government agency by working together. They note (p. 120) that the network has been successful in part because of the strength of some of its member organizations: 'But more so the Network's success results from its bringing communities and grass-roots organizations together based on what unites them in practice: common negative experiences with corporate, military, and government polluters and related economic impacts, coupled with an understanding that much more can be won working together with others than by attempting to fight alone.' The activities of the network have not only strengthened local groups and community resistance and attracted new grassroots organizations, but they have been instrumental in identifying and addressing the larger problems that are shared, in numerous ways, across these diverse communities. In doing so, they have also affected environmental policy at both local and national levels.

The environmental justice movement is seen as a threat (see Waxman 1992; USEPA 1991) because it merges both groups and issues. It brings environmental, economic, and democratic issues to the table, and refuses to break those issues down according to the lines of governmental authority—toxics issues to EPA, workplace issues to OSHA (Occupational Safety and Health Administration), participation issues to state legislators. Like the Lilliputians, the movement has worked together to develop the threads and combine their power, creating the network that has begun to show numerous signs of success. As Penny Newman argues (CCHW 1993: 21), '[w]hen the networks of women of color and poor communities of the U.S. and the networks from around the world merge into a cooperative

issue in the following chapter. Whether or not EPA's intentions were genuine, SNEEJ's influence in the process is apparent. An internal EPA memo on the Environmental Equity Communication Plan included a handwritten note by then Chief of Staff Gordon Binder stating the necessity of a specific 'detailed reply to SW Network . . . being drafted' (USEPA 1991).

network the reverberations will be felt in every corporate board room and governmental stronghold worldwide'. Ambitious, maybe, but actions and responses to date point to its plausibility.

Evaluating the Strategy

Up to this point, I have tried to lay out the motivation, design, and workings of the networked organizational structure in the environmental justice movement, as well as show its possible promise and effectiveness. But it seems suitable at this point to ask a simple question of network organizing: is it a thoroughly workable form? It is possible to list the numerous victories of the US movement: the closure of waste dumps and incinerators, the prevention of others, the establishment of an Office of Environmental Justice in the EPA, the NEJAC, President Clinton's Executive Order on Environmental Justice, and others.[21] But I want to evaluate the network strategy by examining three issues that may be the greatest weakness of the form: the problems of longevity, relationships over distance and difference, and the lack of an overall alternative vision.

First, networks by their very definition are mobile arrangements. Local groups often dissipate after their concern has run its course— after either victory or loss. New groups join and old ones drop out. Projects and campaigns begin and end. Of all of the examples of grassroots environmental action discussed by Gould *et al.* (1996), none embodied a 'sustained resistance'. In each, 'mobilization was sporadic and short-term' (p. 184). Following up on the previous metaphor, what happens when some of the Lilliputians drop their strings? The problem with this lack of staying power is that both governmental agencies and corporations are influenced by longevity; while they can often wait out sporadic protests, they have a much more difficult time ignoring community organizations that have become established and coordinated.

But one strength of the network form is that the contact remains, even if informal. Groups which pull back, or even dissipate, will often be ready for new mobilizations. In one example, a local group in the Southwest was very active in the Campaign for Responsible

---

[21] See the list of general successes compiled by Freudenberg and Steinsapir (1992).

Technology until it dropped out of the network in order to pursue more specific issues of the indigenous peoples of the region. One organizer of the CRT noted the sense of loss that came with this departure, and the effect of the loss of that one link in the larger network. But as the CRT developed a project on the water use of high-tech industry (SWOP/CRT 1997), the group which had dropped out offered input specific to the effects on indigenous populations.

In addition (and related) to the issue of longevity, networks must constantly keep up relations across both distance and difference. Difficulties of this sort come in a number of forms. When very different communities, or groups within communities, come together some may see themselves becoming part of a larger movement, while others remain most firmly associated with their most pressing particular issues. Within networks, solidarity is understood differently by different groups. Hence, a group working on indigenous issues might not see themselves completely aligned with a network which addresses the high-tech industry, even if their respective foci overlap in numerous places.

The point here is that networks should never be considered set or permanent. The political practice of networks is necessarily ongoing; evolution remains a key component. Congruent with notions of pluralism from James and Follett to the present, no unity is final and stable. Networks embody the earliest pluralism's notion of order always in the making, unstable and constantly shifting and changing. This is mirrored in Deleuze and Guattari's (1983) arguments for mobile arrangements, the seriality described by Iris Young (1994), and the 'rhizomatic' pluralism of William Connolly (1995). Examples here might be the expansion of anti-NAFTA environmental and labor organizing into cross-border networks on both issues after the passage of the trade agreement, the move of the CCHW and associated groups into a major campaign on dioxin, and, more generally, the continued development of environmental justice networks—on a variety of issues—as ever more community groups organize around relations among race, class, political power, and environmental contamination.

Difficulties other than the shifting nature of networks often arise, however. Issues of race and gender have strained some relations in the movement. Some place racial differences at the core of the break-up of one of the early major environmental justice networks: the National Toxics Campaign (though others insist the problems of the

NTC centered around organizing strategy and internal relationships). Epstein (1997) discusses difficulties that arise in a movement where the vast majority of local activists and leaders are women, and many regional leaders are men. Obviously, these issues—and it is difficult to determine whether they are minor or widespread—hamper the development and longevity of environmental justice networks. I will return to the discussion of these points in Chapter 7.

Yet another tension in the development of network relations over distance and difference is the relation between the grassroots and the major, mainstream environmental organizations. As noted previously, while grassroots groups are often very critical of the major groups, they have turned to the majors (and their resources) for alliances on specific campaigns and actions. Differences certainly remain between local groups, mainstream organizations, and all that fall in between. The major groups often continue to ignore localized issues, and refrain from participating in them even when asked by locals. But a number of the major groups have learned that, while grassroots groups and networks are suspicious of the mainstream, they *do* appreciate their assistance, as long as it is offered within a respectful process. Hence, the mainstream groups that work most successfully with the grassroots are those that work with the local groups, listen to their concerns, and do not make major moves without consultation with, and direction from, those locals. Generally, and as discussed by Gould *et al.* (1996: pp. 195–6), the most successful efforts are made when alliances are formed between grassroots and larger regional or national organizations; whereas local mobilizations are often short and unsuccessful if the national groups 'countermobilize' against them. Again, I will return to this point in Chapter 7.

Finally, it could be argued that any political struggle or movement that took on the rhizomatic form and decentralized functions of a network would simply become an amalgamation of numerous decentered struggles, incapable of dealing with the 'big pictures' of power, political economy, or the globalization of many environmental issues. On the contrary, the assertion here has been that multiple, localized oppositions are a tactical strength. The key is the application of diverse critiques, approaches, and styles in various places of action. Environmental degradation is not simply the singular product of a lone 'mega-machine' which can easily be unplugged in one place or with one singular changed practice. The targets of the envi-

ronmental movement are varied; and so the movement itself is necessarily decentered and multiple. A tactical defense against numerous
manifestations of environmental degradation and its effects on individuals and communities in varied contexts calls for a variety of local
resistances. As Foucault explains (1978: 96),

> there is no single locus of great Refusal, no soul of revolt, source of all
> rebellions, no pure law of the revolutionary. Instead there is plurality of
> resistance, each of them a special case: resistances that are possible, necessary,
> improbable; others that are spontaneous, savage, solitary, concerted, rampant,
> or violent; still others that are quick to compromise, interested, or sacrificial.

The issues and abuses that form the motivations for political action
need to be targeted at the local level, in the multiplicity of places
where they emerge. The multiplicity of experiences, issues, and
resistances that have developed in the environmental justice movement call for and exemplify diverse approaches to change in varied
venues. The basis of the movement is this composite character, and
the plurality of levels of attack.

The criticism of all of this, of course, is that the focus is on
resistance, and not on large-scale visions of global alternatives. The
notion of resistance itself, goes the argument, is a capitulation to a
rearguard action, and the environmental justice movement is, for the
most part, continuously on the defensive. In addition, the autonomous form of networks makes more concerted proactive campaigns
quite difficult. Certainly, gatherings such as the First National People
of Color Environmental Leadership Summit, and the production of
the principles of environmental justice there, are examples of the
network form devising a long-term vision. But as Di Chiro (1997) has
succinctly noted, within the networked form, it is quite difficult to
work out issues between conferences.

But this is not to say that large-scale critiques, political tactics, or
movements are not possible. On the contrary, the argument here is
that solidarity across locally based groups creates movements that
reach and connect beyond the local and particular. Obviously, there
are similarities among different communities and experiences. Issues
of the power of capital, the market imprisonment of policy, the
exclusion of affected populations from policy-making, the desire
for participation and democratization, and a focus on political process as a way to address both a lack of equity and recognition come
up time and time again in the movement. Networks are assembled

across the connections exposed when dealing with particular issues. And environmental justice networks, based even as they are on resistance, have shown themselves quite capable of flexing fairly large-scale—even global—muscles. Recent cross-border movements around NAFTA, World Bank policy in the Amazon, ozone policy, biodiversity, and the ownership of indigenous knowledge serve as examples.

In addition, it is important to recognize the politics and process of the environmental justice movement as a form of prefigurative politics (Epstein 1988). The form of the movement itself, and its development of this form out of critiques of past social movement organizing, is a living articulation of an alternative form. Networks are not simply a means to an end—and a defensive end at that. They exemplify an attempt at an alternative political structure. In this sense, the movement counters many social movement theorists and left activists who argue that only a unified movement organized around a singular agenda can accomplish significant social change.

Conclusion

Networking and alliance-building have become a major tactic in environmental organizing, especially among grassroots activists and groups. This move has been in response to the limitations of past, liberal pluralist, models of organizing, including the alienation bred by the large, centralized form of the major environmental organizations. It has also been in response to the changing nature of the structures and practices of capital and politics.

Networks begin at the level of the community, with bases in everyday relationships at home, church, work, and play. The organization of networks takes these local realities seriously, and continues the recognition and validation of diverse experiences, even as it links the multiplicity of peoples and issues into alliances. While they may restrict themselves to a local alliance around a local issue, these alliances may also take on a larger, and often more rhizomatic form. Networks expand the notion of environmental locality, as they expose the similarities shared by communities in disparate places.

Networking also goes beyond organizational form; it becomes the mode of organizational function. Decentralization, diversification, and democratization drive networks, as opposed to the centralized and hierarchical practices of past movements and present main-stream organizing. Finally, these networks display a strength and resilience one might not expect from such a decentralized organiza-tion. The plurality of a movement, its diverse tactics, and its numer-ous resources are understood as strategic advantages in organizing.

What the development of networking shows, especially as it has been used in the environmental justice movement, is a new form of movement organizing that is based on the strength of diversity. Dismissed is the standard liberal pluralist model of seeing difference as a hindrance or finding the least common denominator in develop-ing policy. Instead, these networks and alliances recognize the reality and importance of difference, validate multiplicity, and create politi-cal networks of solidarity.

What this initial foray into networks shows is that organizing in environmental justice exemplifies some of the components of a critical pluralism: the acknowledgment of difference and the con-struction of solidarity across these differences. Two crucial questions remain. How exactly does environmental justice *implement* the prac-tices of critical pluralism: what does this new form of critical plural-ism look like in practice, and what does it demand? Those are the central questions of the next chapter. Then, of course, one must address the question of whether critical pluralism works, and evalu-ate the process, its accomplishments, and its prospects. That question is to be addressed in Chapter 7.

6

Communicative Practices and Communicative Demands in the Environmental Justice Movement

A key and necessary component of the ongoing work and success of networked people and organizations is communication between and among various individuals and groups. Issues of communication—from the interpersonal to governmental procedures for public participation—are central to a new generation of pluralism in both theory and practice. As discussed in Chapter 4, the acceptance of multiplicity and situated knowledge necessitates certain communicative practices. Agonistic respect and critical responsiveness (Connolly 1991, 1995), attempts at intersubjective understanding (Benhabib 1992; Habermas 1970*a*, 1970*b*; Honneth, 1992), and inclusive, open discourse free from domination and the possibility of reprisals (Dryzek 1990*a*; Forester 1989; Habermas 1984, 1987*a*) are crucial to the communicative practices of a new critical pluralism.

In the grassroots environmental justice movement, political process is the key to justice, both in terms of environmental equity and in terms of recognition. The acceptance of diversity and the situated experiences of individuals and cultures have fostered the development and demand of more pluralistic and authentic communicative processes in numerous ways. The movement has attempted to employ more open discursive processes internally, paying particular attention to communication within and across groups. And the movement has also made demands with regard to issues of communication and participation on other environmental and activist groups, industry, and government agencies. This chapter will examine both these internal processes and external demands as expressions of critical pluralist practice. First, however, I will survey some of the theoretical examinations of communicative designs, as well as examine the current state of discursive practices in parts of the mainstream of the environmental movement.

Communicative Designs

Beyond the various theories that contribute to a critical pluralism, laid out in Chapter 3, there have been numerous discussions, under various labels, of the communicative aspects of critical pluralist practices. In addition to being criticisms of current institutions and communicative distortions, these discussions focus on the more reconstructive moment of critical theory. One of the basic points of much of the literature on communicatively designed institutions is that taking the real diversity of individuals and groups and their situated experiences seriously demands that discourse be taken seriously as well. Opening the discursive process to people and ideas previously excluded, marginalized, and/or alienated can be accomplished with the development of a number of social and political institutions. While many of these discussions focus on the development of an authentic public sphere (e.g. Cohen and Arato 1992), others attempt to posit possibilities for communicative improvements within the bureaucratic arenas of policy development, planning, administration, and regulation (including Dryzek 1990*a*; Fischer and Forester 1993; Healy 1993; Paehlke and Torgerson 1990*a*).

Dryzek (1990*b*), for example, discusses the implementation of communicative rationality in a participatory 'discursive democracy' that is contrasted with bureaucratic-authoritarian and liberal-democratic political forms. Dryzek argues that 'institutions can be expected to resolve complex problems to the extent they embody principles of free discourse among equals' (1990*b*: 102). Institutions based on discursive design would be ongoing, open sites for communicative interaction—'a public space within which citizens associate and confront the state' (1990*a*: 43). Approximations of discursive designs have been discussed in a number of areas (Handler 1990), including various practices of mediation and dispute resolution (Amy 1987; Cormick 1976; Fisher and Ury 1981), and regulatory negotiation (Harter 1982; Susskind and McMahon 1985).

Numerous authors in planning theory have also been working on institutionalizing participatory designs. Forester (1989) has analyzed communicative distortions in the structures and processes of much contemporary planning, and developed a variety of methods for what he calls 'planning in the face of power'.[1] Healy (1993) has developed ten propositions for 'intercommunicative planning' that have at their base an acknowledgement, respect for, and inclusion of the diverse ways people experience, understand, appreciate, judge, and communicate.

There are a number of advocates of implementing a more open, flexible, discursive policy and administrative process in environmental management specifically.[2] Whereas the current task of conventional environmental administration is seen as 'one of containing and overcoming irrational resistance' to administrative plans (Torgerson and Paehlke 1990: 13), the key characteristic of more discursive environmental administration is openness to and inclusion of the previously excluded and marginalized (Paehlke and Torgerson 1990*b*: 293; Torgerson 1990: 28). Dryzek (1990*b*: 102) insists that, in both policy development and implementation, the 'greening of the administrative state' through discursive design 'enables individuals concerned with different aspects of a complex problem to pool understandings and harmonize actions in light of reciprocal understanding of various issues at stake'. The various components of open and critical discourse allow for diverse experiences and knowledges of specific problems to be shared, discussed, and distilled into administrative arrangements.

The most intriguing examples of such an implementation have been the participatory public inquiries developed by Thomas Berger on the issues of pipeline construction in the Canadian Arctic and the conditions of indigenous peoples in Alaska—both, interestingly, dealing with issues of environmental justice (Berger 1977, 1985). The inquiries were characterized by open access to both the process and the information surrounding the discussions. In the pipeline inquiry, those traditionally underrepresented, such as native groups, rural municipalities, environmental groups, and smaller sustainable businesses were granted funds to participate on a more equal footing with the pipeline companies. All parties were required to share all the

---

[1] For an interesting case study of communicative distortions in environmental planning, see Kemp's (1985) analysis of the public hearing process on Britain's Windscale nuclear waste processing plant.

[2] See e.g. the various contributors to Paehlke and Torgerson 1990*a*.

information they had that was pertinent to the inquiry, enabling each to gain an understanding of the others' knowledge and perspectives. In both cases, Berger encouraged active public participation and took hearings into a variety of indigenous communities. The diverse public, including native peoples communicating their cultural perspectives in their own languages, responded quite actively. The process allowed for stark cultural and ideological differences to be aired in a public arena where intersubjective understanding was a goal, and agonistic respect a means towards it.[3]

In another example, mediation and Alternative Dispute Resolution (ADR) have often been discussed as methods that are designed along more communicative lines than the courts, and have become a popular tool for attempting to resolve environmental disputes (Amy 1987; Bingham 1986; Talbot 1983). Advocates argue that courts do not allow for the full expression of conflict. Mediation, on the other hand, allows environmentalists to argue the real issues at stake, rather than rely on the available legal grounds that may not be at the center of a dispute. Mediation also allows for the creation of 'win-win' situations, rather than the 'win-lose' end of the courts, say supporters (Cormick 1976; Fisher and Ury 1981). ADR generally eschews the more instrumental and alienating methods of the legal system, positing a discursive institutional structure based on open discourse around diverse positions, listening, agonistic respect, and mutually agreeable solutions.

An examination of ADR, however, brings up some important problems and dangers. These problems are not endemic to dispute resolution, but are possible in any attempt to move toward more discursive and participatory institutional designs. Amy (1990) notes that the basic problems with mediation include a lack of both access and authenticity; who is invited remains a matter of power. As one mediator explained, 'I don't ask people who don't have clout to participate in the mediation. This is not public participation, this is cloutful people's participation' (quoted in Amy 1987: 134). Critics also argue that disparities in power and negotiating experience may be strategically employed, leading unsuspecting parties toward their opponent's positions. Distortions of communication are not eliminated in such a setting, but simply hidden behind a conversational

---

[3] For further discussion of Berger's inquiries, see Dryzek 1982, and Torgerson 1986.

facade (Amy 1987, 1990). In addition, lack of information and/or resources is a common obstacle to inclusion in a variety of designs for more open communication. This is the case especially with respect to environmental justice issues and groups (Lee 1993*b*).

While an array of problems may exist in many current attempts to implement communicatively designed and operated institutions, many authors—including critics—continue to emphasize their value. The Berger inquiries, for example, are notable in their attention to these issues, and the building of structures and processes to avoid them. They show that authentic communicative structures are possible. As supporters note, more constant and vigilant attempts to hold communicative experiments up to critical scrutiny could tap their potential and help to create and reinforce the practices of free discourse (Dryzek 1990*a*: 87). As we will see, this has been one of the key tasks of the environmental justice movement.

Creating a Culture of Communication

Before I move on to examine those attempts, it is crucial to note that the development and adoption of more open discursive practices is not limited to more formal institutions, such as the legal system or public administration. Many existing manifestations of open discursive practices are occurring in the *internal* workings and relations of new social and political movements. Many new social movements and new social movement theorists stress the importance of discourse and the creation of democratic public spaces (Cohen 1985: 670; Habermas 1981). The affinity Habermas has for new social movements is not only based on their challenges of the instrumental system's intrusion into the 'lifeworld', but also their potential in the promotion and 'revitalization of buried possibilities for expression and communication' (1981: 36).

The 'prefigurative politics', 'free spaces', and 'symbolic challenge' (Epstein 1988; Evans and Boyte 1986; Melucci 1985) created by movements are characterized by participants and supporters as attempts at more inclusive democratic discourse, an effort to outgrow parochialisms by working with others outside one's usual circle, and the basic discursive and democratic practices of listening, participating, and respecting others. Evaluations of new social movements are often critical of the distance between these ideals and the reality of everyday practices (Breines 1989; Epstein 1988; Miller 1987; Sirianni 1993), but the point here is that the attempt in communicative directions—by both theorists and activists—is an important break from the conventional pluralist model.

Some analysts argue that the cultures of some new social movements have evolved as both an expression and a result of open communication and democratically discursive processes. Melucci's (1985, 1989, 1996) work, for example, centers around both the cooperative creation of identity in new social movements and the symbolic meaning of their internal practices and means. The challenge posed by these movements, he argues, is not only to the particular issues they address, but also to the rationalization of information and information dispersal—both outside and inside the movements (1989: 803–5). Challenging existing instrumentalized communicative practices and posing alternatives are central projects of new social movements.[4]

In attempts to build communicative structures, both institutional design and social movement culture demonstrate that the recognition of the validity and importance of diversity leads to the demand for and practice of particular forms of open, democratic, participatory discourse. There is an obvious tension between discourse and difference, but it is that tension that communicative practices are designed to address. Taking plurality and a critical pluralism seriously necessitates both external, institutional demands and internal, interpersonal practices.

Conventional Environmentalism, Conventional Pluralism

These external demands and internal practices are two of the key factors that help to differentiate the major groups in the US environmental movement, based on a limited notion of interest groups within a liberal pluralism, from the grassroots parts of the move-

---

[4] Epstein (1988, 1991) has written of the culture of the direct-action movement of the 1970s and 1980s, including the development and importance of the internal processes of discussion and the consensus decision-making process. While critical of consensus process as inefficient and impractical for anything other than small groups, Epstein (1991: 270) admits its centrality and its strengths: 'The consensus process has been the direct action movement's illustration of what social relations should be like, in alternative communities in the present and in the society of the future . . . By requiring that everyone participate actively in decision-making it

ment, especially those organized around environmental justice and toxics.

Yet the early successes of the mainstream of the environmental movement were characterized, in part, by aspects of open discourse both internally and in its proposals. Internally, discourse, sharing information, and participation were the norm. The point many refer to as the birth of the second wave of environmentalism—the first Earth Day—was designed as a massive teach-in. Part of the message of that Earth Day was an awareness of the myriad communicative distortions of media and industry. Handbooks for Earth Day included chapters on how to criticize the media presentation of environmental issues and industry promulgation of 'phoney ecologists' (De Bell 1970; Sierra Club 1970). The expanding movement, which both spawned and grew out of Earth Day, had a large grassroots component, mostly populated by environmental amateurs, interns, and volunteers who depended on community knowledge of environmental problems and used accessible language in dealing with those issues. Before mass mailings and mass memberships, open participatory communication was both a demand and a growing practice in the movement.[5]

In the institutional realm, the first generation of environmental protections gained by the burgeoning movement regularly included participatory and discursive components. The major environmental legislation of the era, the National Environmental Policy Act of 1969 (NEPA), while primarily an effort to inject science into the policy process, was 'importantly, even though secondarily, a full disclosure or public participation law' (Caldwell 1982: 74). While critics have argued that the very formalized process induced by NEPA actually stifled growing public participation and meaningful dialogue (see e.g. Fairfax 1978), NEPA spawned participatory mechanisms in the development of, and arguments around, environmental impact

brings differences to the surface that might otherwise remain unexpressed and provides an arena for persuasion and understanding.' The dedication to open discursive processes in the direct-action movement is made obvious, even by some critics, as when a group within it prefaced a pamphlet critical of consensus with the statement that it was meant as 'a starting point for dialogue' (Ryan 1983). See also Ingalsbee (1995) for a description and analysis of the identity, culture, and processes of Earth First!

[5] It is important to note here, however, how limited was the cultural diversity of the movement at this point. On the racial limitations of the movement, see Fox 1981: 324–5, 345–57; Darnovsky 1992.

statements. It also paved the way for legal challenges by environmental groups.[6]

Less technical participatory mechanisms were required under the Resource Conservation and Recovery Act of 1976 (RCRA) and the Comprehensive Environmental Response, Compensation, and Liability Act of 1980 (CERCLA)—both aimed more at environmental hazards than natural resources. RCRA called for 'public participation in the development, revision, implementation and enforcement of any regulation, guideline, information or program', while the language of CERCLA encouraged the establishment of 'community relations programs' to ensure an informed and involved citizenry.[7] As discussed below, the potential of neither of these laws has been fully developed. Still, they demonstrate that notions of discursive design and the validity of diverse public input were, at least initially, taken seriously enough to be included.

While the growing environmental movement celebrated the larger policy victories, their dedication to the specifics of public participation and discursive policy formation was, in fact, minimal. 'Public involvement' was, for the most part, limited to the representatives of the major national environmental and other public interest groups. This being the case, these groups did not fight the frontal attacks on more full public participation waged by the Reagan administration. Eliminated within the EPA were the public involvement budget and staff for the Toxic Substances Control Act (TSCA) and RCRA and the special advisor to the administrator for public participation. Contracts for citizen workshops were canceled, and the funding and staff for public information materials of the Office of Public Affairs was cut (Rosenbaum 1983). In response to these moves by the Reagan administration, the major environmental groups came to focus on maintaining their *own* access, rather than opening up participation to the larger public and to individual communities. They continued their lobbying, legislative agenda, and litigation and refused to challenge limitations on public participation. In effect, they followed a liberal, rather than critical, pluralist agenda, limiting themselves to their role of one of many competing interest groups in the construction of

[6] Litigation, while not a discursively designed process, at least opens the door for increased discussion of an issue, and brings opponents to the table. On the limitations of the legal process on communication, community participation, and empowerment, see esp. Cole 1992, and the special issue of *Race, Poverty, and the Environment* on environmental justice and the law (5: 2–3).

[7] Quotes are from RCRA s. 7004(b), and CERCLA s. 105(9).

policy. As a result of both administrative attacks and movement complacency, the participatory programs won early in the movement 'have come to epitomize administrative marginality . . . usually regarded as embellishments rather than essentials to substantive programs' (p. 177).

Indeed, in more recent years, some of the major groups have actively worked *against* the participation of the public in policy development. Most mainstream environmental leaders, including Jay Hair of the National Wildlife Federation (NWF), supported the 'fast-track' path for NAFTA—which not only excluded public participation, but cut even both houses of Congress out of the specifics of policy-making. Those leaders who supported the treaty dropped a demand for a public commission which would have had the power to enforce environmental standards worked out in a side agreement. In another example, the Environmental Defense Fund (EDF) stepped into the dispute between McDonald's and grassroots groups, including the CCHW, on the issue of styrofoam food containers, forming a task force that excluded grassroots leaders. EDF and McDonald's reached an agreement that fell far short of the demands of those who had raised the issue in the first place (CCHW 1993: 12; Dowie 1995: 139–40).[8] As one activist left out of those negotiations argued, the 'established movement makes decisions and negotiates compromises for others while remaining isolated from where people actually live . . . These communities strongly feel they can speak for themselves . . .' (Newman 1993: 92).

Criticisms of the major environmental groups by grassroots activists have centered not only around the lack of dedication to public participation at the level of policy, but also the lack of participation *inside* these groups, and the alienation this has bred. Mainstream, grassroots, journalistic, and academic environmental writings abound on this issue.[9] The most common complaints include the limitation of participation of members to writing check, the

---

[8] The negotiations between EDF and McDonald's are an example of some of the major groups' foray into a mediation strategy. Often described as part of the 'third wave' of environmentalism—espoused most emphatically by Fred Krupp of the Environmental Defense Fund and Jay Hair of the National Wildlife Federation—mediation with polluters is used hand-in-hand with market incentives. As the McDonald's example shows, this strategy has been used as a method of excluding numerous positions from the debate. See critiques of the third wave in Dowie (1995) and McCloskey (1992).

[9] For a start, see many of the essays in Borrelli 1988; Cockburn and St. Clair 1994; Dowie 1991, 1995; Gottlieb 1993; St. Clair 1995; D. Taylor 1992.

physical distance between mainstream groups and their members as these organizations centralized in Washington, and the attempts to silence dissent in the membership ranks.[10] On the latter, Jeff St. Clair (1995), maverick editor of *Wild Forest Review*, has argued that the surest sign of the decadence of the movement is the suppression of internal dissent: 'Such a decadence now erodes the moral core of the environmental movement. Stray beyond the margins of permitted discourse, publicly critique the prevailing strategy, strike out in a new direction, and the overlords of the environmental movement crack down. They inveigh the insurgents with legalistic maledictions, gag orders, [and] accusations of sedition.' Other grassroots critics of the major groups view their dislocation from the grassroots as an example of 'Washingtonization' (Sale 1993: 55), and the accompanying pro-fessionalization and careerism (Gottlieb 1993: 160). The result, finally, is that the larger organizations are 'alienated and estranged from their membership, and irresponsible to the needs of local communities' (D. Taylor 1992: 44).[11]

Communicative Designs and the Environmental Justice Movement

Many parts of the grassroots environmental movement, especially the environmental justice movement, have come to support critical communicative practices in both their internal workings and their external demands. As activists and organizers Richard Moore and Louis Head have explained, '[i]n contrast to the national liberal establishment, the grassroots movement defined political participation based on those methods that had worked historically: direct action and democratic participation from below' (Moore and Head 1993: 125). Participation means different things to different actors.

---

[10] The geographic issue was especially contentious within Friends of the Earth, and led to the exiting of David Brower. On silencing dissent, the Sierra Club has been battling a membership group (the Association of Sierra Club Members for Environmental Ethics) promoting more internal democracy (Dowie 1995: 216–19). In addition many of the groups who supported NAFTA did so over the objections of both membership and staff.

[11] Again, it should be noted that this is a general critique of the major groups. As discussed in Ch. 5, even within this critical context there are numerous examples of cooperative campaigns between major groups and the environmental justice movement.

For those in the grassroots organizations of the environmental justice movement, it means defining issues, organizing, speaking, and acting for themselves. One of the key rallying cries of the movement has been, 'We speak for ourselves' (Alston 1991). As Dorceta Taylor (1992: 41) argues, this is one of the key reasons why environmental justice groups have become so attractive: 'minorities can, through these groups, set, participate in, or define a new environmental agenda in which they have a real voice'. Voice, and participation, is key to the justice of environmental justice.

In giving voice to more participants, the growing environmental justice movement has become quite aware of its own diversity, and the fact that it is more ideologically inclusive than the more traditional mainstream groups (D. Taylor 1993: 57). As such, it has been quite explicit in addressing the rights and responsibilities of activists communicating with and across this diversity. Cross-cultural communication and understanding, then, has become important in the organizing of the environmental justice movement. It is not just the existence of diversity that makes for strength, but the understanding of others that is necessary for real solidarity. Both the literature and the actions of the movement express the concern for communication, education, and understanding across differences (see M. Taylor 1988).[12] The result has been increased attention to discursive processes within the movement. This is not to say that communication and relations have reached an ideal state; in fact, there have been numerous instances of conflict within the parts of the movement that I discuss here (and I will return to these issues in the final chapter). None the less, it is crucial that organizations within the movement have both dedicated themselves to bettering internal communication and have demonstrated this increased attention in practice. My focus here will be on some of these actual examples.

In April of 1990, the Southwest Organizing Project (SWOP) hosted a 'People of Color Regional Activist Dialogue'. While SWOP is based in Albuquerque, New Mexico, the meeting, dedicated to a range of environmental and economic issues facing people of color and their communities in the Southwest, attracted over one hundred activists from eight states in the region. As the organizers report, the most significant outcome of the meeting was the initiation of a process

---

[12] One of the best examples of this process is practiced by the youth of SNEEJ, who include cultural education as an integral part of the meetings of their diverse group.

of dialogue among Latino-Americans, Asian-Americans, African-Americans, and Native Americans (Moore and Head 1994: 192). The diverse representation 'served as a vehicle to strengthen communications' and the 'dialogue confirmed the need for communication among people of color and the urgency to develop further' such processes (p. 205). This combination of communication and urgency resulted in the founding of the Southwest Network for Environmental and Economic Justice (SNEEJ).

Communication has remained a central concern of the network since this founding in dialogue. SNEEJ notes that local groups that become part of the network are assured the right to be heard, the right to know, the right to respect, and the right to be involved in the decision-making process of the network (SNEEJ 1993). In response, member individuals and groups are expected not only to share information and keep communication open, but are also reminded of the responsibility to recognize, respect, and be understanding of cultural diversity. The policies of the network are not decided by an executive director or a small board, but rather by a Coordinating Council of twenty-three elected at an annual gathering. These internal communicative and participative practices have been integral to both the expansion of the size and mission of the network and its continuing focus on the individual and community concerns that led to its construction.

The care and attention dedicated to communication and discursive process was vividly displayed at the First National People of Color Environmental Leadership Summit in 1991. The Summit was intended to be a forum for process—a place 'where people of color leaders can articulate and share with each other their own realities and their prescriptions for action' (Lee 1992: p. v). The process at the Summit was designed 'to foster mutual support, information exchange, issue clarification, problem solving, agenda development, and network building around the environment' (p. vi). Over 300 delegates participated.

One of the reported hallmarks of the event and its communicative process was the authenticity allowed—people had an opportunity to articulate their concerns on various issues and speak for themselves. Numerous participants have noted that diverse points of view were expressed, trust was built, and mutual respect given. Many have emphasized the importance of this process and its effect on the diverse people involved. Charles Lee reflected that 'one of the most significant elements of the Summit was the lively exchange of information and viewpoints from a gathering of people unprecedented in terms of its racial and geographic diversity' (1992: p. vii). Richard Moore, Co-Director of SWOP, noted that 'trust was crucial to moving forward' (quoted in Lee 1992: p. v). Benjamin Chavis, then Executive Director of the United Church of Christ Commission for Racial Justice and one of the organizers of the Summit, has noted the bond formed at the meeting 'that helped to engender mutual respect and unity' (quoted in Grossman 1994: 273). Robert Bullard has spoken of the exchange between urban African-Americans and rural Native Americans, based both on mutual willingness to listen and a shared sense of loss and struggle, that led each to appreciate further the experiences and beliefs of the other (Bullard 1992).

A microcosm of this process can be seen in the events and discourse leading up to the adoption of the Principles of Environmental Justice at the Summit. As some of its participants have reflected, the process by which the principles came into being 'illustrated the extraordinary degree of openness, patience, dedication, and sacrifice required to foster sufficient trust across immense cultural barriers to create a powerful multiracial, multinational peoples movement' (Madison *et al.* 1992: 49). From the beginning and throughout the discussions at the Summit, the organizers of the conference and the drafting committee of the principles emphasized that the process was to be as important as the outcome (Lee 1992: 61).

Delegates at the Summit were offered the sixth draft of the Principles of Environmental Justice, hammered out over months by a drafting committee. The commitment to the process was tested when a plenary session set for ratification of the principles instead became a discussion of language, framing, differences, and possible additions to the document. Rather than vote on ratification, the plenary instead elected a committee to develop another draft. The committee was charged with taking into consideration all of the spoken and written concerns expressed by the delegates. The process was designed explicitly to give voice, and a respectful ear, to all those who wished to contribute.

Evaluations of the work of the appointed drafting committee acknowledge that an atmosphere of trust, honesty, openness, and respect permeated the committee's discussions. This climate, it is argued, 'served to break down immense barriers and facilitate communication and cooperation which enabled it to arrive at a balanced

articulation of the legitimate interests of the widely disparate conference delegates' (Madison *et al.* 1992: 51). As some of the participants
describe:

> The climate of honesty and openness between members of the Drafting
> Committee was unlike anything many of the participants had ever wit-
> nessed—in having different individuals, who were supposed to be arrayed
> against each other, being generally as concerned about each other and meet-
> ing each other's needs as they were about being heard and having their own
> needs met . . . Despite the regional, ethnic, cultural, age, geographical, and
> experiential differences of the participants, there was, to use one Committee
> member's language, an 'unspoken equality' that bound the group together.
> No Drafting Committee member felt him/herself to be more important than
> any other member. Everybody's ideas were respectfully received and consid-
> ered; nobody felt excluded or unaffirmed. (Madison *et al.* 1992: 51)

The inclusion, openness, and respect of the process were reported
to have eliminated the tendency toward the uncooperative or
unconstructive comments that so often disrupt such attempts at
consensus among differences.[13]

The process exemplified an ongoing agonistic respect—a cultivation of care for others. It also showed the possibility of the development of a unity based in diversity, rather than a push toward
uniformity. As participants have reflected, 'In the dominant society,
difference is often responded to in an adversarial and competitive
manner. Many persons honestly believe that diversity invariably has
to lead to conflict and contentiousness. The Summit demonstrated in
clear and concrete terms that difference can be cooperative instead of
competitive, that diversity can lead to higher harmony rather than
deeper hostility' (Madison *et al.* 1992: 52). The entire process was an
example of the construction of the communicative tools essential for
collaboration across differences: respect, openness, intersubjectivity,
and solidarity.

It also worked. As a result of this process, the number of principles
grew from ten to seventeen and much of the language was altered.

---

[13] It is much easier simply to assert that this type of atmosphere characterized the
Summit than it is to demonstrate such a thing empirically. Once again, my point
here is not that the communicative practices reached a counterfactual ideal, but
that those practices were an important focus of the Summit. In addition, as one of
the common complaints of those involved in the Summit process has been the lack
of voice, ear, and respect from major groups and government, I tend to take
participants at their word that the practices at the Summit were a vast improvement on their everyday experiences with these other entities.

The version returned by the committee was ratified, after a few more minor additions. A preamble was added that emphasized the worth of the process, as it called on participants 'to respect and celebrate each of our cultures, languages and beliefs about the natural world and our roles in healing ourselves' (Lee 1992: p. xiii). The Principles of Environmental Justice have since become an important educational and organizing tool, being reprinted and distributed in numerous outlets.[14]

The basic components of the process practiced at the Summit have become ingrained in many of the relationships in the environmental justice movement. Internally, as I have described with reference to SNEEJ, groups have emphasized the importance of respect, participation, and open communication. The movement, additionally, brings these practices into a number of arenas, from the level of the community, to networking, to the proposed relationship with other environmental groups.

Activists have used a number of strategies to expand the participation of local communities in the environmental justice movement, but an emphasis on respect has been at the center of each. In helping in the organizing around a proposed incinerator in Kettleman City, California, organizers noted that it was 'essential to recognize the element of respect, as simple and as basic as that sounds, because by following that precedent you recognize that you are entering a community with expertise' (Avila 1994). Joe Szakos of Kentuckians for the Commonwealth (KFTC) has argued that 'KFTC wants its members to develop an effective voice on matters concerning them' (CCHW 1993: 50). The point is to value the local knowledge and experience, and to assist in giving it voice.

This care in allowing community voice and expertise to develop is one of the basic reasons for building networks for information dispersal. Rather than step into a community as the holder of technical, health, or legal knowledge, the movement has developed information networks on these issues which help to instill knowledge and self-confidence in community residents. Organizations such as CCHW, the Environmental Justice Resource Center, Environmental Research Foundation, Tulane Environmental Law Clinic, the Deep South Center for Environmental Justice, and the Good Neighbor

---

[14] A list of the Principles of Environmental Justice can be found in Bullard 1994*b*; Dryzek and Schlosberg 1998; Hofrichter 1993*a*; Lee 1992.

Project provide information to, and work with, community activists in a variety of campaigns. This is a distinct rebuttal of the methods of mainstream groups, who, after deciding to take on an issue, would often assume ownership and direction.[15]

With all of the criticism of the tactics, methods, and construction of the major groups, it might be surprising that one of the major goals of the People of Color Environmental Leadership Summit was to initiate a better dialogue between the environmental justice movement and the leaders of the national environmental movement (Lee 1992: p. vi). The participation of mainstream groups, however, was limited, and occurred in terms insisted upon by the grassroots. In the Summit session that included mainstream leaders, Dana Alston of the Panos Institute responded to those leaders' fears of 'disunity' in the movement. While interested in developing partnerships with the national groups, Alston insisted that what the environmental justice movement seeks 'is a relationship based on equity, mutual respect, mutual interest, and justice. We refuse narrow definitions . . . We refuse a paternalistic relationship' (Alston 1992: 103).

Other activists in the movement have praised particular organizations in the mainstream for approaching possible partnerships in just this way. After a few months of discussions between SNEEJ and the National Toxics Campaign (NTC), an Environmental Justice Project was formed between people of color and white environmentalists. It began a program to give grassroots leaders intensive training, which would be brought back to their local communities. SNEEJ also forged a relationship with the Campaign for Responsible Technology to address the environmental and economic impact of the microelectronics industry. As Moore and Head reflect, both partnerships 'involved a process of building trust and mutual respect between two camps' (Moore and Head 1993: 123).[16]

---

[15] Again it should be noted that this is the ideal. Members of local groups in the west not affiliated with SNEEJ have at times expressed resentment of the network, especially its access to resources. But these members also recognize the importance of continued work with SNEEJ, as well as with larger environmental, labor, and other groups. Likewise, some leading academics in the environmental justice movement have noted the difficulties and distrust between some environmental justice resource centers and the community groups they assist, but insist on continuing efforts to inform and empower local communities, and build trusting and respectful relationships with them.

[16] The National Toxics Campaign closed down in 1993, and while accounts of its internal problems differ, issues of race, resources, and organizational structure were central in its difficulties.

Designing and Demanding Communication
and Participation

All of this concern with process and communication by environmental justice activists is more than inwardly focused. The movement organizes as it does in order to strengthen its voice and demand its place in the development of governmental and industry policy.

We have operated from the point of view that in order to sit at the table, the first thing we need to do is bring ourselves together as people of color. We know that if we cannot strengthen our relationships with one another, building a multicultural and multiracial movement to go up against the multinational corporations will be quite difficult. (Moore and Head 1994: 202)

This approach uses community organizing not only for its values and internal rewards, but also as a means of empowering local residents to develop a political base to influence decision-making. The construction of inclusive, participatory decision-making institutions—a 'seat at the table', or equal, informed, respectful participation—is at the center of environmental justice demands. Open, participatory, and democratic process is the key to both environmental equity and cultural recognition.

The grassroots movement is mindful of the many limitations of the policy process and of the environmental effects of exclusion from political and economic decisions. Community members and activists have experienced the limitations and distortions discussed by critical policy theorists. Environmental justice communities are partially defined by their lack of financial resources, and activists have found the acquisition of basic information one of the most difficult tasks of the movement (Lee 1993*b*: 44). The decision-making processes which result in major environmental and economic decisions in minority and low-income communities have also excluded affected populations.

In one case, a Greenpeace activist was arrested for testifying with a Spanish translator during a public hearing on the expansion of a hazardous waste disposal facility in a Mexican-American community. In the case of a proposed hazardous waste incinerator in Kettleman City, California, it was exclusion from participation, in the form of a lack of a Spanish translation of the Environmental Impact Statement, that ultimately led to a court invalidating the process (see Cole 1994*b*). As public interest scientist and editor of *RACHEL's*

Environment and Health Weekly Peter Montague has noted, 'It is now clear that the root cause of pollution and poisoning has been a long string of bad decisions made behind closed doors' (Montague 1993: 14).

Even when the doors are open, environmental justice advocates have found the experience less than ideal. In public hearings supposedly designed to gain community input, activists and concerned community members have often found that neither they nor their testimony are taken very seriously. At times, African-American women have been addressed by their first names, while white women are addressed by full, and formal, names (Krauss 1994: 267). During the campaign to halt a proposed incinerator in South Central Los Angeles, women's concerns were often dismissed as irrational, uninformed, and disruptive. Hamilton (1994: 215) argues that male city and corporate officials 'used gender as the basis for discrediting women's concerns'. During hearings regarding Chem Waste's proposal to build a hazardous waste incinerator in Kettleman City, observers noted the different body language county commissioners expressed when Mexican-American residents and representatives of Chem Waste were at the microphone: patronizing on the one hand, and respectful on the other (Avila 1994). In many ways, then, even the limited public process is uninspired, problematic, and distorted.

In response, the movement has made communicative and participatory demands part of their basic principles and rights. Calls for procedural equity were on par with demands for environmental and social equity. Various principles adopted at the Leadership Summit demand 'the right to participate as equal partners at every level of decision-making including needs assessment, planning, implementation, enforcement and evaluation', affirm 'the fundamental right to political, economic, cultural and environmental self-determination for all peoples', and call for 'public policy [to] be based on mutual respect and justice for all peoples' (Lee 1992: pp. xiii–xiv). As noted by participants and observers alike, a shared and respected role in the decision-making process is the key demand of the movement. Bullard argues that grassroots leaders 'are positioning themselves to become "partners" (not silent or junior partners, but full partners) with environmental policy makers on issues that affect the health of their communities' (Bullard 1994*b*: 7). The right of citizen participation in environmental decision-making is the 'heart of the grassroots movement' and what distinguishes it from the mainstream (Dowie 1995: 135). The movement insists on moving from the limited, and distorted, communicative processes of liberal pluralism, and into more informed, open, ongoing, discursive designs for making policy.

Environmental justice groups, rather than seeking particular and incremental policy changes, are insisting on a fundamental change in the processes of environmental and economic decisions that affect their communities. What we see in the demands of the environmental justice movement is an attempt to implement the kind of participatory and discursive institutional processes discussed by a number of critical policy theorists. The movement uses the ideals of access, inclusion, participation, respect, and empowerment the same way that analysts, such as Kemp (1985: 189), use Habermas's ideal speech situation—as 'both a normative model for the conduct of political discourse and an incisive model of social criticism'. At best, the movement forces institutional change in the direction of pluralist discursive designs; at worst, it exposes the multiple barriers to, and distortions of, democratic discourse in environmental policy-making.

The basic demands of the movement include access to information; participation in assessment, planning, and implementation; and ongoing oversight. The right to know—about such things as chemicals, health risks, worker exposure, and tax breaks for business—has been a central demand in environmental justice disputes. In the battle against a proposed incinerator in South Central Los Angeles, one of the key aims of the Concerned Citizens of South Central was not just to get information themselves, but to get it out into the local community. Public informational hearings were held in order to educate the community, keep people informed about new developments, and intensify public debate on the dispute (Hamilton 1994: 213). The demand is not simply for information, but for the expansion of public discourse to all of those affected by a decision.

The type of information, and the method of its retrieval, is also important to the movement. One of the defining characteristics of the environmental justice movement is its deep suspicion of scientific expertise, and the knowledge of the professionals espousing it (CCHW 1993: 5). From the point of view of many communities, the knowledge that comes from direct experience—situated knowledge—

is a more potent and real form of expertise. An examination of the context of a situation—the community knowledge of an issue—leads to a more full and accurate mapping of a problem. A typical practice of the movement is to *go* to a place and bear witness; such site tours are a regular feature of various environmental justice meetings and conferences. The movement commonly *demands* such visits from companies and governmental agencies making decisions; they are, for example, a regular feature of meetings between the National Environmental Justice Advisory Committee (NEJAC) and the EPA. The point here, of course, is to get those outside of affected communities to understand the perspective of those living in the context of environmental injustice. Along these same lines, the movement has insisted on including community knowledge in assessments of environmental and health conditions. This 'participatory research' or 'popular epidemiology' uses community members to help expose and explain various exposures and environmental illnesses (P. Brown 1992; L. D. Brown and Tandon 1983; Bryant 1995; Gaventa 1991).

One way of implementing a respect for community knowledge is the establishment of environmental justice centers, or 'Communiversities' (Wright 1995). This model would take advantage of the community links forged by historically black colleges and other minority institutions and emphasize 'bilateral understanding and mutual respect between community residents and academicians' (Wright 1995: 64). These centers would engage in not only participatory research, but would also be a conduit for community education on environmental justice issues. The Deep South Center for Environmental Justice at Xavier University in Louisiana, directed by Beverly Wright, serves as an example, as does the Environmental Justice Resource Center at Clark Atlanta University directed by Robert Bullard.

The movement is demanding not only information and involvement in particular research and decisions, but, more importantly, an ongoing community voice in the policy and decision-making processes. Community groups have demanded an ongoing say in how their communities will be developed. The Southwest Organizing Project's (SWOP) 'Community Environmental Bill of Rights', for example, demands the right to participate in choosing which industries will come into communities, and the right to have an open process in which those decisions can be made.

We have the right to participate as equals in all negotiations and decisions affecting our lives, children, homes and jobs . . . We have the right of access without cost to information and assistance that will make our participation meaningful, and to have our needs and concerns be the major factor in all policy decisions. Government agencies at all levels should be responsive to our needs, provide us with necessary data, and include us in all negotiations with polluters. We have the right to sit at the negotiation table. (SWOP 1995: 100)

The demand continues for participation on issues beyond siting. After facilities or industries have located to a town, or have been exposed as polluters, numerous community groups have demanded 'good neighbor agreements', or community/corporate compacts, with companies. These agreements lay out community concerns and what companies and/or government agencies will do about them. They also often call for the establishment of community advisory committees made up of community members, workers, and corporate or government representatives to oversee ongoing monitoring, inspections, and environmental and safety audits of facilities.[17]

What community involvement and oversight in all parts of the policy process guarantee, and what both local government and industry often fear, is this ongoing reflection and renegotiation, akin to what Connolly has described as 'democratic turbulence' (1987: 15; 1991: 200). The end of all of these demands is an ongoing inclusive and discursive design of institutions and policies; the means for achieving this is an ongoing critique of the policy process.

In the academic realm, there have been differences of opinion on the worth and outcome of this type of citizen knowledge and participation in policy. On the one hand, some argue that public participation on issues such as hazardous waste siting leads to extensive polarization among citizens and heightened political conflict (see e.g. Carnes 1982; O'Hare *et al.* 1983). Similarly, some are skeptical of the public's lack of expertise and the additional administrative

---

[17] Examples here include SWOP and the Mountainview Advisory Council's involvement in pushing for increased citizen involvement in the environmental policies at Kirtland Air Force Base (Montague 1989), and agreements signed between Rhone-Poulenc Basic Chemicals Company and Unocal Richmond Refinery and local community organizations—both of which establish ongoing monitoring and oversight by a community-based committee (Lewis 1995). It should be noted that industry and local government will more often reject such community proposals, as have chip manufacturers Intel in Albuquerque, New Mexico (SWOP 1995), and Hyundai in Eugene, Oregon.

complexity of participation (Aberbach and Rockman 1978; Cupps 1977). These arguments often go hand-in-hand with stereotyping activists as selfish, irrational, and emotional NIMBYs (Glaberson 1988; Mazmanian and Morell 1990).[18] Some states, such as Georgia and Arizona, have enacted policy that effectively excludes local or citizen participation in decision-making on various issues (Hadden *et al.* 1993; Wells 1982).

Increasingly, however, there are a number of policy examiners—in addition to those working on the theoretical level—who see a link between increased public knowledge and participation and the development of successful policy (see M. L. P. Elliot 1984; Fiorino 1990; F. Fischer 1993; Kraft 1988; Mazmanian and Morell 1990; Peelle and Ellis 1987; Williams and Matheny 1995). As Matheny and Williams (1988: 42–3) argue, the problems of hazardous waste policy in the US are the product of 'inappropriate democratic processes'. The 'roots of NIMBY', they conclude, 'are in the failure of meaningful public participation.' Conversely, correlations have been noted between improved communication and public participation and the public's willingness to accept even hazardous waste facility siting proposals (M. L. P. Elliot 1984; Ellis and Disinger 1981; F. Fischer 1993; Kraft and Clary 1991).[19] Workable solutions demand both 'extensive interactive communication and participation' and 'new institutional arrangements and guarantees' (Peelle and Ellis 1987). This is the essence of Williams and Matheny's (1995) call for a new 'dialogic' model of public participation in environmental management.

---

[18] It should be noted, however, that Mazmanian and Morell, while critical of what they see as NIMBYs, support public participation. For an interesting comparison of the stereotypes versus the actual views and concerns of grassroots opponents, see Kraft and Clary 1991.

[19] The examinations by M. L. P. Elliot (1984), and F. Fischer (1993) are most interesting here. Elliot's experimental design involved having actual public officials, business owners, environmentalists, and landowners choose from three proposed fictional operators of a waste facility. One operator emphasized technology, another pollution control in the case of an accident, and the third open management and community participation. Elliot found that participants preferred 'strategies that strengthen social control mechanisms to those that strengthen technological control mechanisms' (Elliot 1984: 398). Fischer (1993: 176–7) discusses an actual case of a process that dealt openly with citizen opposition to the siting of a hazardous facility in the Canadian province of Alberta. When given the opportunity to participate, which included citizens hiring their own expert consultants and designing an ongoing monitoring process, resistance to facilities was lessened.

The findings of many of these examiners suggest that the very things the grassroots movement is asking for—access to information, public involvement in decision-making, and community oversight and control of facilities—would help alleviate the current gridlock in much community-level environmental policy-making. Many in the environmental justice movement see the expansion of participation as a way to turn their opposition to hazardous development into support for sustainable development and the public process. Richard Moore has argued that 'we need to build ecologically sound communities in terms of the terrain and infrastructure . . . There should be economic development plans in our communities that would be sustainable in the long term' (quoted in Almeida 1994: 28). Community and worker participation, he notes, is central to a move in this direction. Developing models for participatory and sustainable development is one of the central projects of SNEEJ, the Labor/ Community Strategy Center in Los Angeles (Hamilton 1995: Labor/ Community Strategy Center 1993), and the Sustainable America project in Madison, Wisconsin (Sustainable America 1995), among other environmental and economic justice organizations. With respect, inclusion, and participation, goes the argument, comes the possibility of workable local environmental policy.

Communicating with the EPA

While the demand for more open communication and participation has been made by the environmental justice community into a number of contexts, much of the effort around expanding communication and public participation in environmental justice policy has been focused on the US Environmental Protection Agency (EPA). This attempt to foster a more open policy process reveals some of the resistance and distortions that are to be expected along the way.

A broad focus of the environmental justice movement has been an attempt to get the EPA, first, to admit that there are major inequities in environmental hazards, exposure, and clean-up faced by lower income communities and communities of color,[20] and then to

---

[20] The earliest works focusing on unequal exposure include the volume on *Toxic Wastes and Race* (United Church of Christ 1987), and a study by the US General Accounting Office (1983). On the issue of the EPA's favoritism towards white communities in Superfund clean-ups, see the special issue of the *National Law Journal* (Lavelle and Coyle 1992).

develop a process to involve communities in the construction of environmental policy that affects them. Frustration began quite early with the EPA's refusal to meet with environmental justice leaders. As Benjamin Chavis argued, 'if the EPA had a genuine concern about improving its relationship with the civil rights community, it would engage in a dialogue with the community on some if its critical issues' (quoted in Weisskopf 1992: A15). Through subsequent dealings with the EPA in two administrations, the movement has learnt much about the difference between authentic and inauthentic communication. In finally turning toward these issues, the agency deliberately attempted to quell legitimate concerns, and engaged in a larger public relations campaign, before it began to address the movement's issues of access, voice, respect, and participatory policy-making.

After years of pressure, the EPA in 1992 made what it called an 'initial step' in contributing to the national dialogue on environmental justice with a document on 'environmental equity' (USEPA 1992: 2 vols.).[21] The document showed that the EPA recognized that public access to information and full participation were key issues to be addressed. In addition to the basic inequitable distribution of environmental problems, the report noted that another important category of issues surrounded 'the access of racial minority and low-income communities to the environmental policy making process', including the decision-making in the administration of the agency (i. 8–9). EPA was at the focus of environmental justice organizing both in terms of equity and recognition, with its policy-making processes under particular scrutiny.

The basic problem in the report, however, was that the EPA continually confused (intentionally or not) the communication of information, public relations, and real participation. While noting the importance of what they call 'two-way communication' and informed participation, the final recommendations of the report, and the pilot projects cited, did not reflect real concern in that direction.

The report contains an informative section on how the EPA, ideally, understands communication. 'Risk Communication', as the

---

[21] Even with the choice of the term 'environmental equity', the EPA showed its initial unwillingness to listen to, take seriously, and speak in the language of the grassroots community, which insisted on the use of the more broad term 'justice' rather than equity.

agency defines it, is a 'tangled web, with information flowing in many directions, between multiple sources and audiences, through formal and informal channels, and without explicit goals or objectives' (USEPA 1992: ii. 37).[22] Citing an EPA risk communication manual (USEPA 1989), the report notes that the agency 'does not view risk communication as a one-way street. It recognizes the need to impart information but also to involve the public in the decision-making process. The purpose of risk communication is not to allay the public or merely help them see [the Agency's] point of view.' The report refers to the 'de facto guideline' for risk communication at EPA: Covello and Allen's (1988) document on the *Seven Cardinal Rules of Risk Communication.* These basic rules include accepting and involving the public as a legitimate partner, as people 'have a right to participate in decisions that affect their lives'; involving the community early, 'before important decisions are made'; and listening to the public concerns, which includes the intersubjective admonition to 'identify with your audience and try to put yourself in their place'.

But the conclusions reached by the authors of the Environmental Equity report show a lack of understanding and/or enthusiasm in implementing such suggestions. The emphasis turns to how to communicate not in order to improve two-way communication, but rather in order to improve the image of the EPA. After discussing various rules for authentic participation, the section concludes that a 'good communication process should therefore build trust in the agency, allow the public to influence decisions, and convey the message that issues of concern to the community will be taken seriously' (USEPA 1992: ii. 39). The value of public influence here is sandwiched between two public relations objectives: building trust in the agency and conveying a message. The EPA here demonstrated that its concerns were not around open, respectful communication, democratic participation, and community involvement, but rather the agency's own reputation and image.

The final recommendations of the report echoed this theme. The first recommendation suggests that 'EPA should increase the priority that it gives to issues of environmental equity' (USEPA 1992: i. 25). Yet to show priority, the report suggests only that 'agency managers

---

[22] 'Risk Communication' documents referred to in the section include Chess *et al.* 1988; Covello and Allen 1988; Plough and Krimsky 1987; Sandman 1986.

could make clear statements to EPA staff' and 'signal to outside groups . . . that environmental equity should be given higher priority' (ibid.). While this one-way communication of interest does not display a desire for more open discursive forms of public involvement, recommendation number seven does focus on expanding communication. It suggests that 'EPA should expand and improve the level and forms with which it communicates with racial minority and low-income communities and should increase efforts to involve them in environmental decision-making' (p. 29). To do this, the EPA could help communities get technical assistance, financially support university-based environmental equity centers, improve outreach literature, give staff guidance on communication, hire outreach representatives, translate relevant materials, and develop two-way communication projects (p. 29). Here, most of the recommendations work only to better supply communities with EPA information—necessary, but not sufficient in the eyes of many in the environmental justice movement. The top emphasis of the EPA is on getting the word out; the distant secondary emphasis is on getting communication from communities. There is nothing specific on ensuring an increase in participation in policy development by affected communities.

Finally, the Environmental Equity report ended by describing a number of environmental equity pilot projects (USEPA 1992: i. 32–40). Of the twenty-three projects listed, most focus on information gathering and studies. Four include some education component, and only two note the importance of community participation in environmental initiatives. There is no discussion of community involvement in the development of any of the pilot projects. The EPA, then, had only two pilot projects, nationwide, that included a discursive or communicative component. Certainly, this emphasis does not address the key issues of justice for the movement: real equity, authentic recognition, and active participation.

The environmental justice community, not surprisingly, was quite critical of the report. Much of the criticism centered around the perceived lack of real interest on the part of the EPA. The document appeared lacking in motivation, and included many words like 'could', 'should', and 'attempt', rather than 'must' and 'will'. Many commenting on the report (whose responses to the finished product were included in the supporting document) note their suspicions that the report appears to be 'spin control' and a public relations strategy rather than a substantive effort to address the concerns of affected communities (USEPA 1992: ii. 97, 101, 117; also see Waxman 1992).

Criticism also centered around the fact that the report, while mentioning the importance of communication, was prepared with no input from those who had been working on the issues for years. It left out many of the suggestions of those who had pushed for such a study, failed to recognize the expertise of affected communities, and reflected the 'disrespect and arrogance of the Agency' (USEPA 1992: ii. 88). Certainly all of this should be interpreted as an exercise in distorted communication, rather than an example of the 'cardinal rules' of two-way risk communication.

Environmental justice activists increased their efforts after the 1992 presidential election, and two key leaders, sociologist Robert Bullard and the Reverend Benjamin Chavis, served on the transition team in the natural resources and environment cluster. Key recommendations to the EPA included establishing 'procedures and guidelines that ensure contact with and input from affected communities at the outset of federal evaluation . . . [and] remediation of toxic and hazardous waste sites', and 'expand[ing] the Community Right to Know initiative to include opportunities for communities to be involved in inspections and negotiation or public review of government environmental actions involving siting of industrial facilities' (Ferris 1994: 309, 315). The demand for communication and authentic public involvement in both clean-up of existing sites and the entry of new facilities remained.

In response to many of the criticisms of the Environmental Equity report, the EPA established, in late 1992, a separate Office of Environmental Justice. Beginning to take some of the participatory concerns of critics in the movement seriously after the change in administrations, the agency, in 1993, established the National Environmental Justice Advisory Council (NEJAC). The NEJAC, the majority of whose members are leaders of environmental justice groups and resource centers, was charged with advising, consulting with, and making recommendations to the administrator of the EPA on matters relating to environmental justice. NEJAC established a subcommittee on public participation and accountability, and its first chair, Peggy Saika of the Asian Pacific Environmental Alliance, has described issues of participation as the 'linchpin' of all the NEJAC's recommendations to the EPA (Saika 1995).

President Clinton, responding to the recommendations of the environmental justice community, signed an executive order on environmental justice in February 1994 (White House 1994*a*). The order required all Cabinet departments and agencies dealing with human health and/or the environment to make achieving environmental justice part of their mission. Again, a key section (1-102-b-2) of the executive order, and its accompanying presidential memorandum (White House 1994*b*), addresses communication and participation. Unfortunately, the only request to go beyond existing NEPA participation requirements was a call to translate documents 'when practical and appropriate' and 'work to ensure that public documents, notices, and hearings relating to human health and the environment are concise, understandable, and readily accessible to the public' (sections 5-5b-c). Once again, the distortion and/or confusion of the differences between one-way communication and authentic participation is made evident.

The response of the EPA, its 'Environmental Justice Strategy for Executive Order 12898', quite explicitly lays out the differences between, and need for, the communication of information and authentic participation. Administrator Browner notes in her introduction that an 'informed and involved local community is a necessary and integral part of the process' (USEPA 1995: 1). Browner asserts that the EPA 'will develop strategies to ensure that low-income and minority communities have access to information about their environment— and that they have an opportunity to participate in shaping the government policies that affect their health and environment' (USEPA 1995: 4). As a basic component of an environmental justice strategy, the report calls for the enhancing of communication, partnerships, and co-ordination in order to ensure the input and active participation of stakeholders in environmental decision-making. The communicative and participatory demands of the movement are apparent in Browner's opening.

The problem, however, is in how the EPA sees the implementation of the ideals of open, two-way communication. As with the 1992 Environmental Equity report, the Environmental Justice Strategy concludes with a description of pilot projects (USEPA 1995: 25–32). Of the thirteen listed, four note elements of community participation. While this seems an improvement from 1992,[23] one of the four

---

[23] Interestingly, neither of the communicative pilot projects listed in the 1992 report appear in the 1995 plan.

has only 'hopes of bringing together representatives'; another seems to have 'investors, lenders, developers, and other interested parties' more in mind than community members. A third, a project in Region 6 called 'Partners in Education', sought to get communities involved in environmental issues in the heavily contaminated corridor between Baton Rouge and New Orleans. Soon after its introduction, however, it was relabeled 'Partners in Deception' by one of the largest African-American environmental justice organizations in the country, the Gulf Coast Tenants Organization (1994). The actions of the EPA on communication and participation were in reality a distance from the ideals they set out themselves.[24]

Continued pressure on the EPA by the NEJAC, however, has led to the development of revised procedures on participation. The public participation subcommittee of the NEJAC authored a 'Model Plan for Public Participation' (USEPA 1996*a*) which includes guiding principles, values, and very specific suggestions for the construction of authentic, open, and participatory public process. The model plan expands the notion of participation as communication of information and decisions, and addresses issues of more open, respectful, and intersubjective discourse. Outreach, education, and communications—the modes of EPA's usual one-way communication—are addressed; but they are also exceeded. The EPA is to view environmental justice stakeholders as 'equal partners in dialogue on environmental justice issues', to 'institutionalize public participation', and to 'recognize community knowledge' (USEPA 1996*a*: 2).

An included 'Environmental Justice Public Participation Checklist for Government Agencies' calls for governmental policies and activities to be 'modified to ensure early, effective and meaningful public participation'. Guiding principles in all public meetings should be to 'maintain honesty and integrity throughout the process, recognize community/indigenous knowledge, encourage active community participation, and utilize cross-cultural formats and exchanges' (USEPA 1996*a*: 6). Materials are to be regionalized in order to ensure 'cultural sensitivity and relevance', site-specific advisory boards are to be established, and representation is to include 'all aspects and

---

[24] The minimal projects initially attempted by the EPA ran into other problems, including budget cutting by the Republican-led Congress. The EPA was hampered by the budgetary cuts threatened by the 104th Congress, whose actions resembled in many ways earlier attacks on public participation in environmental policy waged by the Reagan administration.

diversity of the population' (p. 7). The guidelines call for the structure of public meetings to be changed in order to create an atmosphere of equal participation. Panels of experts and head tables are explicitly discouraged (p. 4); rather, agendas are to be constructed with community input, and meetings should be organized to provide an open exchange of ideas.

The Model Plan for Public Participation at the very least shows that the communicative and participatory demands of the movement—expressed through a participatory mechanism, the NEJAC—have been heard and responded to at the EPA. The history of the agency's actions on communication and participation, as well as the tendency towards inertia in the bureaucratic process, leads one to be wary of the proposed guidelines. EPA officials have claimed the NEJAC's model plan 'is used widely by numerous federal and state agencies and has been very well received and adopted by many people' (Knox in summary of May 1996 NEJAC meeting, p. 6-4, s. 3.1). But an inquiry to the Office of Environmental Justice to supply specifics for this claim was answered with a terse 'There has been no formal acceptance' (e-mail, 17 June 1997).

The development of new procedures for public participation in the EPA's recent 'Project XL' allows for an analysis of how community and movement demands have actually been incorporated into the recent policy-making process. Project XL (for eXcellence and Leadership) is an EPA experiment designed to simplify regulatory procedures for manufacturers who use toxic chemicals. The project was initiated by President Clinton, who argued that it was based on the premise 'that in many cases companies know their business a whole lot better than the Government does; that they understand how best to reduce their own pollution' (quoted in Cushman 1996). EPA's first major agreement was with semiconductor manufacturer Intel. In that deal, Intel promised to reduce the total amount of chemicals it releases into the air and groundwater, in exchange for relief from the requirement to file environmental impact reports on its chemical waste, and freedom from acquiring new permits every time it changes its manufacturing process at a new plant in Chandler, Arizona (Sandoval 1996).

A number of environmental groups, coalitions, activists, and academics thoroughly criticized the agreement (CRT 1996a). Part of the critique centered on the specific environmental controls involved in the agreement; the general complaint was that the agreement weakened existing laws and deregulated some pollutants.[25] But the central criticism of EPA's deal with Intel was the process. Both Intel and the EPA claimed that the XL process was open, and included relevant 'stakeholders' from the community. But the Campaign for Responsible Technology, in a sign-on letter of protest to the Intel deal, claims that 'the real reason the Intel XL deal is so flawed is that the "stakeholder process" for developing it was fundamentally flawed. Intel hand-picked the "stakeholder group" which includes only minimal Chandler community representation and no fabrication worker representatives from the plant' (CRT 1996*a*). CRT (1996*b*) circulated a comparison of a number of different community participation models, including the NEJAC's Model Plan for Public Participation, with the process used in the Intel XL agreement. According to that analysis, the XL process fell short of NEJAC's model in key ways: it failed to encourage public participation, seek out and facilitate broad involvement, and design logistics or mechanics to facilitate participation.

Nevertheless, the EPA insisted that the process was legitimate. A press release asserted that '[d]uring the project development, community members were extensively involved. Information on the Intel project was made available to the public from EPA, state and local agencies and several public meetings were held during the development of the project' (USEPA 1996*b*). Intel claimed the complaints came from national groups who were removed from the local process (Sandoval 1996), ignoring the fact that draft guidelines for stakeholder involvement in the XL process explicitly lay out the importance of including national organizations as direct participants (Lund 1996).

Whatever the claims by EPA and Intel, the fact is that over 100 environmental justice groups and activists signed CRT's letter of complaint (CRT 1996*a*) that insisted there were serious problems with the process. An attempt in the US Congress to formalize and extend XL-type deregulation has been met with another grassroots sign-on letter, developed at the 1997 meeting of the CCHW. That letter (SVTC 1997) calls for 'authentic community and worker empowerment' through increased public participation. A set of 'Principles and Tools for Developing a Model Empowerment Strategy' included in the letter was the need for broad (not hand-picked)

---

[25] Some critics have renamed the XL process 'eXtra Lenient'.

community participation, a balance of power in any negotiations, adequate resources and funding to enable participation, and a variety of logistics and mechanics to encourage broad participation. The environmental justice movement has been consistent and thorough in its demands for more authentic, open, and undistorted public participation, and keeps this demand at the center of the movement's concerns.

The experience with Project XL illustrates a very important point. It is crucial to be aware of the power dynamics involved in any proposed communicative structure that includes industry. Critics of environmental mediation (see especially Amy 1987, 1990) have noted how power may corrupt a discourse that is supposed to be open and inclusive. Access, authenticity, and discrepancies in experience may all be manipulated behind a facade of open and participatory communication; and as seen by the response of the CRT to EPA's XL process, the environmental justice movement is very aware, and critical, of these possibilities. In addition, in most instances the power relations *outside* the conversation or participatory mechanism may remain untouched; again, the movement attempts to address this issue by calling for ongoing public participation and, on occasion, third-party oversight of agreements or facilities.

It is too soon to evaluate the full impact of the environmental justice movement's actions. At the least, the environmental justice community has been consulted and expressed its concerns and desires through the NEJAC, and the EPA has shown interest in incorporating these suggestions into the development of *guidelines* for environmental policy-making. That is a step forward in the development of discursive designs and public participation in the agency. The EPA's initial responses to the environmental justice community on the XL process are not encouraging, but it is still too early to tell whether grassroots criticisms and actions will enable the implementation of a new communicative regime at the agency, or whether the EPA will continue to focus more on public relations than public participation.[26]

Critical policy theorists have argued the need for ongoing critical scrutiny of the design and implementation of communicative models

---

[26] It is important to note that there are different responses and levels of dedication to environmental justice issues in various parts of the EPA. For example, while Project XL has not involved the movement, the Community-Based Environmental Protection Initiative (CBEP) has sought input from the environmental justice

in order to tap their potential and create instances of open discourse (Dryzek 1990*a*: 87). The environmental justice movement serves as an example of that constant and vigilant critical scrutiny, as they keep pressure on the EPA to create participatory practices. In a few short years the movement has grown from its role of exclusion to have an impact on the development of policy at the agency. Certainly, that vigilance will need to continue if the movement wishes to see its models of public participation and empowerment implemented at the national level.

Respecting Industry?

The discussion about working with the EPA and industry brings up a crucial question: just how far does a critical pluralism go in recognizing the value of a respect for diverse participation? Grassroots and environmental justice activists face difficult adversaries: government and industry. Many in the movement see various industries and companies just as others see fascists: it is an insult to sit with them, and impossible to talk to them anyway. But the problem with this outlook is that trying to make environmental policy without the representation of toxic polluters not only goes against any notion of pluralism, but it is also thoroughly unrealistic. Industry is a stakeholder, and needs to be involved in discourse.

The components of a critical pluralism—as discussed in Chapter 4—are both voluntary and reciprocal. We need not suffer gladly fools, fascists, fundamentalists, or anyone unwilling to reciprocate an agonistic respect. But it is important that dismissals not be made out of hand. One of the points of valuing a critical pluralism is that as difference confronts itself, change may occur. Approaching and questioning responsible parties in government and industry—engaging them directly in discourse—seems a better tactic for dealing with them than demonizing or confronting them with a closed state of mind.

The problem with the liberal pluralist model is that industry, and, at times of strength, the mainstream environmental groups, have

community. There are also differences on a regional level: while some, such as Region 6, based in Dallas, Texas, are constantly criticized by the movement, others, such as Region 9, based in San Francisco, have demonstrated more of a commitment to environmental justice.

really been the *only* stakeholders that government agencies from the local to the national have involved. Numerous other positions have simply been excluded from discussions, as critics of the liberal pluralist model have argued since the 1960s (Connolly 1969; Wolff 1965).

The central question for an evolution of pluralism is not how to avoid obnoxious voices or destructive stakeholders; instead the point is to get voices and positions recognized and involved that have not been a part of conventional pluralist discourse. The focus is not on who should be excluded in open discourse; rather it is on who *has* been excluded in a pluralist system of limited participation and how to bring them into the process. The aim of a critical pluralism is to expand policy conversations to include the diverse views, perspectives, and understandings that are to be affected. The liberal pluralist model, based on exclusion, has limited conversation. An evolution of the pluralist model demands an expansion of participation.

In the environmental justice movement, for example, the central effort has been to give voice to and involve the victims of environmental destruction and industrial pollution in environmental discourse. One of the accomplishments of the movement has been a move towards the expansion of public hearings and participatory mechanisms. Previously, the interests of industry—the right to pollute, create illness, and make private decisions about communities—were simply assumed. With the expansion of voice and participation in a critical pluralist discourse, those interests are questioned and challenged. The movement has accepted many of the needs of industry; but it also demands an equal representation of its own needs: community participation, a healthy environment, and decent jobs.

Conclusion

Certainly, issues of communication, and authentic public participation, have been central to the environmental-justice community. There has been insistence on open discourse, respect, and intersubjective understanding of difference within the movement—and many examples of implementation. Demands for recognition, access, agonistic respect, and participation in decisions affecting communities have been made on other environmental organizations and the EPA. These internal processes and external demands demonstrate that the movement sees improved communication—manifest in specific discursive practices—as a key strategy of the movement. This, of course, is fitting, as environmental justice is defined not only in terms of environmental equity, but in terms of the recognition of affected individuals and communities. The movement focuses on political process and public participation as a way to gain justice in terms of *both* equity and recognition.

In discussing the communicative practices and demands of the movement, it is important to note that I am not arguing that the movement represents the perfection of the ethics and practices of the critical pluralism that I have laid out. Rather, those practices are a counterfactual ideal to be strived toward, and they are concepts which can be used to critique existing practices in other environmental groups, and in the development of environmental policy. They can also be used as tools for self-reflection in the movement itself. Much of the effort of the environmental justice movement has been in attempts to create less distorted, and more open, participatory modes of communication both *within* the movement and in the companies, communities, and governmental agencies it addresses. In this, the environmental justice movement has both exposed the weakness of, and moved beyond, the tactics of conventional, liberal pluralism, exemplified by many of the mainstream environmental organizations and governmental processes they continually criticize.

Part IV

Conclusion

Environmental Justice and the Prospects for a Critical Pluralism

My task has been to demonstrate the emergence of a new, critical form of pluralism in the realms of both theory and practice. Theoretically, the challenge has been to develop a pluralism that addresses and exceeds the limits of the conventional pluralist model. In practice, the environmental justice movement represents and illustrates just such a politics. This is no liberal interest group; as a movement it embodies a new, critical pluralism.

I began this study by identifying two central questions. The first asks how, from a critical pluralist perspective, we are to acknowledge diversity. In most studies of the environmental movement, as well as the mainstream practice of environmentalism in the US, this has not been a key concern. The second question arises only after the premise of the first is accepted. Once we acknowledge difference, we return to the basic question Mary Follett asked of pluralists early in the century: what is to be done with this diversity? How can we construct political actions and campaigns based in plurality?

I have argued that a return to pluralism is a method for answering these questions. Pluralism in its origins attended to the issue of multiplicity with the acknowledgement of a radical empiricism. Contemporary theorists have returned to this focus in attempts to justify situated knowledges and embodied objectivity. The components of a critical pluralism which come from this acknowledgement of difference, including network arrangements and communicative ethics, can be constructed from a variety of sources—both self-declared pluralists and others who would surely eschew the label.

The environmental justice movement has been motivated by what many see as the limits of the conventional pluralist model of the mainstream. In its base in diversity, its networked structure, and its communicative practices and demands, the movement exemplifies the attempt to design political practices beyond what one would expect from a standard interest group in the liberal pluralist model. What I have attempted to do in this study is explore, draw out, and make explicit an evolving form of pluralist political practice that is inherent in the movement.

In addition to the question of difference, the environmental justice movement brings the issue of the conception of justice to the fore of a new pluralist politics. The movement is based on a critique of the inequity in the distribution of environmental hazards and risks, but, importantly, it demonstrates an insistence on recognition and participation as key to a thorough conception of justice. The focus on procedural equity—the processes by which environmental inequities will be addressed in both the movement itself and in larger political and policy practices—adds another dimension to the question of what to do with difference. If the new pluralism exhorts us to listen and respect difference, the environmental justice movement demonstrates that these types of concerns with recognition and inclusion are not necessarily *separate* from concern with equitable distribution. Process is not elevated *above* content, or inequitable environmental risks, but it is just as central. The movement shows that these two conceptions of justice, often seen at odds in the recent theoretical literature, can be brought together in political practice. If social movements were the impetus to the academic study of 'identity politics', those same social movements should also be examined to address the incorrect assertion that politics that arise out of identity ignore or downplay issues of social equity.

In evaluating the move to critical pluralism in political practice, a number of questions arise about its value, its sustainability, and its breadth. I want to deal with each of these issues, though more in an attempt to open the discussion than close it, as the movement— young as it is—has not yet been subject to much evaluation.

But Does It Work?

The central questions of this study have revolved around diversity and political practice, but this has begged another central question: is such a political practice successful? The focus, in other words, has been mainly on the prefigurative practices rather than the strategic orientation of critical pluralism. Beyond the attractiveness of practice based on an enthusiasm for plurality, a network of grassroots activists and organizations, and dedication to communicative and participatory ethics, does such a practice have a *strategic* advantage? Can it—bottom line—deliver the goods (or at least keep the bads out of the community)?

It is not very difficult to make the claim that over the past few years the environmental justice movement has been quite successful. One need only look at the alternative: the lack of accomplishments of the mainstream model. As discussed in Chapter 1, the liberal model reached the pinnacle of success in 1992, with its access to the new administration, yet it is generally agreed that in the first Congressional session of that administration the movement fared worse than in any of the last twenty years (Cockburn and St. Clair 1994; Dowie 1995; Montague 1995). And things have gotten only worse since then (Cushman 1995; Gerstenzang 1995; Knickerbocker 1996; Reisner 1995).

Conversely, the environmental justice and anti-toxics movements, using the form and strategy of critical pluralism, have had numerous successes in the past decade. The organization of toxics networks began soon after Love Canal, with the founding of the CCHW in response to the grassroots need for information on toxins, tactics, and industries. The protest seen as the founding moment in the fight against environmental racism—in Warren County, North Carolina, in 1982—was itself a synthesis of civil-rights and environmental movements. This networked form of organization has expanded with the growth of environmental justice as a movement; and the evolution from isolated communities to connected ones has, in fact, worked quite well in pushing for, and accomplishing, the aims of environmental justice.

Lois Gibbs, of the CCHW, has repeatedly stated that the main goal of the network is to 'stop up the toilet', and make sure that there would be no 'away' for toxic wastes. National surveys by various state environmental agencies, the EPA, and even industry consulting firms all show the same story: that numerous new threatening facilities have been proposed, but hardly more than a handful of them were actually sited and built (McCoy and Associates 1986, 1990; Szasz 1994, 114–15). In fact, on the issue of toxic waste disposal and incineration, the total national disposal capacity has actually decreased every year (Szasz 1994: 115). Industry recognizes this is not due to overregulation or government interference, but organized community opposition. As such, industry has been faced with the option that communities have insisted on: a move toward lowering the production of toxic wastes.

On another front, the environmental justice movement has forced the EPA to re-evaluate its conception of community participation. The National Environmental Justice Advisory Council oversees the actions of each EPA region, and confronts the agency at each of its meetings.[1] As a result of the President's Executive Order on Environmental Justice (White House 1994*a*, 1994*b*), every Cabinet department has been required to reflect on how their activities affect environmental justice issues. And, like their allies in the CCHW, numerous environmental justice organizations have been successful in keeping toxic facilities out of their communities and forcing industry and/or the EPA to begin cleaning up neighborhoods and compensating victims. In addition, there have been numerous successful attempts at implementing community participation in the oversight of hazardous facilities (Citizens for a Better Environment 1996; Lewis 1995). And in a precedent-setting decision that may affect the future of environmental justice claims in the US, a three-judge panel of the US Nuclear Regulatory Commission (NRC) in 1997 denied a permit sought by the state of Louisiana for a uranium enrichment plant. The judges specifically noted that 'racial bias played a role in the selection process', and that the NRC failed to take into account the provisions of the President's Executive Order on Environmental Justice (USNRC 1997).

These types of instrumental 'success' of the grassroots have not been central to this study, as the focus has been on evaluating the values behind, and the practices within, the movement. Still, one need only cursorily compare the stated goals and accomplishments of the mainstream environmental movement with those of environmental justice to see that the latter appears to be as successful, if not more so, in realizing its instrumental goals. The movement is fairly new, however, and a more long-term empirical comparison of the strategic goals and accomplishments of different parts of the movement is surely called for.

Implicit in this preliminary evaluation is the possibility that it is the *form* of organizing that has led to its instrumental successes. As discussed in Chapter 5, it is crucial to note that any success of the

---

[1] See the Summaries of the NEJAC meetings, available from the EPA's Office of Environmental Justice. Executive summaries are available on the World Wide Web: http://www.prcemi.com:80/nejac/publicat.html

decentralized networking strategy may be related to the shift in how capital and political power are organized. The liberal pluralist model may be workable when issues are centered at the national level; but environmental issues are not located simply on this one level. The network model may be more successful because more of the crucial environmental decisions that affect everyday life are made at a variety of levels—both local and regional, in terms of community and corporate decisions, and global, in terms of the expanding 'freedom' of transnationals (Brecher and Costello 1994a). Networking may both mirror the construction of environmental problems by the globalizing economy, and mirror the need to act at numerous political levels as the national state becomes just one site of contestation among many. For both of these developments in capital and political power, the liberal pluralist model is simply inadequate. We live in an age of shrinking budgets, of the disempowerment of government oversight, and of the growing power of transnational capital. But we also live in an age which has increased the ease of grassroots communication and coordination. With this technology, organizations can not only cooperate, but networks of NGOs can have an effect on global environmental discourse (Dryzek 1997; Wapner 1996). Again, the times themselves both illustrate and demonstrate the need and value of a new form of pluralist organizing.

If this is the case, the evidence will continue to grow in support of the strategic value of networking. And, indeed, networks have been increasingly developing around a variety of issues. In the past few years, for example, new networks of community organizations have developed around issues of dioxin, mining, oil refineries, the Mexican maquiladora, semiconductor plants, nuclear waste transport and disposal, indigenous intellectual property rights, economic globalization, and others. These parts of the environmental movement are relatively new, and it is too early to evaluate their instrumental impact. Again, a long-term examination of the strategic value of different forms of organizing should be on the agenda of those who study the environmental movement.

Staying Power

The environmental justice movement is not the first movement to attempt some forms of prefigurative political practice. The Student

Non-Violent Coordinating Committee (SNCC), Students for a Democratic Society (SDS), portions of the feminist movement, the direct-action movement, and others have all partially defined themselves with the use of some form of communicative ethics.

The common, and convincing, critique of these movements is that they failed to keep up such practices in the face of diversification in political style, strategies, and memberships (see, e.g. Miller 1987; Sirianni 1993; Stoper 1989). These studies suggest that these movements had difficulty keeping tensions in check between their democratic ideals and leadership needs as well as between their prefigurative and strategic orientations. The latter has been the central issue in Breines's (1989) study of the new left and Sirianni's (1993) examination of pluralism in the history of the feminist movement.

Sirianni's study ends on a positive note, as he argues that diversifying feminist theory and organizational practice has helped to re-examine and enrich pluralism—much as I have argued regarding parts of the environmental movement. Still, the history of many new social movements does not imbue one with a sense of optimism for the staying power of environmental justice.

With a sense of the history of past social movements, two simple questions arise about the environmental justice movement that I have not addressed to this point. First, are the tensions that ripped apart past movements reasserting themselves in the environmental justice community? And second, will these tensions eventually do the movement in, as they did in the experiences of SNCC and SDS? As discussed in Chapters 5 and 6, the environmental justice movement has focused seriously on both prefigurative politics and strategic ends. The explicit attempts to deal with diversity in both, and keep the tension between them minimal, has been a defining characteristic of the movement. One cannot answer questions regarding the staying power of the movement; it is simply too early to tell whether the management of this tension, and the equal attention to both moments, will persist. At this time, we can only note the dedication participants of the environmental justice movement place on avoiding 'past organizing mistakes' (Almeida 1994: 26).

Admittedly, that is no guarantee. SDS, which later fell apart into factionalization, had quite open, participatory, and fluid origins. Miller's (1987) close reconstruction of the events leading up to the release of the Port Huron Statement shows the importance SDS placed on communicative ethics, the incorporation of difference, and the need for statements that are open rather than doctrinaire. The events were not too unlike those around the construction of the principles of environmental justice described here in Chapter 6. If SDS shows how an organization based on communicative principles can eventually implode under the pressure of diversification (among other things), are we to expect the same from environmental justice?

I would argue that the environmental justice movement has at least three things going for it that will help it resist repeating past failures. First, and most crucially, there is an understanding of the importance of local power, autonomy, and organization. Part of the problem with SNCC and SDS stemmed from the focus on national organization and the tension between the universal and the particular, or between organization and local action (Miller 1987; Stoper 1989). In eschewing a large national organization for environmental justice in favor of local autonomy and coordinated action, the current movement has organized in a way that might help avoid this central, recurring problem. In fact, the focus on the empowerment of local groups, as opposed to a national organization, was one of the responses to the organizing lessons of the past.

A similar focus on diversity and coordination has been discussed by Staggenborg (1989) in the context of the women's movement.[2] Her argument is that successful social movements include a variety of organizational structures, each making different types of contribution. The diversity in styles, perspectives, forms of organization, and action are a strength—they reach disparate constituencies and serve different purposes. Organizations that I have discussed in the environmental justice movement, such as SNEEJ and CCHW, do not dictate the organizational form or process of individual member groups. These larger bodies will offer plenty of organizing advice, but do not interfere with the organizational decisions of locals. As we have seen in the discussion of those organizations, the availability of varied forms and actions has allowed for the inclusion of a diverse membership.

Second, and related, this focus on autonomy demonstrates the attempt to pluralize and democratize political realms outside the boundaries of the state. Numerous authors from varied perspectives

---

[2] See also the discussion in Sirianni (1993: 304–9).

have emphasized the importance of civil society, subpolitics, differential politics, etc., in strengthening democracy (see e.g. Beck 1992; Cohen and Arato 1992; Cohen and Rogers 1995, Dryzek 1996b, Fraser 1995). Pluralism began as an attempt to legitimize the political nature of groups outside the state; a critical pluralism has evolved to focus not only on the sub- or extra-state *site* of political practice, but the very form and make-up of the political process in those sub-national spheres. For environmental justice, the targets of pluralization and democratization are numerous and varied. Beyond the sphere of institutional success at the state level, the movement has focused on the construction of a diverse and integrated environmental justice community, the inclusion of environmental justice issues in environmental and civil-rights discourse, and the implementation of critical and democratic pluralist practices within the movement itself.

The third strength that may help environmental justice avoid the movement problems of the past is its devotion to a particular notion of unity and its embodiment in the form of networks. Mary Follett's attempt to define a unity that differed from uniformity has been reawakened in environmental justice. The development of solidarity across both similarities and differences, the ability to form networks with those like and unlike, and the simultaneous celebration of unity and difference in the movement are advances from past movements that eventually insisted on an exclusionary, unitary form of unity. In addition to this exemplification of a critical pluralist form of unity, the flexibility of these networks also works to keep the tensions between centralization and locality in check by constructing a larger organization for evolving strategic needs, rather than as an end in itself. The argument has been made that alliances among diverse groups are central to the growth of a postmodern feminist movement (Fraser and Nicholson 1990). The environmental justice community has not only begun this work, but it has also laid down some of the key aspects of such a structure in its own movement.

This is not to say that conflict in the movement does not, and will not, exist. Tensions have surfaced, for example, around issues of race, gender, and resources—as one might expect in such a diverse movement. Epstein (1995, 1997) discusses the racial tensions involved in the very definition of the term 'environmental justice'. Some minority activists have pressured white activists and academics to leave the articulation of issues of environmental justice solely to people of color (Epstein 1995: 7). Several see the term as exclusively devoted to the problems faced by communities of color; while others insist on the cross- or inter-racial nature of environmental injustices (Epstein 1997: 80–2). Epstein also documents complaints that have come forward of the way SNEEJ insists on all groups in its network being represented by people of color—even if their memberships are over-whelmingly white (pp. 78–9).[3] These difference, I would assert, come from the various conceptions of justice held by the environmental justice community. The argument in support of more autonomy by people of color is that communities and groups of color need to organize independently—at least initially—in order for those groups to be empowered and recognized. Once this element of justice is realized, defenders of this model argue, more integrated cooperation will follow. In this sense, it could be argued that these are not necessarily racial or gender conflicts, as Epstein argues, but conflicts that arise from groups prioritizing conceptions of justice differently (equity, recognition, or process first?). It is also crucial to note here that there is nothing in this model of organizing that rules out cooperative networks and arrangements with predominantly white communities or organizations. Those, in fact, are quite numerous in the environmental justice movement; the CCHW, the Campaign for Responsible Technology, and the National Oil Refinery Action Network stand as examples here.

Tensions have also come about around the competition between grassroots groups for scarce resources. Some activists and groups within the diverse network that makes up SNEEJ have complained that the resources of the network go to those groups or communities which 'cry loudest', which often happen to be the groups or commu-nities which already have some resources at their disposal. And re-cently, even academics of color with long histories of activism in the environmental justice movement have had strained relationships with local groups who see them as removed from the community.[4] All of these tensions have the potential to threaten the continuation

---

[3] The racial tensions cut both ways: in my own research, a white member of an active group in a western city told me that all the media, government, and foundation attention is paid to groups primarily of people of color, which were, in his mind, neither as broad nor as effective as his own group.

[4] These conflicts have been minor, and my only knowledge of them is from unofficial and off-the-record comments. There have been no public or printed discussions, as I have seen, of these issues.

and growth of the movement. They may escalate—or they may be discussed, recognized, and resolved. I think it is important to emphasize that the ethics that form the base of the movement—a recognition of difference, a respect for diverse positions, and an attempt to develop a solidarity still based in that difference—offer a place from which communication and dialog about these tensions may begin. The new pluralist toolbox certainly offers more in this direction than that of conventional liberal pluralism. It is also important to note that the existence of these tensions pales in comparison with the construction and accomplishments of a movement that has brought together such a rich variety of people, strategies, and organizations.

It certainly will be necessary to pay attention to the development of various tensions and their effects over time. One would hope that the memory and understanding of the history of past movements will help conflicts like these from threatening the movement. Again, it is possible that the very structure and communicative practices that I have described will help the movement to address such conflicts constructively. The ongoing practices and performance of the environmental justice movement, in dealing with each of these and other tensions that come with difference, will be nothing less than a test of a new form of pluralism.

The Future of Critical Pluralism and Environmentalism

In examining the development of a new form of pluralism in political practice, the focus here has been on the structures and practices of the environmental justice movement. While this movement is diverse, and includes those working at the grassroots on race, class, and gender issues in the maldistribution of environmental problems and risks, the environmental movement as a whole in the US is, of course, much more broad. While I have focused on the differences between the major organizations and the grassroots environmental justice movement in order to contrast a traditional picture of pluralist politics with a new, more critical pluralist set of practices, the movement is more complex than this simple dichotomy. As discussed in Chapter 2, the US environmental movement is certainly diverse, and its differences cannot be contained by simplified classification systems. All sorts of issue-oriented groups, local, regional, and national groups, and groups representing various ideological points of view contribute to the larger sense of 'environmentalism'.

But even given this diversity, it is difficult to deny that one sector of the movement—the major organizations that have been part of the Big Ten—serve as a focal point for environmentalism in the US. Those groups are seen as representing the movement, and are recognized as such by political leaders, governmental agencies, and the media alike. While the diversity of the movement as a whole is real, the dichotomy I draw does exist both in the popular representation of the movement, and in the minds of those at the grassroots who see the limitations of the major groups in structure, strategy, and make-up.

The challenge for environmentalism as a whole in the US is to incorporate the difference that exists throughout the movement. The problem, similar to the one noted by Diani in his examination of the Italian environmental movement (1995: 175), is that there has not been much done, or resources invested, in the building of links between and among the diverse sectors of the movement in the US. In other words, while the movement for environmental justice has constructed a new form of pluralist politics, there has been little in the way of network-building and the development of communicative relations in the contemporary US environmental movement as a whole. The task of building a strong movement is based in difference, recognition, and the acknowledgement of these as a strategic advantage. The connection among groups in the US—especially between the large, well-funded major organizations and the smaller, resource-poor grassroots—does not, generally, illustrate a critical pluralist relationship.

This is not to say that this type of association is not possible. There have been some examples of synergistic relations between the majors and grassroots—tensioned, yet productive arrangements on particular issues. As discussed in Chapter 5, there is a long history of such fruitful collaboration, and there are myriad grassroots campaigns—on issues such as oil-refinery pollution, semiconductor manufacturing, waste-dump siting, water pollution, and urban transportation—that have been assisted by major organizations such as the National Resources Defense Council and the Environmental Defense Fund. The National Wildlife Federation has worked with a number of groups in Michigan on environmental justice and health issues. Greenpeace has a long history of involvement in environmental justice issues, including a key battle against a toxic waste incinerator in Kettleman City, California. Sierra Club has joined in a number of grassroots campaigns on environmental justice, mostly offering resources to underfunded local groups.[5] Even the Nature Conservancy has been involved in a local battle on a semiconductor manufacturing facility nextdoor to one of its heritage sites.

While the major groups are often criticized for taking over issues, exaggerating their role for public relations reasons, or their sometimes paternalistic attitude toward environmental justice issues and activists,[6] there are numerous, and growing, examples of cooperative endeavors between environmental justice groups and the major organizations. The key to these relations is an understanding of the justice of environmental justice on the part of the major groups, and an attention not just to the end goal of a particular environmental agreement or policy, but to the *process* of such a battle.

These working relationships are crucial, as they form the foundation of the possible expansion of new pluralist ethics and political strategies into the greater environmental movement. They offer one possible way the environmental justice movement can overcome its most potent problem: the lack of resources of the disempowered and marginalized communities most subject to environmental inequity. And, perhaps more importantly, they offer the environmental movement as a whole a way out of its limited and conventional pluralist approach, into a realm of a more diverse, participatory, effective, and just environmentalism.

[5] Hopefully, the rejection by the membership of the Sierra Club of a hostile anti-immigration policy will aid in the continued building of relationships.

[6] Two African-American women—one a lawyer, the other a Superior Court Judge—resigned from the Sierra Club Legal Defense Fund (now Earthjustice Legal Defense Fund) in 1995, citing this continuing paternalism as their motivation.

Bibliography

Aberbach, Joel D., and Bert A. Rockman (1978). 'Administrators' Beliefs about the Role of the Public: The Case of American Federal Executives', *Western Political Quarterly*, 31: 502–22.

Ackelsberg, Martha (1988). 'Communities, Resistance, and Women's Activism: Some Implications for a Democratic Polity', in Ann Bookman and Sandra Morgen, eds., *Women and the Politics of Empowerment*. Philadelphia: Temple University Press.

Adams, John, *et al.* (1985). *An Environmental Agenda for the Future*. Washington, DC: Island Press.

Adorno, Theodor (1973 [1966]). *Negative Dialectics*. New York: Continuum.

Almeida, Paul (1994). 'The Network for Environmental and Economic Justice in the Southwest: Interview with Richard Moore', *Capitalism, Nature, Socialism*, 5/1: 21–54.

Alston, Dana (1990). *Taking Back Our Lives: A Report to the Panos Institute on Environment, Community Development and Race in the United States*. Washington, DC: The Panos Institute.

——ed. (1991). *We Speak for Ourselves: Social Justice, Race, and Environment*. Washington, DC: The Panos Institute.

——(1992). 'Moving Beyond the Barriers', in Charles Lee, ed., *Proceedings: The First National People of Color Environmental Leadership Summit*. New York: United Church of Christ Commission for Racial Justice.

Amy, Douglas (1987). *The Politics of Environmental Mediation*. New York: Columbia University Press.

——(1990). 'Environmental Dispute Resolution: The Promise and the Pitfalls', in Norman J. Vig and Michael E. Kraft, *Environmental Policy in the 1990s*. Washington, DC: Congressional Quarterly Press.

Anthony, Carl, and Luke Cole (1990). 'A Statement of Purpose', *Race, Poverty, and the Environment*, 1/1: 1–2.

Anthony, Carl, Ben Chavis, Richard Moore, Vivien Li, Scott Douglas, and Winona LaDuke (1993). 'A Place at the Table: A Sierra Roundtable on Race, Justice, and the Environment', *Sierra*, May–June: 51–8, 90–1.

Aronowitz, Stanley (1992). 'Reflections on Identity', *October*, 61: 91–103.

Austin, Regina, and Michael Schill (1991). 'Black, Brown, Red, and Poisoned: Minority Grassroots Environmentalism and the Quest for Eco-Justice', *Kansas Journal of Law and Public Policy*, 1: 69–82.

Avila, Magdalena (1992). 'David vs. Goliath', *Crossroads/Forward Motion*, 11/2: 13–15.

Avila, Magdelena (1994). Personal Communication.

Bachrach, Peter, and Morton Baratz (1962). 'The Two Faces of Power', *American Political Science Review*, 56: 947–52.

Banfield, Edward (1961). *Political Influence*. New York: Free Press.

Barker, Ernest (1957 [1915]). 'The Discredited State', in Ernest Barker, *Church, State, and Education*. Ann Arbor: University of Michigan Press.

Beck, Ulrich (1992). *Risk Society: Toward a New Modernity*. London: Sage.

——(1995). *Ecological Enlightenment: Essays on the Politics of the Risk Society*. Englewood Cliffs, NJ: Humanities Press.

——Anthony Giddens, and Scott Lash (1994). *Reflexive Modernization: Politics, Tradition, and Aesthetics in the Modern Social Order*. Palo Alto, Calif.: Stanford University Press.

Benhabib, Seyla (1986*a*). *Critique, Norm, and Utopia: A Study of the Foundations of Critical Theory*. New York: Columbia University Press.

——(1986*b*). 'The Generalized and the Concrete Other: Toward a Feminist Critique of Substitutionalist Universalism', *Praxis International*, 5/4: 402–24.

——(1992). *Situating the Self: Gender, Community and Postmodernism in Contemporary Ethics*. New York: Routledge.

——ed. (1996*a*). *Democracy and Difference: Contesting Boundaries of the Political*. Princeton: Princeton University Press.

——(1996*b*). 'Toward a Deliberative Model of Democratic Legitimacy', in Seyla Benhabib, ed., *Democracy and Difference: Contesting the Boundaries of the Political*. Princeton, NJ: Princeton University Press.

Bentley, Arthur (1908). *The Process of Government: A Study of Social Pressures*. Chicago: University of Chicago Press.

Berger, Thomas R. (1977). *Northern Frontier, Northern Homeland: Report of the MacKenzie Valley Pipeline Inquiry*. Toronto: James Lorimer.

——(1985). *Village Journey: The Report of the Alaska Native Review Commission*. New York: Hill and Wang.

Bernstein, Richard (1983). *Beyond Objectivism and Relativism*. Philadelphia: University of Pennsylvania Press.

——(1987). 'One Step Forward, Two Steps Backward: Rorty on Liberal Democracy and Philosophy', *Political Theory*, 15: 538–63.

——(1990). 'Rorty's Liberal Utopia', *Social Research*, 57: 31–72.

Bickford, Susan (1996). *The Dissonance of Democracy: Listening, Conflict, and Citizenship*. Ithaca, NY: Cornell.

Bingham, Gail (1986). *Resolving Environmental Disputes: A Decade of Experience*. Washington, DC: The Conservation Foundation.

Bohman, James (1995). 'Public Reason and Cultural Pluralism: Political Liberalism and the Problem of Moral Conflict', *Political Theory*, 23/2: 253–79.

Borrelli, Peter, ed. (1988). *Crossroads: Environmental Priorities for the Future*. Covelo, Calif.: Island Press.

Brecher, Jeremy, and Tim Costello, eds. (1990). *Building Bridges: The Emerging*

Grassroots Coalition of Labor and Community. New York: Monthly Review Press.

————(1994*a*). *Global Village or Global Pillage: Economic Reconstruction From the Bottom Up*. Boston: South End Press.

————(1994*b*). 'The Lilliput Strategy: Taking on the Multinationals', *The Nation*, 259/21: 757–60.

Breines, Wini (1989). *Community and Organization in the New Left, 1962– 1968: The Great Refusal*. 2nd edn. New Brunswick, NJ: Rutgers University Press.

Brody, Charlotte (1994). 'The New Deal: CCHW's New Organizing Model Takes Form', *Everyone's Backyard*, 13/4: 11–13.

Brown, L. D., and R. Tandon (1983). 'Ideology and Political Economy in Inquiry: Action Research and Participatory Research', *The Journal of Applied Behavioral Science*, 19: 277–94.

Brown, P. (1992). 'Popular Epidemiology and Toxic Waste Contamination: Lay and Professional Ways of Knowing', *Journal of Health and Social Behavior*, 33: 267–81.

Brown, Wendy (1993). 'Wounded Attachments', *Political Theory*, 21: 390–410.

Bryant, Bunyan (1995). 'Issues and Potential Policies and Solutions for Environmental Justice: An Overview', in Bunyan Bryant, ed., *Environmental Justice: Issues, Policies, and Solutions*. Covelo, Calif.: Island Press.

——and Paul Mohai, eds. (1992). *Race and the Incidence of Environmental Hazards: A Time for Discourse*. Boulder, Colo.: Westview Press.

Bullard, Robert D. (1990). *Dumping in Dixie: Race, Class, and Environmental Quality*. Boulder, Colo.: Westview Press.

——(1992). Keynote Address. People for Community Recovery Conference. Chicago, 17 October.

——ed. (1993*a*). *Confronting Environmental Racism: Voices from the Grassroots*. Boston: South End Press.

——(1993*b*). 'Anatomy of Environmental Racism and the Environmental Justice Movement', in Robert Bullard, ed., *Confronting Environmental Racism: Voices from the Grassroots*. Boston: South End Press.

——ed. (1994*a*). *People of Color Environmental Groups 1994–95 Directory*. Atlanta: Environmental Justice Resource Center.

——(1994*b*). 'Environmental Justice at Home and Abroad', in Robert Bullard, ed., *People of Color Environmental Groups 1994–95 Directory*. Atlanta: Environmental Justice Resource Center.

——ed. (1994*c*). *Unequal Protection: Environmental Justice and Communities of Color*. San Francisco: Sierra Club Books.

Butler, Judith (1990). *Gender Trouble: Feminism and the Subversion of Identity*. New York: Routledge.

Cable, Sherry, and Charles Cable (1995). *Environmental Problems, Grassroots Solutions: The Politics of Grassroots Environmental Conflict*. New York: St Martin's.

Caldwell, Lynton (1982). *Science and the National Environmental Policy Act.* Tuscaloosa: University of Alabama Press.

——(1990). *Between Two Worlds: Science, the Environmental Movement, and Policy Choice.* Cambridge: Cambridge University Press.

Callicott, J. Baird (1990). 'The Case against Moral Pluralism', *Environmental Ethics*, 12: 99–124.

Calpotura, Francis, and Rinku Sen (1994). 'PUEBLO Fights Lead Poisoning', in Robert D. Bullard, ed., *Unequal Protection: Environmental Justice and Communities of Color.* San Francisco: Sierra Club Books.

Campaign for Responsible Technology (1996*a*). 'Intel XL Action Alert', E-mail, 11 November 1996.

——(1996*b*). 'Comparison of Community Participation Models with the Intel XL Project', San Jose, Calif.: CRT.

Capek, Sheila (1993). 'The "Environmental Justice" Frame: A Conceptual Discussion and an Application', *Social Problems*, 40/1: 5–24.

Carnes, Sam A. (1982). 'Confronting Complexity and Uncertainty: Implementation of Hazardous Waste Policy', in Dean E. Mann, ed., *Environmental Policy Implementation.* Lexington, Mass.: Lexington Books.

Caulfield, Henry P. (1989). 'The Conservation and Environmental Movements: An Historical Analysis', in James P. Lester, ed., *Environmental Politics and Policy: Theories and Evidence.* Durham, NC: Duke University Press.

Chavis, Benjamin F., Jr. (1993). 'Foreword', in Robert D. Bullard, ed., *Confronting Environmental Racism: Voices from the Grassroots.* Boston: South End Press.

Chess, Caron, Billie Jo Hance, and Peter M. Sandman (1988). *Improving Dialogue with Communities: A Short Guide for Government Risk Communication.* Trenton, NJ: New Jersey Department of Environmental Protection.

Citizen's Clearinghouse for Hazardous Waste (1989). *Everybody's Backyard*, 7/2: 1.

——(1990). *Everybody's Backyard*, 8/1: 2.

——(1993). *Ten Years of Triumph.* Falls Church, Va.: Citizen's Clearinghouse for Hazardous Waste.

——(1996). 'People's Environmental Impact Study Won', in *Conference on Environmental Justice* [ecojustice@igc.apc.org]. 6 February.

Cockburn, Alexander, and Jeffrey St. Clair (1994). 'After Armageddon: Death and Life for America's Greens', *The Nation*, 259/21: 760–5.

Cohen, Jean L. (1985). 'Strategy or Identity: New Theoretical Paradigms and Contemporary Social Movements', *Social Research*, 52: 663–716.

——and Andrew Arato (1992). *Civil Society and Political Theory.* Cambridge, Mass.: MIT Press.

Cohen, Joshua (1993). 'Moral Pluralism and Political Consensus', in David Copp, Jean Hampton, and John Roemer, eds., *The Idea of Democracy.* Cambridge: Cambridge University Press.

——(1996). 'Procedure and Substance in Deliberative Democracy', in Seyla

Benhabib, ed., *Democracy and Difference: Contesting the Boundaries of the Political*. Princeton, NJ: Princeton University Press.

——and Joel Rogers (1995). *Associations and Democracy*. London: Verso.

Coker, Francis W. (1921).'The Technique of the Pluralist State', *American Political Science Review*, 15: 186–213.

Cole, Luke (1992). 'Empowerment as the Key to Environmental Protection: The Need for Environmental Poverty Law', *Ecology Law Quarterly*, 19: 619–83.

——(1994*a*). 'Environmental Justice Litigation: Another Stone in David's Sling', *Fordham Urban Law Journal*, 21: 523.

——(1994*b*). 'The Struggle of Kettleman City for Environmental Justice: Lessons for the Movement', *Maryland Journal of Contemporary Legal Issues*, 5: 67.

——(1994*c*). 'Civil Rights, Environmental Justice and the EPA: The Brief History of Administrative Complaints Under Title VI', *Journal of Environmental Law and Litigation*, 9: 309–98.

——(1995). 'Community-Based Administrative Advocacy Under Civil Rights Law: A Potential Environmental Justice Tool for Legal Services Advocates', *Clearinghouse Review*, 29: 360.

Collette, Will (1993). *How to Deal with a Proposed Facility*. Falls Church, Va.: Citizen's Clearinghouse for Hazardous Waste.

Cone, Marla (1997). 'Civil Rights Suit Attacks Trade in Pollution Credits', *Los Angeles Times*, 23 July 1997: A1.

Connolly, William, ed. (1969). *The Bias of Pluralism*. New York: Atherton.

——(1987). *Politics and Ambiguity*. Madison: University of Wisconsin Press.

——(1991). *Identity/Difference: Democratic Negotiations of Political Paradox*. Ithaca, NY: Cornell University Press.

——(1995). *The Ethos of Pluralization*. Minneapolis: University of Minnesota Press.

Cormick, Gerald (1976). 'Mediating Environmental Controversies: Perspectives and First Experience', *Earth Law Journal*, 2: 215–24.

Cotgrove, Stephen (1982). *Catastrophe or Cornucopia*. Chichester: John Wiley & Sons.

Cotkin, George (1990). *William James, Public Philosopher*. Baltimore: John Hopkins Press.

Covello, Vincent, and Frederick Allen (1988). *Seven Cardinal Rules of Risk Communication*. Washington, DC: EPA.

Crenshaw, Kimberle, ed. (1995). *Critical Race Theory*. New York: New Press.

Crenson, Matthew (1971). *The Un-Politics of Air Pollution*. Baltimore: John Hopkins Press.

Cupps, Steven (1977). 'Emerging Problems of Citizen Participation', *Public Administration Review*, 37: 478–87.

Cushman, John H., Jr. (1995). 'Moderates Soften G.O.P. Agenda on Environment', *New York Times*, 24 October: A1.

Cushman, John H., Jr. (1996). 'E.P.A. Innovates at Big Arizona Factory', *New York Times*, 20 November: A10.

Dahl, Robert (1961). *Who Governs?* New Haven Conn.: Yale University Press.

——(1967). *Pluralist Democracy in the United States*. Chicago: Rand McNally.

Darnovsky, Marcy (1992). 'Stories Less Told: Histories of U.S. Environmentalism', *Socialist Review*, 22/4: 11–54.

Davies, James C. (1963). *Human Nature in Politics: The Dynamics of Political Behavior*. New York: Wiley.

DeBell, Garret, ed. (1970). *The Environmental Handbook*. New York: Ballantine/ Friends of the Earth.

De Lauretis, Teresa (1988). *Technologies of Gender*. Bloomington, Ind.: Indiana University Press.

Deleuze, Gilles, and Felix Guattari (1983). *Anti-Oedipus: Capitalism and Schizophrenia*. Minneapolis: University of Minnesota Press.

————(1987). *A Thousand Plateaus: Capitalism and Schizophrenia*. Minneapolis: University of Minnesota Press.

Devall, Bill, and George Sessions (1985). *Deep Ecology: Living as if Nature Mattered*. Layton, UT: Gibbs M. Smith.

Diani, Mario (1992). 'The Concept of Social Movement', *Sociological Review*, 40: 1–25.

——(1995). *Green Networks: A Structural Analysis of the Italian Environmental Movement*, Edinburgh: Edinburgh University Press.

Di Chiro, Giovanna (1992). 'Defining Environmental Justice: Women's Voices and Grassroots Politics', *Socialist Review*, 22/4: 93–130.

——(1995). 'Nature as Community: The Convergence of Environment and Social Justice', in William Cronon, ed., *Uncommon Ground: Rethinking the Human Place in Nature*. New York: Norton.

——(1997). 'Local Actions, Global Expertise: Remaking Environmental Expertise', presented in the on-line conference on *Cultures and Environments: On Cultural Environmental Studies*, June 1997. Sponsored by the Washington State University American Studies Department.

Diggins, John (1994). *The Promise of Pragmatism*. Chicago: University of Chicago Press.

Di Stefano, Christine (1988). 'Dilemmas of Difference: Feminism, Modernity, and Postmodernism', *Women and Politics*, 8/3–4: 1–24.

Dowie, Mark (1991).'American Environmentalism: A Movement Courting Irrelevance', *World Policy Journal*, 9: 67–92.

——(1995). *Losing Ground: American Environmentalism at the Close of the Twentieth Century*. Cambridge, Mass.: MIT Press.

Dryzek, John (1982). 'Policy Analysis as a Hermeneutic Activity', *Policy Sciences*, 14: 309–29.

——(1990a). *Discursive Democracy: Politics, Policy, and Political Science*. Cambridge: Cambridge University Press.

——(1990b). 'Designs for Environmental Discourse: The Greening of the

Administrative State?' in Robert Paehlke and Douglas Torgerson, eds., *Managing Leviathan: Environmental Politics and the Administrative State.* Peterborough, Ontario: Broadview Press.

——(1993). 'Policy Analysis and Planning: From Science to Argument', in Frank Fischer and John Forester, eds., *The Argumentative Turn in Policy Analysis and Planning.* Durham, NC: Duke University Press.

——(1995). 'Political and Ecological Communication', *Environmental Politics*, 4: 13–30.

——(1996*a*). *Democracy in Capitalist Times: Ideals, Limits, and Struggles.* New York: Oxford University Press.

——(1996*b*). 'Political Inclusion and the Dynamics of Democratization', *American Political Science Review*, 90/1: 475–87.

——(1997). *Politics of the Earth: Environmental Discourses.* London: Oxford.

——and David Schlosberg (1995). 'Disciplining Darwin: Biological Ideas in the History of Political Science', in John Dryzek, James Farr, and Stephen Leonard, eds., *Political Science in History: Research Programs and Political Traditions.* Cambridge: Cambridge University Press.

——and David Schlosberg, eds. (1998). *Debating the Earth: The Environmental Politics Reader.* Oxford: Oxford University Press.

Dunlap, Riley E., and Angela G. Mertig (1992). 'The Evolution of the U.S. Environmental Movement from 1970 to 1990: An Overview', in Riley and Mertig, eds., *American Environmentalism: The U.S. Environmental Movement, 1970–1990.* Philadelphia: Taylor & Francis.

Eckersley, Robyn (1989). 'Green Politics and the New Class: Selfishness or Virtue?', *Political Studies* 37: 205–23.

Edwards, David (1988). 'Toleration and Mill's Liberty of Thought and Discussion', in Susan Mendus, ed., *Justifying Toleration: Conceptual and Historical Perspectives.* Cambridge: Cambridge University Press.

Eisenberg, Avigail (1995). *Reconstructing Political Pluralism.* Albany, NY: SUNY Press.

Elliot, Michael L. Poirier (1984). 'Improving Community Acceptance of Hazardous Waste Facilities Through Alternative Systems for Mitigating and Managing Risk', *Hazardous Waste*, 1: 397–410.

Elliot, W. Y. (1924). 'The Pragmatic Politics of Mr. H. J. Laski', *American Political Science Review*, 18: 251–75.

Ellis, Ellen Deborah (1920). 'The Pluralistic State', *American Political Science Review*, 14: 393–407.

Ellis, Richard, and J. Disinger (1981).'Project Outcomes Correlate with Public Participation Variables', *Journal of Water Pollution Control Federation* (Nov.).

Environmental Careers Organization (1992). *Beyond the Green: Redefining and Diversifying the Environmental Movement.* Boston: Environmental Careers Organization (ECO).

Epstein, Barbara (1985). 'The Culture of Direct Action: Livermore Action Group and the Peace Movement', *Socialist Review*, 15: 31–61.

Epstein, Barbara (1988). 'The Politics of Prefigurative Community: The Non-Violent Direct Action Movement', in Mike Davis and Michael Sprinker, eds., *Reshaping the U.S. Left: Popular Struggles in the 1980s*. London: Verso.

——(1991). *Political Protest and Cultural Revolution: Nonviolent Direct Action in the 1970s and 1980s*. Berkeley: University of California Press.

——(1995). 'Grassroots Environmentalism and Strategies for Social Change', *New Political Science*, 32: 1–24.

——(1997). 'The Environmental Justice/Toxics Movement: Politics of Race and Gender', *Capitalism, Nature, Socialism*, 8/3: 63–87.

Evans, Sara, and Harry Boyte (1986). *Free Spaces: The Sources of Democratic Change in America*. New York: Harper and Row.

Fairfax, Sally (1978). 'A Disaster in the Environmental Movement', *Science*, 199: 743–8.

Fay, Brian (1987). *Critical Social Science: Liberation and its Limits*. Ithaca, NY: Cornell University Press.

Ferris, Deeohn (1994). 'A Call for Justice and Equal Environmental Protection', in Robert D. Bullard, ed., *Unequal Protection: Environmental Justice and Communities of Color*. San Francisco: Sierra Club.

Fiorino, Daniel (1990). 'Citizen Participation and Environmental Risk: A Survey of Institutional Mechanisms', *Science, Technology, and Human Values*, 15: 226–43.

Fischer, Claude S. (1977). *Networks and Places: Social Relations in the Urban Setting*. New York: Free Press.

Fischer, Frank (1993). 'Citizen Participation and the Democratization of Policy Expertise: From Theoretical Inquiry to Practical Cases', *Policy Sciences*, 26: 165–87.

——and John Forester, eds. (1993). *The Argumentative Turn in Policy Analysis and Planning*. Durham, NC: Duke University Press.

Fisher, Roger, and William Ury (1981). *Getting to Yes*. Boston: Houghton Mifflin.

Flax, Jane (1987). 'Postmodernism and Gender Relations in Feminist Theory', *Signs*, 12/4: 621–43.

Follett, Mary Parker (1918). *The New State: Group Organization and the Solution of Popular Government*. New York: Longmans, Green and Co.

——(1924). *Creative Experience*. New York: Longmans, Green and Co.

——(1942). *Dynamic Administration*. New York: Harper and Brothers.

Foreman, Dave (1991). *Confessions of an Eco-Warrior*. New York: Harmony Books.

Forester, John (1989). *Planning in the Face of Power*. Berkeley: University of California Press.

Foster, John Bellamy (1994). *The Vulnerable Planet: A Short Economic History of the Environment*. New York: Monthly Review Press.

Foucault, Michel (1978). *The History of Sexuality*. Vol. i. *An Introduction*. New York: Random House.

——(1979). *Discipline and Punish: The Birth of the Prison*. New York: Random House.

——(1980). *Power/Knowledge*. New York: Pantheon Books.

——(1983). 'On the Genealogy of Ethics: An Overview of Work in Progress', in Hubert Dreyfus and Paul Rabinow, eds., *Michel Foucault: Beyond Structuralism and Hermeneutics*. Chicago: University of Chicago Press.

——(1988*a*). *The History of Sexuality*. Vol. iii. *The Care of the Self*. New York: Random House.

——(1988*b*). 'The Ethic of Care For the Self as a Practice of Freedom', in James Bernauer and David Rasmussen, eds., *The Final Foucault*. Cambridge, Mass.: MIT Press.

——(1988*c*). 'The Masked Philosopher', in Lawrence D. Kritzman, ed., *Michel Foucault: Politics, Philosophy, Culture*. New York: Routledge.

Fox, Stephen (1981). *The American Conservation Movement: John Muir and his Legacy*. Madison: University of Wisconsin Press.

Fraser, Nancy (1995). 'Politics, Culture, and the Public Sphere: Toward a Postmodern Conception', in Linda Nicholson and Steven Seidman, eds., *Social Postmodernism: Beyond Identity Politics*. Cambridge: Cambridge University Press.

——(1997). *Justice Interruptus: Critical Reflections on the 'Postsocialist' Condition*. New York: Routledge.

——and Linda J. Nicholson (1990). 'Social Criticism without Philosophy: An Encounter Between Feminism and Postmodernism', in Linda J. Nicholson, ed., *Feminism/Postmodernism*. New York: Routledge.

Freeman, Jo (1975). *The Politics of Women's Liberation*. New York: McKay.

Freudenberg, Nicholas (1984). *Not in Our Backyards! Community Action for Health and the Environment*. New York: Monthly Review Press.

——and Carol Steinsapir (1992). 'Not in Our Backyards: The Grassroots Environmental Movement', in Riley E. Dunlap and Angela G. Mertig, eds., *American Environmentalism: The U.S. Environmental Movement, 1970–1990*. Philadelphia: Taylor & Francis.

Friends of the Earth (1990). 'The Whiteness of the Green Movement', *Not Man Apart*, 20/2: 14–17.

Gaventa, John (1980). *Power and Powerlessness: Quiescence and Rebellion in an Appalachian Valley*. Chicago: University of Illinois Press.

——(1991). *Participatory Research in North America*. New Market, Tenn.: Highlander Center.

Gerlach, Luther P., and Virginia H. Hine (1970). *People, Power, and Change: Movements of Social Transformation*. Indianapolis: Bobbs-Merrill.

Gerstenzang, James (1995). 'G.O.P. Clouds the Future of Environmental Protections', *Los Angeles Times*, 25 December: A1.

Gibbs, Lois (1982). *Love Canal: My Story*. Albany, NY: State University of New York Press.

Giddens, Anthony (1994). *Beyond Left and Right: The Future of Radical Politics.* Stanford: Stanford University Press.

Gilligan, Carol (1982). *In a Different Voice.* Cambridge, Mass.: Harvard University Press.

Glaberson, William (1988). 'Coping in the Age of "Nimby"'. *New York Times,* 19 June: C1.

Goldman, Benjamin A. (1996). 'What is the Future of Environmental Justice?' *Antipode,* 28/2: 122–41.

Goodin, Robert (1992). *Green Political Theory.* Cambridge: Polity Press.

Gore, Al (1992). *Earth in the Balance: Ecology and the Human Spirit.* New York: Plume.

Gottlieb, Robert (1990). 'An Odd Assortment of Allies: American Environmentalism in the 1990s', *Gannett Center Journal,* 4/3: 37–47.

Gottlieb, Robert (1993). *Forcing the Spring: The Transformation of the American Environmental Movement.* Washington, DC: Island Press.

Gould, Carol (1978). *Marx's Social Ontology.* Cambridge, Mass.: MIT Press.

Gould, Kenneth (1991). 'The Sweet Smell of Money: Economic Dependency and Local Environmental Political Mobilization', *Society and Natural Resources,* 4: 133–50.

Gould, Kenneth, Allan Schnaiberg, and Adam Weinberg (1996). *Local Environmental Struggles: Citizen Activism in the Treadmill of Production.* Cambridge: Cambridge University Press.

Gray, Chris Hables, and Steven Mentor (1995). 'The Cyborg Body Politic', in Chris Hables Gray, ed., *The Cyborg Handbook.* New York: Routledge.

Greider, Katherine (1993). 'Against All Odds', *City Limits,* 18/7: 34–8.

Grossman, Karl (1994). 'The People of Color Environmental Summit', in Robert D. Bullard, ed., *Unequal Protection: Environmental Justice and Communities of Color.* San Francisco: Sierra Club.

Gulf Coast Tenants Organization (1994). 'EPA Partners in Deception', in *Conference on Environmental Justice* [ecojustice@igc.apc.org]. 29 November.

Gunnell, John (1993). *The Descent of Political Theory: The Genealogy of an American Vocation.* Chicago: University of Chicago Press.

——(1995). 'The Declination of the "State" and the Origins of American Pluralism', in James Farr, John S. Dryzek, and Stephen T. Leonard, eds., *Political Science in History: Research Programs and Political Traditions.* Cambridge: Cambridge University Press.

Habermas, Jurgen (1970*a*). 'On Systematically Distorted Communication', *Inquiry,* 13: 205–18.

——(1970*b*). 'Toward a Theory of Communicative Competence', *Inquiry,* 13: 360–75.

——(1981). 'New Social Movements', *Telos,* 49: 33–7.

——(1984). *The Theory of Communicative Action.* Vol. i. *Reason and the Rationaliztion of Society,* tr. Thomas McCarthy. Boston: Beacon.

——(1987*a*). *The Theory of Communicative Action.* Vol. ii. *Life-World and System:*

A Critique of Functionalist Reason, tr. Thomas McCarthy. Boston: Beacon.

——(1987*b*). *The Philosophical Discourse of Modernity*. Cambridge, Mass.: MIT Press.

——(1990*a*). 'Discourse Ethics: Notes on a Program of Philosophical Justification', in Seyla Benhabib and Fred Dallmayr, eds., *The Communicative Ethics Controversy*. Cambridge, Mass.: MIT Press.

——(1990*b*). 'Justice and Solidarity: On the Discussion Concerning Stage 6', in Thomas E. Wren, ed., *The Moral Domain: Essays in the Ongoing Discussion between Philosophy and the Social Sciences*. Cambridge, Mass.: MIT Press.

——(1992). *Postmetaphysical Thinking*. Cambridge, Mass.: MIT Press.

——(1994). 'Struggles for Recognition in the Democratic Constitutional State', in Charles Taylor, ed., *Multiculturalism: Examining the Politics of Recognition*. Princeton: Princeton University Press.

Hadden, Susan G., Joan Veillette, and Thomas Brandt (1993). 'State Roles in Siting Hazardous Waste Disposal Facilities: From State Preemption to Local Veto', in James P. Lester and Ann O'M. Bowman, eds., *The Politics of Hazardous Waste Management*. Durham, NC: Duke University Press.

Hall, Stuart (1987). 'Minimal Selves', in *The Real Me: Postmodernism and the Question of Identity*. London: ICA Documents 6.

Hamilton, Alexander, James Madison, and John Jay (1961). *The Federalist Papers*. New York: New American Library.

Hamilton, Cynthia (1990). 'Women, Home and Community: The Struggle in an Urban Environment', *Race, Poverty, and the Environment*, 1/1: 3.

——(1994). 'Concerned Citizens of South Central Los Angeles', in Robert D. Bullard, ed., *Unequal Protection: Environmental Justice and Communities of Color*. San Francisco: Sierra Club.

——(1995). 'Toward a New Industrial Policy', in Bunyan Bryant, ed., *Environmental Justice: Issues, Policies, and Solutions*. Covelo, Calif.: Island Press.

Handler, Joel (1990). *Law and the Search for Community*. Philadelphia: University of Pennsylvania Press.

Haraway, Donna (1988). 'Situated Knowledges: The Science Question in Feminism as a Site of Discourse on the Privilege of Partial Perspective', *Feminist Studies*, 14/3: 575–99.

——(1991 [1985]). 'A Cyborg Manifesto: Science, Technology, and Socialist-Feminism in the Late Twentieth Century', in *Simians, Cyborgs, and Women: The Reinvention of Nature*. New York: Routledge.

Harding, Sandra (1986). *The Science Question in Feminism*. Ithaca, NY: Cornell University Press.

Harter, Philip (1982). 'Negotiating Regulations: A Cure for Malaise', *Georgetown Law Journal*, 71: 1–118.

Hartsock, Nancy (1987). 'Foucault on Power: A Theory for Women?', in Monique Leijenaar, ed., *The Gender of Power: A Symposium*. Leiden: Vakgroep Vrouwenstudies/Vena. Reprinted in Linda Nicholson, ed., *Feminism/Postmodernism*. New York: Routledge, 1990.

Harvey, David (1991). 'Flexibility: Threat or Opportunity?', *Socialist Review*, 21/1: 65–77.

Hays, Samuel P. (1982). 'From Conservation to Environment: Environmental Politics in the US since World War II', *Environmental Review*, 6: 14–41.

——(1987). *Beauty, Health and Permanence: Environmental Politics in the United States, 1955–1985*. Cambridge: Cambridge University Press.

Haywood, Terry (1990). 'Working Class Feminism: Creating a Politics of Community, Connection, and Concern', Ph.D. dissertation, The Graduate School and University Center of the City University of New York.

Healy, Patsy (1993). 'Planning Through Debate: The Communicative Turn in Planning Theory', in Frank Fischer and John Forester, eds., *The Argumentative Turn in Policy Analysis and Planning*. Durham, NC: Duke University Press.

Hofrichter, Richard, ed. (1993*a*). *Toxic Struggles: The Theory and Practice of Environmental Justice*. Philadelphia: New Society.

——(1993*b*). 'Cultural Activism and Environmental Justice', in Hofrichter, ed., *Toxic Struggles: The Theory and Practice of Environmental Justice*. Philadelphia: New Society.

Honig, Bonnie (1996). 'Difference, Dilemmas, and the Politics of Home', in Seyla Benhabib, ed., *Democracy and Difference: Contesting the Boundaries of the Political*. Princeton, NJ: Princeton University Press.

Honneth, Axel (1992). 'Integrity and Disrespect: Principles of Morality Based on the Theory of Recognition', *Political Theory*, 20: 187–201.

hooks, bell (1984). *Feminist Theory from Margin to Center*. Boston: South End Press.

Hoy, Suellen (1995). *Chasing Dirt: The American Pursuit of Cleanliness*. Oxford: Oxford University Press.

Ingalsbee, Timothy (1995). 'Earth First!: Consciousness and Action in the Unfolding of a New-Social-Movement'. Doctoral dissertation, Department of Sociology, University of Oregon.

Inglehart, Ronald (1971). 'The Silent Revolution in Europe: Intergenerational Change in Post-Industrial Societies', *American Political Science Review*, 65: 991–1017.

——(1981). 'Post-Materialism in an Environment of Insecurity', *American Political Science Review*, 75: 880–900.

——(1990). *Culture Shift in Advanced Industrial Society*. Princeton, NJ: Princeton University Press.

James, William (1890). *Principles of Psychology*, i. New York: Henry Holt and Co.

——(1975 [1907]). *Pragmatism*. Cambridge, Mass.: Harvard University Press.

——(1976 [1912]). *Essays in Radical Empiricism*. Cambridge, Mass.: Harvard University Press.

——(1977 [1909]). *A Pluralistic Universe*. Cambridge, Mass.: Harvard University Press.

——(1978). *Essays in Philosophy*. Cambridge, Mass.: Harvard University Press.

——(1979 [1896]). *The Will to Believe and Other Essays in Popular Philosophy*. Cambridge, Mass.: Harvard University Press.

——(1985 [1902]). *The Varieties of Religious Experience*. Cambridge, Mass.: Harvard University Press.

——(1987). *Essays, Comments, and Reviews*. Cambridge, Mass.: Harvard University Press.

Jordon, Grant (1990). 'The Pluralism of Pluralism: An Anti-theory?', *Political Studies*, 38: 286–301.

Kariel, Henry S. (1955). 'The New Order of Mary Parker Follett', *Western Political Quarterly*, 8: 425–40.

——(1961). *The Decline of American Liberalism*. Stanford, Calif.: Stanford University Press.

Karliner, Joshua (1997). *The Corporate Planet: Ecology and Politics in the Age of Globalization*. San Francisco: Sierra Club Books.

Kaufman-Osborn, Timothy V. (1993). 'Teasing Feminist Sense from Experience', *Hypatia*, 8/2: 124–44.

Kemp, Ray (1985). 'Planning, Public Hearings, and the Politics of Discourse', in John Forester, ed., *Critical Theory and Public Life*. Cambridge, Mass.: MIT Press.

Kerr, Mary Lee, and Charles Lee (1993). 'From Conquistadores to Coalitions', *Southern Exposure*, 21/4: 8–19.

Kitschelt, Herbert P. (1986). 'Political Opportunity Structures and Political Protest: Anti-Nuclear Movements in Four Democracies', *British Journal of Political Science*, 16: 57–85.

Knickerbocker, Brad (1996). 'Why the G.O.P. Changed Little in Environment', *Christian Science Monitor*, 2 January: 1.

Kowalewski, David, and Karen L. Porter (1992). 'Ecoprotest: Alienation, Deprivation, or Resources?', *Social Science Quarterly*, 73: 523–34.

Kraft, Michael E. (1988). 'Evaluating Technology through Public Participation: The Nuclear Waste Disposal Controversy', In Michael E. Kraft and Norman J. Vig, eds., *Technology and Politics*. Durham, NC: Duke University Press.

——and Bruce B. Clary (1991). 'Citizen Participation and the Nimby Syndrome: Public Response to Radioactive Waste Disposal', *Western Political Quarterly*, 44: 299–328.

Krauss, Celene (1994). 'Women of Color on the Front Line', in Robert D. Bullard, ed., *Unequal Protection: Environmental Justice and Communities of Color*. San Francisco: Sierra Club.

Kuehls, Thom (1995). *The Space of Eco-Politics*. Minneapolis: University of Minnesota Press.

Labor/Community Strategy Center (1993). *Reconstructing Los Angeles from the Bottom Up*. Los Angeles: Labor/Community Strategy Center.

LaChapelle, Dolores (1994). 'The Rhizome Connection', in David Clarke

Burks, ed., *Place of the Wild: A Wildlands Anthology*. Covelo, Calif.: Island Press.

Laclau, Ernesto (1990). *New Reflections on the Revolution of Our Time*. London: Verso.

——and Chantal Mouffe (1985). *Hegemony and Socialist Strategy: Toward a Radical Democratic Politics*. London: Verso.

Lake, Robert W. (1996). 'Volunteers, Nimbys, and Environmental Justice: Dilemmas of Democratic Practice', *Antipode*, 28/2: 160–74.

Laski, Harold (1917). *Studies in the Problem of Sovereignty*. New Haven, Conn.: Yale University Press.

——(1921). *Foundations of Sovereignty*. New York: Harcourt, Brace and Company.

Lavelle, Marianne, and Marcia Coyle (1992). 'Unequal Protection', *The National Law Journal*, 21 September.

Lee, Charles, ed. (1992). *Proceedings: The First National People of Color Environmental Leadership Summit*. New York: United Church of Christ Commission for Racial Justice.

——(1993*a*). 'From Los Angeles, East St. Louis, and Matamoros: Developing Working Definitions of Urban Environmental Justice', *Earth Island Journal*, 84: 39–42.

——(1993*b*). 'Beyond Toxic Wastes and Race', in Robert Bullard, ed., *Confronting Environmental Racism: Voices from the Grassroots*. Boston: South End Press.

——(1996). *Environmental Justice, Urban Revitalization, and Brownfields: The Search for Authentic Signs of Hope*. Washington, DC: NEJAC.

Leonard, Stephen T. (1990). *Critical Theory in Political Practice*. Princeton, NJ: Princeton University Press.

Lewis, Sanford (1995). *Precedents for Corporate-Community Compacts and Good Neighbor Agreements*. Waverly, Mass.: The Good Neighbor Project.

Lindblom, Charles (1965). *The Intelligence of Democracy: Decision Making through Mutual Adjustment*. New York: Free Press.

——(1977). *Politics and Markets*. New York: Basic Books.

——(1982). 'The Market as Prison', *Journal of Politics*, 44: 324–36.

Lorde, Audre (1984). *Sister Outsider*. Trumansburg, NY: Crossing Press.

Lowi, Theodore (1969). *The End of Liberalism*. New York: Norton.

Luke, Timothy W., and Stephen K. White (1985). 'Critical Theory, the Informational Revolution, and an Ecological Path to Modernity', in John Forester, ed., *Critical Theory and Public Life*. Cambridge, Mass.: MIT Press.

Lukes, Steven (1974). *Power: A Radical View*. London: Macmillan Press.

Lund, Lisa (1996). *Superior Environmental Performance for Project XL Facilities: Draft 11/29/96*. Washington, DC: USEPA Office of Policy, Planning, and Evaluation.

Lynch, Barbara Deutsch (1993). 'The Garden and the Sea: U.S. Latino Environmental Discourses and Mainstream Environmentalism', *Social Problems*, 40/1: 108–24.

Lynch, Sue Greer (1993). 'Larger than Locals: The Critical Link', in Citizen's Clearinghouse for Hazardous Waste, *Ten Years of Triumph*. Falls Church, Va.: Citizen's Clearinghouse for Hazardous Waste.

Lyotard, Jean-François (1984). *The Postmodern Condition*. Minneapolis: University of Minnesota Press.

McAdam, Doug (1988). *Freedom Summer*. Oxford: Oxford University Press.

McCarthy, John, and Mayer Zald (1977). 'Resource Mobilization and Social Movements: A Partial Theory', *American Journal of Sociology*, 82: 1212–41.

McCarthy, Thomas (1990). 'Ironist Theory as a Vocation: A Response to Rorty', *Critical Inquiry*, 16: 644–55.

McCloskey, Michael (1992). 'Twenty Years of Change in the Environmental Movement: An Insider's View', in Riley Dunlap and Angela G. Mertig, eds., *American Environmentalism: The U.S. Environmental Movement, 1970–1990*. Philadelphia: Taylor & Francis.

McClure, Kirstie (1990). 'Difference, Diversity, and the Limits of Toleration', *Political Theory*, 18/3: 361–91.

—— (1992). 'On the Subject of Rights: Pluralism, Plurality, and Political Identity', in Chantal Mouffe, ed., *Dimensions of Radical Democracy*. London: Verso.

McCoy and Associates, Inc. (1986). '1986 Outlook for Commercial Hazardous Waste Management Facilities: A Nationwide Perspective', *Hazardous Waste Consultant* (Mar./Apr.): 4.1–6.

—— (1990). '1990 Outlook for Commercial Hazardous Waste Management Facilities: A Nationwide Perspective', *Hazardous Waste Consultant* (Mar./Apr.): 4.1–6.

Mclennan, Gregor (1995). *Pluralism*. Minneapolis: University of Minnesota Press.

Madison, Isaiah, Vernice Miller, and Charles Lee (1992). 'The Principles of Environmental Justice: Formation and Meaning', in Charles Lee, ed., *Proceedings: The First National People of Color Environmental Leadership Summit*. New York: United Church of Christ Commission for Racial Justice.

Manley, John (1983). 'Neo-Pluralism: A Class Analysis of Pluralism I and Pluralism II', *American Political Science Review*, 77: 368–83.

Matheny, Albert R., and Bruce A. Williams (1988). 'Rethinking Participation: Assessing Florida's Strategy for Siting Hazardous Waste Disposal Facilities', in Charles E. Davis and James P. Lester, eds., *Dimensions of Hazardous Waste Politics and Policy*. New York: Greenwood Press.

Mazmanian, Daniel, and David Morell (1990). 'The "NIMBY" Syndrome: Facility Siting and the Failure of Democratic Discourse', in Norman J. Vig and Michael E. Kraft, eds., *Environmental Policy in the 1990s*. Washington, DC: Congressional Quarterly Press.

Mead, George (1932). *Philosophy of the Present*. La Salle, Ill.: Open Port Press.

Mead, George (1938). *The Philosophy of the Act*. Chicago: University of Chicago Press.

Melosi, Martin, ed. (1980). *Pollution and Reform in American Cities, 1870–1930*. Austin, Tex.: University of Texas Press.

Melucci, Alberto (1985). 'The Symbolic Challenge of Contemporary Movements', *Social Research*, 52/4: 789–816.

——(1989). *Nomads of the Present*. Philadelphia: Temple University Press.

——(1996). *Challenging Codes: Collective Action in the Information Age*. Cambridge: Cambridge University Press.

Mendus, Susan, ed. (1988). *Justifying Toleration: Conceptual and Historical Perspectives*. Cambridge: Cambridge University Press.

Merchant, Carolyn (1985). 'The Women of the Progressive Conservation Crusade, 1900–1915', in Kendall E. Bailes, ed., *Environmental History: Critical Issues in Comparative Perspective*. Lanham, Md.: University Press of America.

Milbrath, Lester (1984). *Environmentalists: Vanguard for a New Society*. Albany, NY: State University of New York Press.

Miller, James (1987). *Democracy is in the Streets: From Port Huron to the Siege of Chicago*. New York: Simon and Schuster.

Miller, Vernice D. (1993). 'Building on Our Past, Planning for Our Future: Communities of Color and the Quest for Environmental Justice', in Richard Hofrichter, ed., *Toxic Struggles: The Theory and Practice of Environmental Justice*. Philadelphia: New Society.

Mohanty, S. (1989). 'Us and Them: On the Philosophical Bases of Political Criticism', *Yale Journal of Criticism*, 2/2: 1–31.

Montague, Peter (1989). 'What We Must Do', *The Workbook*, 14/3: 90–110.

——(1993). 'After Ten Years: Reason for Hope', in Citizen's Clearinghouse for Hazardous Waste, *Ten Years of Triumph*. Falls Church, Va.: Citizen's Clearinghouse for Hazardous Waste.

——(1995). 'Big Picture Organizing, Part 5: A Movement in Disarray', *Rachel's Environment and Health Weekly*, No. 425.

Moore, Richard, and Louis Head (1993). 'Acknowledging the Past, Confronting the Future: Environmental Justice in the 1990s', in Richard Hofrichter, ed., *Toxic Struggles: The Theory and Practice of Environmental Justice*. Philadelphia: New Society.

————(1994). 'Building a Net that Works: SWOP', in Robert D. Bullard, ed., *Unequal Protection: Environmental Justice and Communities of Color*. San Francisco: Sierra Club Books.

Mouffe, Chantal (1988). 'Radical Democracy: Modern or Postmodern?', in Andrew Ross, ed., *Universal Abandon: The Politics of Postmodernism*. Minneapolis: University of Minnesota Press.

——(1990). 'Radical Democracy or Liberal Democracy?', *Socialist Review*, 20/2: 57–66.

——(1992a). 'Democratic Citizenship and the Political Community', in Chantal Mouffe, ed., *Dimensions of Radical Democracy*. London: Verso.

——(1992*b*). 'Citizenship and Political Identity', *October*, 61: 28–32.

——(1996). 'Democracy, Power, and the "Political"' in Seyla Benhabib, ed., *Democracy and Difference: Contesting the Boundaries of the Political.* Princeton, NJ: Princeton University Press.

Naples, Nancy (1992). 'Activist Mothering: Cross-Generational Continuity in the Community Work of Women from Low-Income Urban Neighborhoods', *Gender and Society*, 6/3: 441–63.

Nash, Roderick (1982). *Wilderness and the American Mind.* 3rd edn. New Haven, Conn.: Yale University Press.

National Environmental Justice Advisory Council (1996). *Summary of the Meeting of the National Environmental Justice Advisory Council: May 29–31, 1996.* Washington, DC: U.S. EPA Office of Environmental Justice.

Newman, Peggy (1993). 'The Grassroots Movement for Environmental Justice: Fighting For Our Lives', *New Solutions*, 3/4: 87–95.

—— (1994). 'Beyond the Neighborhood—Women Working for Multi-Ethnic, Multi-Issue Coalitions', *The Workbook*, 19/2: 93–5.

Nicholson, Linda, ed. (1990). *Feminism/Postmodernism.* London: Routledge.

Norton, Bryan G. (1991). *Toward Unity among Environmentalists.* Oxford: Oxford University Press.

O'Brien, William (1993). 'Network Effect: Door to Door, City by City, PICO Helps Communities Organize', *The Neighborhood Works*, 16/6: 32–4.

Offe, Clause (1985). 'New Social Movements: Challenging the Boundaries of Institutional Politics', *Social Research*, 52: 832–8.

O'Hare, Michael, Lawrence Bacow, and Debra Sanderson (1983). *Facility Siting and Public Opposition.* New York: Van Nostrand.

Oliver, Patsy Ruth (1994). 'Living on a Superfund Site in Texarkana', in Robert D. Bullard, ed., *Unequal Protection: Environmental Justice and Communities of Color.* San Francisco: Sierra Club Books.

O'Riordan, Timothy (1976). *Environmentalism.* London: Pion.

Paehlke, Robert (1988). 'Democracy, Bureaucracy, and Environmentalism', *Environmental Ethics*, 10: 291–308.

—— (1989). *Environmentalism and the Future of Progressive Politics.* New Haven, Conn.: Yale University Press.

——and Douglas Torgerson, eds. (1990*a*). *Managing Leviathan: Environmental Politics and the Administrative State.* Peterborough, Ontario: Broadview Press.

————(1990*b*). 'Environmental Politics and the Administrative State', in Robert Paehlke and Douglas Torgerson, eds., *Managing Leviathan: Environmental Politics and the Administrative State.* Peterborough, Ontario: Broadview Press.

Pardo, Mary (1990). 'Mexican American Women Grassroots Community Activists: "Mothers of East Los Angeles"', *Frontiers*, 11/1: 1–7.

Peelle, Elizabeth, and Richard Ellis (1987). 'Beyond the "Not-In-My-Backyard" Impasse', *Forum for Applied Research and Public Policy*, 2: 68–77.

Perry, Ralph Barton (1948). *The Thought and Character of William James.* Cambridge, Mass.: Harvard.

Petulla, Joseph M. (1980). *American Environmentalism: Values, Tactics, Priorities.* College Station, Tex.: Texas A&M University Press.

Phillips, Anne (1993). *Democracy and Difference.* University Park, Pa.: Pennsylvania University Press.

Philp, Mark (1985). 'Michel Foucault', in Quentin Skinner, ed., *The Return of Grand Theory in the Human Sciences.* Cambridge: Cambridge University Press.

Plotkin, Sidney (1990). 'Enclave Consciousness and Neighborhood Activism', in Joseph M. Kling and Prudence S. Posner, eds., *Dilemmas of Activism: Class, Community, and the Politics of Local Mobilization.* Philadelphia: Temple University Press.

Plough, A., and S. Krimsky (1987). 'The Emergence of Risk Communication Studies: Social and Political Context', *Science, Technology and Human Values,* 12: 4–10.

Polsby, Nelson W. (1963). *Community Power and Political Theory.* New Haven, Conn., Yale University Press.

Pulido, Laura (1996). *Environmentalism and Social Justice: Two Chicano Struggles in the Southwest.* Tucson: University of Arizona Press.

Quinby, Lee (1990). 'Ecofeminism and the Politics of Resistance', in Irene Diamond and Gloria Feman Orenstein, eds., *Reweaving the World: The Emergence of Ecofeminism.* San Francisco: Sierra Club.

Reagon, Bernice Johnson (1983). 'Coalition Politics: Turning the Century', in *Home Girls: A Black Feminist Anthology.* New York: Kitchen Table/Women of Color Press.

Reisner, Marc (1995). 'Government by Chainsaw', *New York Times,* 16 November: A25.

Rogin, Michael (1987). *Ronald Reagan, The Movie, and Other Episodes in Political Demonology.* Berkeley: University of California Press.

Rorty, Richard (1983). 'Post-Modernist Bourgeois Liberalism', *Journal of Philosophy,* 80: 583–9.

——(1985). 'Solidarity or Objectivity?', in John Rajchman and Cornel West, eds., *Post-Analytic Philosophy.* New York: Columbia University Press.

——(1986a). 'The Contingency of Community', *London Review of Books,* 24 July: 10–14.

——(1986b). 'Thugs and Theorists: A Reply to Bernstein', *Political Theory,* 15/4: 564–80.

——(1989). *Contingency, Irony, and Solidarity.* Cambridge: Cambridge University Press.

Rosenbaum, Walter A. (1983). 'The Politics of Public Participation in Hazardous Waste Management', in James P. Lester and Ann O'M. Bowman, eds., *The Politics of Hazardous Waste Management.* Durham, NC: Duke University Press.

——(1985). *Environmental Politics and Policy.* Washington: Congressional Quarterly Press.

Rothman, Hal (1998). *The Greening of a Nation? Environmentalism in the United States since 1945*. Fort Worth, Tex.: Harcourt Brace.

Rozek, Victor (1994). 'A Gathering of Warlords', *Wild Forest Review*, March: 22–5.

Ruddick, Sara (1980). 'Maternal Thinking', *Feminist Studies*, 6/3: 342–67.

Ruffins, Paul (1992). 'Defining a Movement and a Community', *Crossroads/Forward Motion*, 11/2.

Ryan, Howard (1983). *Blocking Progress: Consensus Decision-Making in the Anti-Nuclear Movement*. Oakland, Calif.: Overthrow Cluster of Livermore Action Group.

Saika, Peggy (1995). Personal Communication.

St. Clair, Jeffrey (1995). 'Cashing Out: Corporate Environmentalism in the Age of Newt', Paper given as part of panel on Foundation/Corporate Control Over Environmental Organizations, Public Interest Law Conference, Eugene, Oreg. 11 March 1995.

Sale, Kirkpatrick (1993). *The Green Revolution: The American Environmental Movement 1962–1992*. New York: Hill and Wang.

Sandbach, Francis (1980). *Environment, Ideology, and Policy*. Montclair: Allanheld, Osmun Publishers.

Sandel, Michael (1982). *Liberalism and the Limits of Justice*. Cambridge: Cambridge University Press.

Sandman, Peter M. (1986). *Explaining Environmental Risk: Some Notes on Environmental Risk Communication*. Washington, DC: Office of Toxic Substances, EPA.

Sandoval, Ricardo (1996). 'Intel to be its own Pollution Watchdog', *San Jose Mercury News*, 20 November: 1A.

Scarce, Rik (1990). *Eco-Warriors: Understanding the Radical Environmental Movement*. Chicago: The Noble Press Inc.

Schlosberg, David (1995). 'Communicative Action in Practice: Inter-subjectivity and New Social Movements', *Political Studies*, 43: 291–311.

Schnaiberg, Allan (1980). *The Environment: From Surplus to Scarcity*. Oxford: Oxford University Press.

Schumaker, Paul (1991). *Critical Pluralism, Democratic Performance, and Community Power*. Lawrence, Kan.: University Press of Kansas.

Schwab, Jim (1994). *Deeper Shades of Green: The Rise of Blue-Collar and Minority Environmentalism in America*. San Francisco: Sierra Club Books.

Scott, Joan (1991). 'The Evidence of Experience', *Critical Inquiry*, 17: 773–97.

——(1992). 'Multiculturalism and the Politics of Identity', *October*, 61: 12–19.

Seigfried, Charlene Haddock (1996). *Pragmatism and Feminism: Reweaving the Social Fabric*. Chicago: University of Chicago Press.

Shabecoff, Philip (1990). 'Environmental Groups Told they are Racists in Hiring', *New York Times*, 1 February: A1.

——(1993). *A Fierce Green Fire: The American Environmental Movement*. New York: Hill and Wang.

Sierra Club (1970). *Ecotactics: The Sierra Club Handbook for Environmental Activists*. New York: Pocket Books.

Silicon Valley Toxics Coalition (1997). *Sign-on Letter Opposing Environmental De-regulation and Supporting Community and Worker Empowerment*. San Jose, Calif.: SVTC. (Website: http://www.svtc.org/svtc/leiberman.htm, accessed 2 Jan. 1998.)

Sirianni, Carmen (1993). 'Learning Pluralism: Democracy and Diversity in Feminist Organizations', in John W. Chapman and Ian Shapiro, eds., *Democratic Community: NOMOS XXXV*. New York: New York University Press.

Southwest Network for Environmental and Economic Justice (1993). *Southwest Network for Environmental and Economic Justice*. Albuquerque, N.Mex.: SNEEJ.

Southwest Organizing Project (1995). *Intel Inside New Mexico: A Case Study of Environmental and Economic Injustice*. Albuquerque, N.Mex.: SWOP.

——and the Campaign for Responsible Technology (1997). *Sacred Waters*. Albuquerque, N.Mex.: Southwest Organizing Project.

Spelman, Elizabeth (1988). *Inessential Woman*. Boston: Beacon.

Sprout, Harold, and Margaret Sprout (1978). *The Context of Environmental Politics*. Lexington, Ky.: University Press of Kentucky.

Staggenborg, Suzanne (1989). 'Stability and Innovation in the Women's Movement: a Comparison of Two Movement Organizations', *Social Problems*, 36/1: 75–93.

Stoper, Emily (1989). *The Student Nonviolent Coordinating Committee: The Growth of Radicalism in a Civil Rights Organization*. Brooklyn, NY: Carlson.

Susskind, Lawrence, and Gerard McMahon (1985). 'The Theory and Practice of Negotiated Rulemaking', *Yale Journal of Regulation*, 3: 133–65.

Sustainable America (1995). *Metro Futures: A High-Wage, Low-Waste, Democratic Development Strategy for America's Cities and Inner Suburbs*. Madison: Sustainable America.

Szakos, Joe (1993). 'Multi-Issue Success in Kentucky', in Citizen's Clearinghouse for Hazardous Waste, *Ten Years of Triumph*. Falls Church, Va.: Citizen's Clearinghouse for Hazardous Waste.

Szasz, Andrew (1994). *EcoPopulism: Toxic Waste and the Movement for Environmental Justice*. Minneapolis: University of Minnesota Press.

——and Michael Meuser (1997). 'Environmental Inequalities: Literature Review and Proposals for New Directions in Research and Theory', *Current Sociology*, 453: 99–120.

Talbot, Allan (1983). *Settling Things: Six Case Studies in Environmental Mediation*. Washington, DC: Conservation Foundation.

Tarrow, Sidney (1994). *Power in Movement: Social Movements, Collective Action and Politics*. Cambridge: Cambridge University Press.

Taylor, Bron, ed. (1995). *Ecological Resistance Movements: The Global Emergence of Radical and Popular Environmentalism*. Albany, NY: State University of New York Press.

Taylor, Charles (1994). *Multiculturalism: Examining the Politics of Recognition.* Princeton, NJ: Princeton University Press.

Taylor, Dorceta (1992). 'Can the Environmental Movement Attract and Maintain the Support of Minorities?', in Bunyan Bryant and Paul Mohai, eds., *Race and the Incidence of Environmental Hazards: A Time for Discourse.* Boulder, Colo: Westview Press.

——(1993). 'Environmentalism and the Politics of Exclusion', in Robert D. Bullard, ed., *Confronting Environmental Racism: Voices from the Grassroots.* Boston: South End Press.

Taylor, Linda (1988). 'The Importance of Cross-Cultural Communication between Environmentalists and Land-Based People', *The Workbook*, 13/3: 90–100.

Taylor, Michael (1982). *Community, Anarchy, and Liberty.* Cambridge: Cambridge University Press.

Torgerson, Douglas (1986). 'Between Knowledge and Politics: Three Faces of Policy Analysis', *Policy Sciences*, 19: 33–59.

——(1990). 'Obsolescent Leviathan: Problems of Order in Administrative Thought', in Robert Paehlke and Douglas Torgerson, eds., *Managing Leviathan: Environmental Politics and the Administrative State.* Peterborough, Ontario: Broadview Press.

—— and Robert Paehlke (1990). 'Environmental Administration: Revising the Agenda of Inquiry and Practice', in Robert Paehlke and Douglas Torgerson, eds., *Managing Leviathan: Environmental Politics and the Administrative State.* Peterborough, Ontario: Broadview Press.

Tronto, Joan (1993). *Moral Boundaries: A Political Argument for an Ethic of Care.* New York: Routledge.

Truax, Hawley, ed. (1990). 'Beyond White Environmentalism: Minorities and the Environment', *Environmental Action*, 21: 19–30.

Truman, David (1960). *The Governmental Process: Political Interests and Public Opinion.* New York: Knopf.

United Church of Christ Commission for Racial Justice (1987). *Toxic Wastes and Race in the United States: A National Report on the Racial and Socio-Economic Characteristics of Communities with Hazardous Waste Sites.* New York: United Church of Christ.

United States Environmental Protection Agency (1979). *Siting of Hazardous Waste Management Facilities and Public Opposition* (SW-809). Washington, DC: Government Printing Office.

——(1989). *Workshop on Risk Communication Manual.* Washington, DC: EPA.

—— (1991). *Memorandum on Draft Environmental Equity Communication Plan.* Washington, DC: EPA.

——(1992). *Environmental Equity: Reducing Risk for All Communities*, 2 vols. Washington, DC: Government Printing Office.

——(1995). *Environmental Justice Strategy for Executive Order 12898.* Washington, DC: EPA.

United States Environmental Protection Agency (1996*a*). *The Model Plan for Public Participation*. Washington, DC: EPA Office of Environmental Justice.
——(1996*b*). *US EPA Press Release: EPA Administrator, Intel Corporation Sign Final Project XL Agreement*. Washington, DC: Environmental Protection Agency; 19 November.

United States General Accounting Office (1983). *Siting of Hazardous Waste Landfills and their Correlation with Racial and Economic Status of Surrounding Communities*. Washington, DC: Government Printing Office.

United States Nuclear Regulatory Commission (1997). *Final Initial Decision— Louisiana Energy Services*. USNRC, Atomic Safety and Licensing Board, Docket No. 70-3070-ML (1 May 1997).

Van Liere, Kent D., and Riley E. Dunlap (1980). 'The Social Bases of Environmental Concern: A Review of Hypotheses, Explanations, and Empirical Evidence', *Public Opinion Quarterly*, 44: 181–97.

Waldron, Jeremy (1988). 'Locke: Toleration and the Rationality of Persecution', in Susan Mendus, ed., *Justifying Toleration: Conceptual and Historical Perspectives*. Cambridge: Cambridge University Press.

Wapner, Paul (1996). *Environmental Activism and World Civic Politics*. Albany, NY: State University of New York Press.

Waxman, Congressman Henry A. (1992). 'Environmental Equity Report is Public Relations Ploy: Internal Memoranda Reveal Report to be Misleading', press release, 24 February.

Wellman, Barry, Peter J. Carrington, and Alan Hall (1988). 'Networks as Personal Communities', in Barry Wellman and S. D. Berkowitz, eds., *Social Structures: A Network Approach*. Cambridge: Cambridge University Press.

Wells, Donald (1982). 'Site Control of Hazardous Waste Facilities', *Policy Studies Review*, 1/4: 728–35.

Weisskopf, Michael (1992). 'EPA's Two Voices on Pollution Risks to Minorities', *Washington Post*, 9 March: A15.

West, Cornel (1989). *The American Evasion of Philosophy: A Genealogy of Pragmatism*. Madison: University of Wisconsin Press.

White, Stephen K. (1991). *Political Theory and Postmodernism*. Cambridge: Cambridge University Press.

White House (1994*a*). Executive order 12898, 'Federal Actions to Address Environmental Justice in Minority Populations and Low-Income Populations.'
——(1994*b*). Presidential memorandum accompanying executive order 12898, 'Federal Actions to Address Environmental Justice in Minority Populations and Low-Income Populations.'

Williams, Bruce A. and Albert R. Matheny (1995). *Democracy, Dialogue, and Environmental Disputes: The Contested Languages of Social Regulation*. New Haven, Conn.: Yale University Press.

Williams, Michael (1993). 'Building Bridges . . . Plan the Span', *Everyone's Backyard*, 12/4: 18.

Williams, Patricia (1991). *The Alchemy of Race and Rights*. Cambridge, Mass.: Harvard.

Wolff, Robert (1965). 'Beyond Tolerance', in Wolff, B. Moore, and H. Marcuse, eds., *A Critique of Pure Tolerance*. Boston: Beacon.

——Barrington Moore, and Herbert Marcuse, eds. (1965). *A Critique of Pure Tolerance*. Boston: Beacon.

Wright, Beverly (1995). 'Environmental Justice Equity Centers: A Response to Inequity', in Bunyan Bryant, ed., *Environmental Justice: Issues, Policies, and Solutions*. Covelo, Calif.: Island Press.

——Pat Bryant, and Robert D. Bullard (1994). 'Coping with Poisons in Cancer Alley', in Robert D. Bullard, ed., *Unequal Protection: Environmental Justice and Communities of Color*. San Francisco: Sierra Club Books.

Young, Iris Marion (1986). 'The Ideal of Community and the Politics of Difference', *Social Theory and Practice*, 12/1: 1–26.

——(1990). *Justice and the Politics of Difference*. Princeton, NJ: Princeton University Press.

——(1994). 'Gender as Seriality: Thinking about Women as a Social Collective', *Signs*, 193: 713–38.

——(1996). 'Communication and the Other: Beyond Deliberative Democracy', in Seyla Benhabib, ed., *Democracy and Difference: Contesting the Boundaries of the Political*. Princeton, NJ: Princeton University Press.

Zald, Mayer N., and John D. McCarthy, eds. (1987). *Social Movements in an Organizational Society*. New Brunswick, NJ: Transaction Books.

Index